GREA...
ON CA...
THE 21ST
CENTURY

STEVEN RANSOM

 Credence Publications

Great News on Cancer in the 21st Century

"Our great grandchildren will look back at this period and wonder how we could condemn one third of the population to the disease, when for the last 50 years we've had good evidence that much of cancer could be eradicated."

Ross Hulme Hall, chairman
Dept. Biochemistry, McMaster University

"An excellent, well researched book, congratulations! You have presented the position exceptionally clearly as it is regarding mainstream and alternative. I will be certainly directing all my cancer patients to your site." **Bill Reeder, Registered Medical Practitioner MB. ChB. Member of ACNEM, AIMA, NZIMA, NZNMA. (Nutritional and Natural Medicines Associations of Australia and NZ)**

"Dear Steve, I must blame you for a sleepless night. Just brilliant! I have been immersing myself in all of this information for a while now but never have I found it written so well.... So, thank you! You certainly gave myself and my family members something to think about. Keep up the brilliant work." **Ledonna James**

"Mr Ransom, I share your thoughts and I applaud you for your courage for bringing us this book. The most dangerous place on Planet Earth is the hospital - next is the doctor's office - followed closely by the dentist's office." **Frank D Wiewel, Former Chairman, Pharmacological and Biological Treatments Committee, Office of Alternative Medicine (OAM), US National Institutes of Health (NIH)**

"Dear Steve, Thank God you wrote this book! The senseless deaths of the past for the sake of a buck is so sinful I cannot express the grief I feel knowing all of this. No one in my family has this dreadful affliction and I hope they never do. Thank you, thank you, thank you." **Eddie Matthews**

"This informative and empowering book shows that the main beneficiaries of cancer treatment are the medical and pharmaceutical interests, while most cancer patients continue to suffer and die of this spreading disease - and not only despite conventional treatment, but often because of it! This book should be required reading for anyone who values his or her health." **John J Moelaert - author of The Cancer Conspiracy**

Table of contents

The Cancer Jungle

Cancer... what is it? Such fear surrounds it. The conventional approach to cancer treatment is to kill the cancer cell, either by surgical removal or toxic treatment (chemicals or radiation). None of the current conventional treatments for cancer addresses its cause. Because of this, recurrence rates are high and cancer mortality rates have not dropped overall. Some patients know this and begin a search on their own for alternatives. They can soon find themselves in unchartered territory - lost in the cancer jungle. Told by their physicians that there are a lot of quacks out there pushing false hope, many cancer patients are torn between complying with their doctor and listening to others whisper in their ear about someone who overcame cancer with some alternative treatment. Can cancer be treated successfully outside of establishment medicine? If you have been diagnosed with cancer, it is a critical time in your life. It can be so difficult to know whom to trust.

Some great news!

This book has been written as a guide through the cancer jungle. It is divided into two sections. In Part One, we take a realistic look at the conventional cancer treatments on offer today and ask what role might be played by cancer doctors and cancer medicines in the human cancer death toll. We also examine the foundations of the industry in general. In Part Two, we look at the work carried out by qualified scientists and doctors dedicated to promoting a greater knowledge of non-toxic, natural cancer treatments – despite some very fierce opposition from certain quarters. We also look at the wonderful testimonies of those who are alive and well today because of non-conventional cancer treatment. There really is some great news on cancer in the 21st century!

Part 1
Death by Doctoring?

"What you don't know can hurt you."
Samuel Epstein, MD

Nothing new under the sun

Every year in the UK, 200,000 people are diagnosed with cancer and 152,500 die.[1] In the US, the annual death rate for this disease is approximately 547,000.[2] Staying with America, 184,000 women are diagnosed with breast cancer every year and the deaths in both the UK and US from breast cancer are recorded at around 54,000 per annum. Collectively speaking, all these deaths are recorded as cancer deaths.

But how many of these deaths are really attributable to cancer itself? How many deaths should in fact be recorded as 'death by doctoring'? When we consider that conventional treatment consists almost entirely of radiation, chemotherapy, surgery and the long-term application of toxic pharmaceuticals - treatments which are well known for their life-threatening side-effects, then the question becomes all the more legitimate. On chemotherapy, for instance, note the following from Allen Levin MD:

"Most cancer patients in this country die of chemotherapy. Chemotherapy does not eliminate breast, colon, or lung cancers. This fact has been documented for over a decade, yet doctors still use chemotherapy for these tumours."[3]

The extraordinary evidence to substantiate Levin's observations, together with many other damning statements on conventional cancer treatments, are presented for the reader in the following pages. In any argument, one of the most critical issues is balance. Are both sides to the issue being presented fairly to the public? Throughout the book, we examine the much-publicised story of UK media personality, the late John Diamond, who opted for conventional treatment. What does his story tell us? John was known for his critical attitude towards many of the more popular alternative therapies. We look at some aspects of the alternative approach to cancer and ask if his criticisms were entirely undeserved.

---

[1] UK Cancer Research Campaign, www.crc.org.uk/cancer/cs_mortality1.html
[2] "Cancer – The Social Impact":
http://yakko.bme.virginia.edu/biom304/notes/cancer.htm
[3] Levin, Allen, *The Healing of Cancer*, Marcus Books, 1990

£6,800,000 a day

We hear from those within the cancer establishment who cite the conventional *cut, burn and dissolve* techniques as ugly and inhumane, and from those who seriously question the amounts of money being invested in conventional cancer today. Given the depressingly low recovery rate most experience when choosing the conventional path, are these observations and indictments justified? In the UK alone, £2.8billion a year is spent in the conventional cancer emporium. That's roughly £6,800,000 a day. US spending on cancer is ten times this figure.

We also hear from those who defied conventional wisdom and opted for non-toxic, non-conventional cancer treatments, with remarkable results. From the known range of anti-cancer treatments available, this story focuses primarily on the naturally occurring substances Vitamin B17 and Vitamin C, and their use in conjunction with a solid program of nutrition. Vitamin B17 in particular has been attracting a great deal of attention recently, despite concerted efforts by some parties to suppress or distort all positive reporting on this vitamin.

Some may baulk at the accusation that a concerted suppression of successful, non-conventional cancer treatments has been taking place. We must realise however, that with global spending on conventional cancer running into hundreds of billions of dollars annually, any news of a successful, non-pharmaceutical anti-cancer approach might be expected to upset the status quo.

Isn't it right we know?

As mentioned, there is great news on cancer treatment in the 21st century! And you can, of course, go straight to Part Two. But this would mean reading only one half of a fascinating story. As world-renowned toxicologist Dr Samuel Epstein states, *"What you don't know can hurt you."* At the very least, isn't it a basic responsibility to ascertain whether there really is such a thing as 'death by doctoring'?

By way of introduction to this subject, we travel back a few hundred years to the bedside of King Charles II, where fourteen of the most eminent physicians in the land are earnestly 'reviving' the king from a stroke.

King Charles II, 1685
Curiously, his strength seemed to wane

"The king was bled to the extent of a pint from a vein in his right arm. Next, his shoulder was cut into and the incised area was sucked of an additional 8oz of blood. An emetic and a purgative were administered followed by a second purgative followed by an enema containing antimony, sacred bitters, rock salt, mallow leaves, violets, beetroot, camomile flowers, fennel seeds, linseed, cinnamon, cardamom seed, saffron, cochineal and aloes.

The king's scalp was shaved and a blister raised. A sneezing powder of hellebore was administered. A plaster of burgundy pitch and pigeon dung was applied to the feet. Medicaments included melon seeds, manna, slippery elm, black cherry water, lime flowers, lily of the valley, peony, lavender, and dissolved pearls. As he grew worse, forty drops of extract of human skull were administered, followed by a rallying dose of Raleigh's antidote. Finally Bezoar Stone was given.

Curiously, his Majesty's strength seemed to wane after all these interventions and, as the end of his life seemed imminent, his doctors tried a last-ditch attempt by forcing more Raleigh's mixture, pearl julep and ammonia down the dying King's throat. Further treatment was rendered more difficult by the king's death." [4]

We can be sure that the physicians gathered around the King's bed were all leaders in their particular field - royalty and presidents do not settle for anything less. But with hindsight, we can now see the hideous error of their therapeutics. Today, the skull-drops, the ammonia and the pigeon dung have long since disappeared from the conventional arsenal, but what will we say in a few years' time when we look back on the 'highly respected' cancer therapeutics of 2002? Will we dare to venture that there is nothing new under the sun?

---

[4] Buckman, Robert, *Magic Or Medicine*, Pan Books, 1994

John Diamond, 2001
Have we really progressed further?
"He's been poisoned, blasted, had bits lopped off him, been in remission, felt lumps grow again, been given shreds of hope, had hope removed." [5]

Many thousands of people were touched by John Diamond's regular *Times* newspaper column, giving stark and brutal insight into living with throat cancer. In a witty and very down-to-earth manner, John's remarkable column explored numerous life-with-cancer issues, including the ups and considerably more downs in body and mind during radiation treatment, the effects of his illness upon the wider family, the rediscovery of everyday wonders previously taken for granted, and his distaste for numerous cancer clichés such as 'brave John' and 'staying positive'. He replied,

"I am not brave. I did not choose cancer. I am just me, dealing with it."

and

"Whenever somebody told me how good a positive attitude would be for me, what they really meant was how much easier a positive attitude would make it for them."

He was also well known for his castigation of almost all non-orthodox treatments and for his willingness to submit to all that the medical orthodoxy had to offer – a service that even he, a conventional advocate, had variously described as *"pay-as-you-bleed"* and *"surgical muggings"*.

For me, the most memorable images of John were captured in the BBC's *Inside Story* – a television program that followed John during a year of treatment, showing him clearly suffering. An operation on John's throat caused him to lose his voice, which, as a popular broadcaster, was a serious blow. Later, through surgery and radiation treatment, he would lose most of his tongue, and with it all sense of

---

[5] Gerrard, Nicci, *Sunday Observer*, 14th May 2001

taste and the ability to eat properly - a double blow, given that he was married to TV super-cook Nigella Lawson.

In his extraordinary book *C: Because Cowards Get Cancer Too* (which I could not put down), John Diamond writes: *"He who didn't realise what a boon an unimpaired voice was, who ate his food without stopping to think about its remarkable flavour, who was criminally profligate with words, who took his wife and children and friends for granted - in short, he who didn't know he was living."* [6]

John died in March 2001, aged 47, after having suffered for four years. In his death, he joined sports presenter Helen Rollason, Ian Dury, Roy Castle, Cardinal Basil Hume, Linda McCartney, ex-Beatle George Harrison and, most recently, actor John Thaw, along with 152,500 others in the UK who succumb annually to the cancer ordeal. Kate Law of the Cancer Research Campaign said that John's story helped to bring cancer out of the closet in Britain. John's writings certainly brought home the ugliness of conventional treatment. But the more informed in the cancer debate who have read John's columns and book will have recognised that John's writings, brilliant though they were, did not bring out the full story of cancer at all.

---

[6] Diamond, John, *C: Because Cowards Get Cancer Too*, Vermilion Press, 1999

Chemotherapy - fraught with risks and side-effects

"Cured yesterday of my disease, I died last night of my physician." **Matthew Prior**

Consider the following statement from French cancer specialist, Professor Charles Mathe:

"If I contracted cancer, I would never go to a standard cancer treatment centre. Cancer victims who live far from such centres have a chance."[7]

Walter Last, writing in *The Ecologist*, reported recently:

"After analysing cancer survival statistics for several decades, Dr Hardin Jones, Professor at the University of California, concluded '...patients are as well, or better off untreated.' Jones' disturbing assessment has never been refuted."[8]

Consider this from Dr Albert Braverman in the *Lancet*:

"Many... oncologists recommend chemotherapy for virtually any tumour, with a hopefulness undiscouraged by almost invariable failure."[9]

And this from Alan C Nixon, former president of the American Chemical Society:

"...as a chemist trained to interpret data, it is incomprehensible to me that physicians can ignore the clear evidence that chemotherapy does much, much more harm than good."[10]

---

[7] Mathe, Charles, *Scientific Medicine Stymied*, Medicines Nouvelles, 1989
[8] *The Ecologist*, Vol.28, No.2, March/April 1998
[9] Braverman, Albert, "Medical oncology in the '90's", *Lancet*, p.901, August 1991
[10] Day, Phillip, *Cancer: Why We're Still Dying To Know The Truth*, Credence Publications, 1999

And this from Dr Thomas Dao, writing in the *New England Journal of Medicine*:

"Despite widespread use of chemotherapies, breast cancer mortality has not changed in the last 70 years." [11]

Ferocious chemistry

Chemotherapy is an invasive and toxic treatment able supposedly to eliminate cancer cells. Unfortunately its ferocious chemistry is not able to differentiate between the cancerous cell and the healthy cells in the surrounding tissue. Put simply, many conventional chemotherapy drugs are intravenously administered poisons which have been designed to target cells that multiply the most rapidly. Many beneficial cells are killed in the process. Repeated chemotherapy and radiation treatments will kill the whole body by degrees.

The immune system is hit particularly hard by chemotherapy and often does not recuperate enough adequately to protect from common illnesses, which can then lead to death. Some 67% of people who die during cancer treatment, do so through opportunistic infections arising as a direct result of the immune system failing because of the aggressive and toxic nature of the drugs. [12] What is this if it is not death by doctoring?

Side-effects

The side-effects from chemotherapy and radiation are extensive. They can include dizziness, skin discolouration, sensory loss, audio-visual impairment, nausea, diarrhoea, loss of hair, loss of appetite, leading to malnutrition, loss of sex drive, loss of white blood cells, permanent organ damage, organ failure, internal bleeding, tissue loss, cardiovascular leakage (artery deterioration), to name but a few.

Vincristin is a commonly applied chemotherapy agent. Its side-effects include rapid heart-beat, wheezing or difficulty breathing, skin rash or swelling, fever or chills, infection, unusual bleeding or bruising,

---

[11] Dao, Thomas, *New England Journal of Medicine*, March 1975, 292, p.707
[12] The Home of Orthomolecular Oncology:
http://www.canceraction.org.gg/index2.htm

abdominal or stomach cramps, loss of movement, loss of muscle coordination, spasms, fits, seizures and convulsions. The full list can be viewed at the web address below.[13]

Another common drug is Actinomycin-D. Again, the side-effects are horrendous and can be viewed at the reference below.[14] They include hair-loss, anaemia, low white platelet count, nausea, sickness, diarrhoea and liver failure. These drugs are just two of large family of 'chemotherapeutics' which are being prescribed every day in hospitals across the world – and in very large quantities.

Death on legs

Two years ago, registered nurse Hazel was diagnosed with breast cancer. She described her chemotherapy as the worst experience of her life.

"This highly toxic fluid was being injected into my veins. The nurse administering it was wearing protective gloves because it would burn her skin if just a tiny drip came into contact with it. I couldn't help asking myself, 'If such precautions are needed to be taken on the outside, what is it doing to me on the inside?' From 7pm that evening, I vomited solidly for two and a half days. During my treatment, I lost my hair by the handful, I lost my appetite, my skin colour, my zest for life. I was death on legs." [15]

The hazards posed by chemotherapy drugs coming into contact with the skin are discussed shortly. And we shall be hearing more from Hazel later, although under very different circumstances! It seems though that with chemotherapy, we have once again been visited by King Charles' abominable treatments, again being administered by the most skilled, most learned physicians in the land. John Diamond noted that it was only when he began his radiation treatment that he began to feel really ill.[16]

---

[13] http://healthanswers.telstra.com/drugdata/appco/00070129.asp
[14] http://www.tirgan.com/actinomy.htm
[15] Testimony on file at Credence.
[16] Diamond, John, op. cit.

Senior cancer physician Dr Charles Moertal of the Mayo Clinic in the US stated:

"Our most effective regimens are fraught with risks and side-effects and practical problems; and after this price is paid by all the patients we have treated, only a small fraction are rewarded with a transient period of usually incomplete tumour regressions...." [17]

Dr Ralph Moss is the author of *The Cancer Industry* - a detailed account of the world of conventional cancer politics and practice. Interviewed live on the Laurie Lee show in 1994, Moss stated:

"In the end, there is no proof that chemotherapy actually extends life in the vast majority of cases, and this is the great lie about chemotherapy, that somehow there is a correlation between shrinking a tumour and extending the life of a patient." [18]

OK for you, but not for me!
Scientists based at McGill Cancer Centre sent a questionnaire to 118 lung cancer doctors to determine what degree of faith these practising cancer physicians placed in the therapies they administered. They were asked to imagine that they themselves had cancer and were asked which of six current trials they would choose. 79 doctors responded, of which 64 would not consent to be in any trial containing cisplatin - one of the common chemotherapy drugs they were trialling, (current worldwide sales are around $110,000,000 a year). 58 of the 79 found that all the trials in question were unacceptable due to the ineffectiveness of chemotherapy and its unacceptably high degree of toxicity.[19] Cisplatin is a class 2 carcinogen and all containers of the drug require a label indicating poisonous and corrosive contents.[20]

After spending over 30 years researching cancer survival statistics, Dr Hardin Jones, who was a professor of medical physics and

---

[17] Griffin, G Edward, *World Without Cancer*, American Media Publications, 1996
[18] Day, Phillip, *Cancer: Why We're...*, op. cit
[19] Ibid.
[20] The chemistry of cisplatin at www.ch.ic.ac.uk/local/projects/s_liu/Html/Frames.html

physiology at the University of California at Berkeley, came to the following conclusion:

"My studies have proven conclusively that untreated cancer victims usually live up to four times longer than treated individuals. For a typical type of cancer, people who refused treatment lived for an average of twelve and a half years. Those who accepted surgery and other kinds of treatment lived an average of only three years." [21]

These words were contained in Jones' paper, "A Report on Cancer", which he delivered – ironically - to the American Cancer Society's 11th Annual Science Writers' Conference in New Orleans, Louisiana, on 7th March 1969.

Chemotherapy - a scientific wasteland
The following extract is taken from Dr Tim O'Shea, writing for 'The Doctor Within':

"A German epidemiologist from the Heidelberg and Mannheim Tumour Clinic, Dr Ulrich Abel, has done a comprehensive review and analysis of every major study and clinical trial of chemotherapy ever done. His conclusions should be read by anyone who is about to embark on the Chemo Express. To make sure he had reviewed everything ever published on chemotherapy, Abel sent letters to over 350 medical centres around the world asking them to send him anything they had published on the subject. Abel researched thousands of articles: it is unlikely that anyone in the world knows more about chemotherapy than he.

The analysis took him several years, but the results are astounding: Abel found that the overall worldwide success rate of chemotherapy was 'appalling' because there was simply no scientific evidence available anywhere that chemotherapy can 'extend in any appreciable way the lives of patients suffering from the most common organic cancers.' Abel emphasises that chemotherapy rarely improves the quality of life. He describes chemotherapy as 'a scientific wasteland' and states that at least 80 percent of chemotherapy

---

[21] Jones, Hardin, "A Report on Cancer", delivered to the American Cancer Society's 11th Annual Science Writers' Conference in New Orleans, Louisiana, 7th March 1969

administered throughout the world is worthless, and is akin to the 'emperor's new clothes' - neither doctor nor patient is willing to give up on chemotherapy even though there is no scientific evidence that it works!" [22]

No mainstream media even mentioned this comprehensive study.

Chemotherapy can cause cancer

An amazing admission is made on a website supported by the US National Cancer Institute. Giving the reader information on the treatment of Wilms' tumour (a rare form of cancer affecting the kidney, especially in children) the site goes on to state:

"When very high doses of chemotherapy are used to kill cancer cells, these high doses can destroy the blood-forming tissue in the bones (the bone marrow). If very high doses of chemotherapy are needed to treat the cancer, bone marrow may be taken from the bones before therapy and frozen until it is needed. Following chemotherapy, the bone marrow is given back through a needle in a vein. This is called autologous bone marrow re-infusion.

Radiation therapy uses x-rays or other high-energy rays to kill cancer cells and shrink tumours. Radiation for Wilms' tumour usually comes from a machine outside the body (external radiation therapy). Radiation may be used before or after surgery and/or chemotherapy.

After several years, some patients develop another form of cancer as a result of their treatment with chemotherapy and radiation. Clinical trials are ongoing to determine if lower doses of chemotherapy and radiation can be used." [23]

Dr Henry Rosenberg has made an extensive study of the carcinogenic effects of chemotherapy. A detailed list of referenced papers demonstrating these effects is included in the appendices to this book. A full list of the major licensed chemotherapy drugs is found at The Drug Centre. Readers considering chemotherapy are encouraged

---

[22] O'Shea, Tim, "Chemotherapy - an unproven procedure":
www.thedoctorwithin.com/index20.html
[23] http://www.cancerlinksusa.com/kidney/wilm/treatment.htm

to visit the site and research the information on side-effects found there.[24]

An equally uninspiring message on chemotherapy is delivered in this recent report:

"Chemo Slightly Extends Brain Cancer Survival - *Adding chemotherapy to the treatment of some patients with aggressive brain tumours may make a modest difference in their survival, UK researchers report.... While 40% of radiation-only patients lived one year, 46% of chemotherapy patients did. Overall, chemotherapy patients lived about 2 months longer than patients given radiation alone, the researchers note. 'This small but clear improvement in survival from chemotherapy encourages further study of drug treatment of these tumours,' the researchers write..."* [25]

An extra two months! Not exactly fantastic news, is it? And what about quality of life? What suffering will be endured by the patient on chemotherapy for those extra 8 weeks?

So, what exactly is chemotherapy and where did it originate? Its extraordinarily low success rate in the treatment of cancer comes as no surprise when we realise that this treatment actually began life as a biological/chemical agent for use in war.

---

[24] The Drug Centre:
www.cancerpage.com/centers/Drug/chemodrugs.asp
[25] The full report can be found at Yahoo News:
http://story.news.yahoo.com/news?tmpl=story&u=/nm/20020322/hl_nm/cancer_c
hemotherapy_1

Medicine or chemical warfare?

WARNING: Leukeran (chlorambucil) can severely suppress bone marrow function. Chlorambucil is a carcinogen in humans.
label on a Glaxo chemotherapy bottle

Mustard gas
During the Second World War, a ship carrying mustard gas exploded. In the autopsies carried out on the crew-members, it was noticed that exposure to the mustard gas had caused destruction of fast growing tissue and had slowed down the reproduction of white blood cells. It was surmised that since cancer grew raidly, these poisons could kill cancer tissue swiftly.[26]

Fighting for breath
Mustard gas was one of the most lethal of the poisonous chemicals used during the war. Almost odourless when breathed in, it can take up to twelve hours to wreak its havoc. Yperite, its main constituent, is so powerful that only small amounts have to be added to high-explosive shells in order to render them 'effective'. Once in the soil, mustard gas remains active for several weeks. Victims present skin blisters, sore eyes and violent vomiting.

Mustard gas causes internal and external bleeding and attacks the bronchial tubes, stripping off the mucous membrane. This is extremely painful and most soldiers had to be strapped to their beds. It usually took a person four or five weeks to die of mustard gas poisoning. On the effects of mustard gas, one nurse, Vera Brittain, wrote:

"Sometimes in the middle of the night we have to turn people out of bed and make them sleep on the floor to make room for the more seriously ill ones who have come down from the line. We have heaps of gassed cases at present: there are 10 in this ward alone. I wish those people who write so glibly about this being a holy war, and the orators who talk so much about going on, no matter how long the war lasts and what it may mean, could see a case - to say nothing of

---

[26] Moelaert, John, *The Cancer Conspiracy*, Moelaert Publications, June 1999

10 cases of mustard gas in its early stages - could see the poor things all burnt and blistered all over with great suppurating blisters, with blind eyes - sometimes temporarily, sometimes permanently - all sticky and stuck together, and always fighting for breath, their voices a whisper, saying their throats are closing and they know they are going to choke." [27]

The scientists were right; exposure to these gases did kill cancerous tissue, but, as Ralph Moss states in his book *Questioning Chemotherapy*:

"The amount of toxic chemicals needed to kill every last cancer cell was found to kill the patient long before it eliminated the tumour." [28]

While these poisons and the ones that followed did cause some tumours to shrink, these reductions in mass did not increase the lifespan of the patients and the patients' quality of life suffered enormously. This is no wonder, as we can now see that taking chemotherapy is equivalent to being exposed to chemical warfare. On this point, authors of *Toxicity of Chemotherapy*, M C Perry and J W Yarbo note:

"Almost without exception, every drug developed for four decades that is active against cancer has produced side-effects that are reminiscent of the outgrowth of these agents from research on chemical warfare." [29]

Ralph Moss again:

"I remembered the story of a celebrated Sloan-Kettering chemotherapist who, when he found out that he had advanced cancer, told his colleagues, 'Do anything you want - but no chemotherapy....' It was an open secret that an official of Sloan-Kettering sent his mother to Germany for unconventional treatment." [30]

---

[27] Brittain, Vera, *A Testament of Youth*, Penguin reprint, October 1994
[28] Moss, Ralph W, *Questioning Chemotherapy: A Critique of the Use of Toxic Drugs in the Treatment of Cancer*, Equinox Press, 1995
[29] Perry, M C & J W Yarbo, *Toxicity of Chemotherapy*, Grune & Stratton, 1984
[30] Moss, Ralph, op. cit.

In an article entitled "Chemotherapy: Snake-Oil Remedy?" Dr Martin F Shapiro explained that while

"...some oncologists inform their patients of the lack of evidence that treatments work, others may well be misled by scientific papers that express unwarranted optimism about chemotherapy. Still others respond to an economic incentive. Physicians can earn much more money running active chemotherapy practices than they can providing solace and relief to dying patients and their families." [31]

WARNING

The following label accompanies the GlaxoSmithKline cancer drug Alkeran:

WARNING: Alkeran (melphalan) should be administered under the supervision of a qualified physician experienced in the use of cancer chemotherapeutic agents. Severe bone marrow suppression with resulting infection or bleeding may occur. Melphalan is leukemogenic in humans. Melphalan produces chromosomal aberrations in vitro and in vivo and, therefore, should be considered potentially mutagenic in humans.

DESCRIPTION: ALKERAN (melphalan), also known as L-phenylalanine mustard, phenylalanine mustard, L-PAM, or L-sarcolysin, is a phenylalanine derivative of nitrogen mustard.... [32]

And Glaxo's leukaemia drug Leukeran has the following label attached to the bottle:

WARNING: Leukeran (chlorambucil) can severely suppress bone marrow function. Chlorambucil is a carcinogen in humans. [33]

---

[31] "Chemotherapy - Snake Oil Remedy?" *Los Angeles Times*, 9th January, 1987
[32] Alkeran product information: www.glaxowellcome.com/pi/alktabs.pdf
[33] Leukeran product information:
www.accessdata.fda.gov/scripts/cder/onctools/labels.cfm?GN=chlorambucil

Danger! Toxic spill!

The burning and scarring [below] is the result of a spill of chemotherapy onto the bare hand. Is it any wonder that people are worried about what might be happening to their insides as chemotherapy is intravenously fed into the body? Is it any wonder that chemotherapy nurses wear protective gloves? Is it any wonder that so high a percentage of oncologists refuse to submit to the treatments they advocate to their patients? Hazel had every right to be concerned about the internal damage taking place as she was being intravenously administered chemotherapy for her breast cancer.

Go immediately to the Emergency Room

The following information is taken from a medical college website, specialising in bone marrow transplant accompanied by chemotherapy

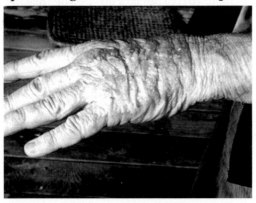

'support'. The site is not for the faint-hearted. This particular text discusses the procedures in place to dispense with clothing and other contaminated apparatus after a chemotherapy spill. The lady overleaf is wearing the regulatory, full-protective suit to deal with such a spill.

"Contaminated pads and towelling, the outer pair of gloves, and shoe covers are placed in the first chemo waste disposal bag, which is then knotted and placed in the second waste disposal bag.

The remaining protective clothing and gloves are placed in the second chemo waste bag.

Goggles can be reprocessed and are bagged separately in a zip-lock bag and sent to pharmacy with the chemo spill kit after they are removed. The chemo waste bags must be sealed securely and disposed

of in the biohazard waste containers. A "Medication Incident Report"
must be filled out after any chemotherapy spill.

If skin comes in to contact with the drug:

> *Remove gloves and protective clothing.*
> *Rinse the contaminated area thoroughly with warm water.*
> *Wash thoroughly with soap and rinse again with warm water.*
> *If skin is not broken, wipe affected area thoroughly with gauze saturated with a diluted 0.05% chlorine bleach solution and rinse with warm water. If the skin is broken, use 3% hydrogen peroxide. Wash off with warm water.*
> *Note the drug(s) that made contact, as there may be a specific antidote.*
> *Go immediately to the Emergency Room."* [34]

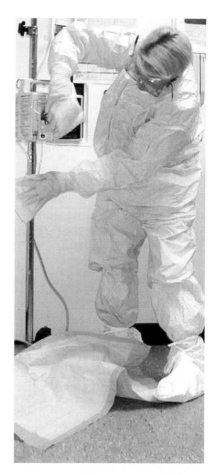

This is what is pumped into the patient undergoing conventional chemotherapy treatment. We are reminded of Professor Charles Mathe, who stated:

"If I contracted cancer, I would never go to a standard cancer treatment centre. Cancer victims who live far from such centres have a chance."

---

[34] http://www2.mc.duke.edu/9200bmt/ChemoSpill7.htm

Are these people really dying of cancer?

Having had opportunity briefly to examine the toxicity of some conventional cancer treatments, we can return to that earlier question, 'How many of these deaths are really attributable to cancer itself? How many deaths should in fact be recorded as 'death by doctoring?' Dr Mollie Hunter wrote a letter recently to Professor Michael Gearin-Tosh which was published in the UK *Daily Telegraph*.[35] Dr Hunter was writing about an experience with one of her patients who had been receiving chemotherapy for her myeloma cancer and steroids for the effects of her chemotherapy:

"I got to see her in only the last stage of her illness when she kept getting repeated bronchitis. The steroids she was on not only lowered her immune system but collapsed her vertebrae so that her spine curved and her chin was on her chest and she could not breathe. She really died of respiratory failure due to her curvature of the spine, due to her steroid treatment, but I signed the death certificate myeloma. It made me wonder at the time how often the true cause of death is recorded, i.e. the treatment and not the underlying illness." [36]

How much longer can we continue to sanction chemotherapy and similar toxic interventions as frontline cancer treatments? And why aren't we asking more questions of establishment medicine? In the face of such disastrous therapeutics, what keeps us in our current state of passivity?

Are there some subtle dynamics at work?

---

[35] Gearin-Tosh, Michael, "How Dare I Question the Experts?" *Daily Telegraph*, 14th March 2002

[36] Oxford Don Professor Michael Gearin-Tosh was diagnosed with incurable bone marrow cancer eight years ago and had read conventional medical literature which gave him no more than about a year to live. Gearing Tosh is alive and well today as a result of refusing conventional treatment and following a nutritional protocol. He has written about his experience in a book entitled *Living Proof*, Scribner Publications, 2002; see also Gearin-Tosh, Michael, "How dare I Question the Experts?" *Daily Telegraph*, 14th March 2002

Our hereditary submissive attitude?

"I kind of went into a trance and although something didn't feel quite right, I found myself nodding to chemotherapy." **Hazel**

Whilst in the main dismissing the *'alternativist'* treatments (as he called them) and writing in a generally confident manner about his trust in the conventional medical paradigm, John Diamond would sometimes waver:

"What if those denying alternativists were right? What if the truth was that no life had ever been saved by radiotherapy and that there was every chance that my cancer would be made worse by it being irradiated? What if the truth, as pronounced by a couple of book,s was that the main effect of cancer surgery was to release stray cancer cells into the body, allowing them to set up home elsewhere?... I turned to the medical books for solace and got none." [37]

Talk with cancer patients and one soon discovers that many of them report that they have an uncomfortable gut feeling that there must somehow be a better way forward. Yet they still find themselves returning to their oncologist for more of the same 'uncomfortable' treatment. Why is this, when there are, as we shall see, well-founded, non-conventional and non-toxic treatments available?

Surely, one significant factor is our hereditary submissive attitude to the medical orthodoxy and its archetypal symbolism – the white coat, the stethoscope, the years of knowledge represented in those framed diplomas. Every artefact speaks of us being in the hands of experts. On top of this, there is the added pressure that can be exerted upon the patient at the point of diagnosis by the cancer physician.

"We must move aggressively"

In his essay entitled *The $200 Billion Scam,* Jeff Kamen reports on how a cancer diagnosis was delivered to Kathy Keeton, the late wife of *Penthouse* magazine magnate, Bob Guiccione:

---

[37] Diamond, John, op. cit.

"I'm sorry," she remembers her doctor saying, *"It's a very rare form of the disease. It's the nature of this kind of cancer that it takes off at a gallop, and metastasises quickly, so we need to act quickly and get you started on chemotherapy at once. We have some of the best people in the world in this field. I urge you to let me get you into their expert care. There is no time to waste. This form of cancer is often fatal, and quickly so. Untreated, you have six weeks to live. We really must move aggressively with the chemo."* [38]

Here is Gawie Marx's story:

"A week before my planned vacation to Miami and the Caribbean, I noticed a big bruise on my right upper leg, and decided to see my doctor because it looked awful. For some reason the doctor decided to take a full blood count. He told me he would let me have the results the next afternoon. At that stage I did not even know what a full blood count was! I was still sleeping the next morning, when Dr Petersen phoned me and instructed me to go and see a certain Professor Peter Jacobs. He actually told me the Professor was waiting for me. I was still not concerned, because I did not feel sick.

Prof Jacobs told me I had acute promyelocytic leukaemia (APL). He told me I was very sick and he had to start treatment immediately. I did not listen to what he was saying - I could not believe I had cancer. I told him there was nothing wrong with me - I was feeling fine. But that was not the case. My white cell count was 0.7 and my platelets 6. I was admitted into hospital the same afternoon and had my first platelet transfusion.

My folks and my one brother were with me that evening and the following day my youngest brother and his family came down from Johannesburg to see me. The treatment I was going to receive consisted of a course of all-trans-retinoic acid for 3 months, followed by 3 rounds of 7-day continuous Ara-C with 3 days of idarubicin chemotherapy." [39]

---

[38] www.kathykeeton-cancer.com
[39] Marx, Gawie, "My Cancer Story":
http://www.george.co.za/leukaemia/story.html

Hazel recalls a similar rushed experience:

"Basically, I was in shock from the diagnosis. I was sitting there, with the doctor saying that this treatment was the best available and that it was actually a matter of life or death that I received it. My husband was sitting next to me, telling me that I needed to go along with it. I kind of went into a trance and although something didn't feel quite right, I found myself nodding to chemotherapy."[40]

And in Janet's story, we discover a particularly hurried and pressurised encounter with the establishment:

"It all started when I went into the gynaecology clinic on base for very heavy bleeding, which was unusual for me. This was on Thursday, 4th May. They said that they couldn't see anything because of all the blood, but that there was definitely something wrong with my cervix. They stressed how important it was that I see a cancer specialist off-base within the next couple of days. That really scared me. I left there more freaked out than when I went in, with no answers.

On Monday, 8th May, I went down to Salt Lake to see a specialist oncologist. After my examination, he had Dee and I come into his office. He determined that it was cervical cancer and that he believed it was still stage 1 and I would not be able to have any more kids. Of course that hit me very hard. He said I needed a radical hysterectomy, which is more drastic than a regular hysterectomy.... they take out a lot more tissue, etc. He scheduled my surgery for that Thursday, 11th May.

The surgery took 4 hours. They removed my cervix, uterus, ovaries, 20-some-odd lymph nodes, and a bunch of tissue surrounding the uterus. All went well. A couple of days after my surgery, my pathology report came back. They got all the cancer from my cervix. The cancer had already started to spread to the lymph nodes, but they believe they removed all that as well. The tumour they removed was about the size of a golf ball.

---

[40] Testimony on file at Credence.

I was in the hospital for a week. I came home Wednesday, 17th May. I cannot believe that just 6 months before all this, I had a normal pap done. I don't understand. The Doctor said that I had some really nasty cancer cells. It just progressed so fast. I am just soooo thankful that it was found when it was. If I would've waited 6 more months for my annual exam, I just know that the cancer would've been too far gone to stop. I just know it.

On Monday, 10th July, I began both radiation therapy and chemotherapy. The reason for me having to go through both the radiation and the chemotherapy is that it increases my survival rate to around 85%. My chemo doctor said that if I decided not to get treated, the chances of it coming back were pretty high and that if it did, it would take my life. Scary thought, so, needless to say, I decided to do it." [41]

Most definitely, the power imbalance that exists in all doctor-patient relationships, (whence the term 'shrink' in psychiatry) is a key agent in determining the direction of treatment. As we shall see, there is plenty of evidence to suggest that Janet, Hazel, Gawie and countless other cancer patients are being coerced into a one-sided regime, in which perfect valid treatment options are not being made available to them - options that do not involve such drastic medical intervention.

A sea of conflicting information
Shock and fear at point of diagnosis, combined with the powerful influence inherent in the doctor/patient relationship, is one aspect of the equation. The move away from conventional cancer treatment towards non-conventional treatments is also being hampered by the vast sea of confusing, conflicting and often bizarre information posing as 'helpful' alternative cancer advice. Take the Internet, for instance. A first-time patient, or someone just plain interested in researching cancer, can soon become thoroughly confused and disheartened. Some four thousand links come up under "alternative cancer treatment" alone!

---

[41]" My Cancer Story":
http://www.independent-thoughts.com/jrygh/cancer.htm

But an anxious patient, without the luxury of a clear guide to hand, and with no time to separate the wheat from the chaff, turns off his computer. He is faced with having to make decisions based solely on his own somewhat overwhelming and probably demoralising Internet search, together with a kind of blind, desperate faith that, somehow, the well-qualified oncologist has got to be right, *"... and didn't he warn us that there were a lot of Internet 'cancer kooks' out there wanting your money?"* The patient then finds himself right back at square one and, by default, the chemotherapy suggested earlier seems overall to be the 'safest' bet. In the view of health reporter Phillip Day, author of *'Cancer: Why We're Still Dying to Know The Truth'*, *"Many people just gulp, enter the cancer tunnel and hope they come out the other end."*

Genuine treatments do exist!

Despite the fact that an Internet search can quite easily generate confusion, there is actually a wealth of well-documented, credible information available on the web on natural, efficacious treatments for a variety of serious illnesses, including cancer - information that in some instances has been on record for many years. But information on such treatments is not widely known in the public domain. This is because genuine medicine has often had to fight tremendously hard to be clearly heard. And there are particular reasons why this has been so.

Before discussing specific natural cancer treatments in more depth, it is important that we briefly examine the reasons for the current levels of confusion surrounding genuine natural medicine as a whole. Sometimes, it is not so much *where* to look for genuine treatment and advice, as *how* to look for it. Wilful distortion, negative propaganda campaigns, unwitting stupidity - you name it. Conventional and alternative, it's taking place on both sides of the fence. We must learn to read between the lines.

The merchants

"If man were to throw his entire medicine cabinet into the sea, it would be better for man and worse for the fishes." **Oliver Wendell Holmes**

In its long, hard battle for proper recognition, genuine natural treatments for serious illnesses have always had to fight on two fronts. Firstly, they have had to do battle with the drug merchants, who use every trick in the book to undermine any genuine treatments not under their own jurisdiction. And they will employ all means possible to disseminate their damaging disinformation on *'the non-conformists and their wares'* as far and wide as possible in order to protect their own lucrative market. No department, private or public, is beyond the reach of the merchants' all-consuming influence.

Thriller writer John Le Carré spent many years working in the British Foreign Office and knows the politics of big business very well. His most recent book, *The Constant Gardener*, focuses on the corrupt nature of the pharmaceutical industry. Interviewed on the subject, Le Carré stated:

"Big Pharma is engaged in the deliberate seduction of the medical profession, country by country, worldwide. It is spending a fortune on influencing, hiring and purchasing academic judgment to a point where, in a few years' time, if Big Pharma continues unchecked on its present, happy path, unbought medical opinion will be hard to find."[42]

The following report, dated February 2002, comes from the *Journal of The American Medical Association*:

Most Doctors Who Set Guidelines Have Industry Ties: *The vast majority of doctors involved in establishing national guidelines on disease treatment have financial ties to the pharmaceutical industry that could potentially sway their*

---

[42] Interview with John Le Carré, *The Nation*, New York, 9th April 2001

recommendations and inappropriately influence thousands of other physicians, a new study concludes.

Eighty-seven percent of guideline authors had some type of relationship with drug companies, yet these often were not disclosed, according to survey responses from 100 authors of guidelines published from 1991 to 1999 for common diseases such as diabetes, high blood pressure and asthma.

More specifically, 38% of respondents said they had served as employees or consultants for pharmaceutical companies and 58% had received financial support for medical research. In addition, 59% had links with drug companies whose medications were considered in the particular guidelines they authored. [43]

Selling sickness

The *British Medical Journal* recently featured an article entitled "Selling Sickness: the Pharmaceutical Industry and Disease-Mongering". The report, which readers are strongly advised to read for themselves, reveals the calculated manner in which unnecessary fear of disease is instilled into the public mind, in order then to market equally unnecessary drugs and related pharmaceutical services. In the introduction to their study, the *BMJ* authors state:

"There's a lot of money to be made from telling healthy people they're sick. Some forms of medicalising ordinary life may now be better described as disease-mongering: widening the boundaries of treatable illness in order to expand markets for those who sell and deliver treatments. Pharmaceutical companies are actively involved in sponsoring the definition of diseases and promoting them to both prescribers and consumers. The social construction of illness is being replaced by the corporate construction of disease....

Although some sponsored professionals or consumers may act independently and all concerned may have honourable motives, in many cases the formula is the same: groups and/or campaigns are

---

[43] Stenson, Jacqueline, "Most Doctors Who Set Guidelines Have Industry Ties", *JAMA*, 5th February 2002. Full article at:
www.curezone.com/art/read.asp?ID=119&db=1&C0=13

orchestrated, funded, and facilitated by corporate interests, often via their public relations and marketing infrastructure. A key strategy of the alliances is to target the news media with stories designed to create fears about the condition or disease and draw attention to the latest treatment. Company-sponsored advisory boards supply the 'independent experts' for these stories, consumer groups provide the 'victims' and public relations companies provide media outlets with the positive spin about the latest 'breakthrough' medications." [44]

Through information taken from leaked documents and other sources, the authors single out GlaxoSmithKline, Merck, Pfizer and Roche – all leading pharmaceutical companies - as engaging in this practice to one degree or another. The authors summarise their report as follows:

> ➤ *"Some forms of 'medicalisation' may now be better described as 'disease-mongering' - extending the boundaries of treatable illness to expand markets for new products.*
> ➤ *Alliances of pharmaceutical manufacturers, doctors, and patients groups use the media to frame conditions as being widespread and severe.*
> ➤ *Disease-mongering can include turning ordinary ailments into medical problems, seeing mild symptoms as serious, treating personal problems as medical, seeing risks as diseases, and framing prevalence estimates to maximise potential markets.*
> ➤ *Corporate funded information about disease should be replaced by independent information."*

For those interested in the extent to which this brazen form of 'marketing' has penetrated and 'shaped' our collective understanding of illness and disease, readers are encouraged to obtain a copy of the Credence title, *Plague, Pestilence and the Pursuit of Power*. In this book, the reader discovers that engendering a heightened fear of minor

---

[44] Moynihan, Ray, Heath, Iona & David Henry, "Selling Sickness: the pharmaceutical industry and disease-mongering", *British Medical Journal Online*, BMJ, 13th April 2002

illnesses and disease is a useful political tool for profit and control and is being used to influence public reaction in a wide variety of ways.

A great number of profitable oncology services are now being offered to a fearful population – a population whose understanding of cancer has been 'shaped' almost entirely by those who sell and deliver treatments. *Great News on Cancer in the 21ˢᵗ Century* reveals the extent to which establishment medicine has been teaching us *what* to think about cancer but not *how*.

Forever 'unproven'

G Edward Griffin is the author of *World Without Cancer*. On the approval and licensing of non-pharmaceutical cancer treatments, he states:

"Therefore - and mark this well - as long as the present laws remain, the only substances that ever will be 'approved' for cancer therapy will be proprietary. No substance from nature will ever be legally available for cancer or any other disease unless its source can be monopolised or its processing patented. No matter how safe and effective it may be, and no matter how many people are benefited, it will forever be relegated to the category of 'unproven' therapies. As such, freely available cures from nature will always be illegal to prescribe, to promote, and in many cases even to use."[45]

In opposition to the incessant drive by big business to dominate our health choices, Dr Matthias Rath provides another non-populist summary of the primary ethics of the merchant's house:

"Throughout the 20th century, the pharmaceutical industry has been constructed by investors, the goal being to replace effective but non-patentable natural remedies with mostly ineffective but patentable and highly profitable pharmaceutical drugs. The very nature of the pharmaceutical industry is to make money from ongoing diseases. Like other industries, the pharmaceutical industry tries to expand its market - that is, to maintain ongoing diseases and to find new diseases for their drugs. Prevention and cure of

---

[45] Griffin, G Edward, *World Without Cancer*, American Media Publications, Los Angeles, 1997

diseases damage pharmaceutical business and the eradication of common diseases threatens its very existence.

Therefore the pharmaceutical industry fights the eradication of any disease at all costs. The pharmaceutical industry itself is the main obstacle, why today's most widespread diseases are further expanding, including heart attacks, strokes, cancer, high blood pressure, diabetes, osteoporosis and many others. Pharmaceutical drugs are not intended to cure diseases. According to health insurers, over 24,000 pharmaceutical drugs are currently marketed and prescribed without any proven therapeutic value.[46] According to medical doctors' associations, the known, dangerous side-effects of pharmaceutical drugs have become the fourth leading cause of death after heart attacks, cancer and strokes.[47]

Millions of people and patients around the world are defrauded twice: A major portion of their income is used to finance the exploding profits of the pharmaceutical industry. In return, they are offered a medicine that does not even cure."[48]

More vested interests

In an eye-opening book entitled *Reclaiming our Health: Exploding the Medical Myth and Embracing the Source of True Healing*, author John Robbins has collated some interesting statistics:

The Cancer Industry
Percentage of cancer patients whose lives are reliably saved by chemotherapy - 3%

Evidence to show that, for the majority of cancers, chemotherapy exerts a significant positive influence on survival or quality of life - none

Percentage of oncologists who said that if they developed cancer they would not participate in chemotherapy trials due to "the

---

[46] *AOK Magazine*, April 1998
[47] *Journal of the American Medical Association*, 15th April 1998
[48] Opening statement on European Directive on Vitamin Supplements
www.drrath.com

ineffectiveness of chemotherapy and its unacceptable degree of toxicity" - 75%

Percentage of people with cancer in the United States who receive chemotherapy - 75%

Company that accounts for nearly half the chemotherapy sales in the world - Bristol-Meyers Squibb

Chairman of the Board, Bristol-Meyers Squibb - Richard L Gelb

Richard L Gelb's other job - Vice-Chairman, Memorial Sloan-Kettering Cancer Center

Director, Bristol-Meyers Squibb - James D Robinson III

James D Robinson III's other job - Chairman of the Board, Memorial Sloan-Kettering Cancer Center

Director, Ivax, Inc. Chemotherapeutics - Samuel Broder

Samuel Broder's other job (until 1995) - Executive Director, the National Cancer Institute.[49]

Organised medical crime
Dr Richard Schulze has spent many years speaking out against the pharmaceutical cartels and promoting personal responsibility in healthcare. One of his more famous sayings is *"Getting well is easy, it's the getting sick that takes years of constant, dedicated, hard work."* When he was 11, his father died in his arms of a massive heart attack. At 14, his mother also died of a heart attack. They were both only 55 years old. At 16 years of age, Richard was diagnosed with a genetic incurable heart deformity.

After curing himself of this so-called incurable disease through changes in his lifestyle (and no surgery), he set out on a mission to help

---

[49] Robbins, John, *Reclaiming our Health: Exploding the Medical Myth and Embracing the Source of True Healing*, Kramer Publications, 1998

others. Schulze had first-hand experience of being in the clutches of the orthodoxy and determined to set out to do something about alerting the wider world to some of its perils. Dr Schulze now travels the world, delivering his message:

"Over 200 years ago, Ben Rush, who signed the Constitution of the United States, warned that we needed to include a medical freedom clause in the Constitution. He said if we didn't it was likely that one group of doctors would monopolise healthcare by passing legislation to outlaw other types of doctors and systems of medicine.

This is exactly what happened. Over the last 80 years, organised medical groups and pharmaceutical companies, using lawyers, bribes, lobbyists, insurance companies and the strong arm of the Food and Drug Administration, have been very busy. They have corrupted elected officials to pass laws to remove any competition. They have crushed Natural Doctors, Natural Medicine and Self-Care. Their goal is to monopolise healthcare and make us dependent on medical doctors and pharmaceutical drugs. It almost worked!

We have watched them pass more and more laws restricting our rights. They have made many healing herbs, foods and even nutrients illegal. Natural health professionals who flourished a few decades ago are now barred by law to practise, and natural doctors, holistic healers, health food store-owners and even family members of the sick have been arrested and jailed for using natural remedies. If you disagree with your doctor regarding the medical treatment of your children, they can be taken away from you, put in a foster home, and you can be arrested for endangering the health and welfare of your child.

There are many people who are jailed every year, put there for disagreeing with medical doctors and their policies. Organised medical crime has gone so far, they have outlawed words for other health professionals to use, such as 'Diagnose' and 'Cure'. Just by using these words you can be arrested for practising medicine without a license." [50]

---

[50] Dr Schulze's Natural Healing Crusade: www.whale.to/v/shulze1.html

It seems that the delivery system of 21st century conventional healthcare is being bought and taught to think of treatment and prevention of disease in pharmaceutical terms only. The current move by the European Parliament to restrict the nutritional supplement market is a case in point. In its sights are over 300 vitamins, minerals, herbs and other nutrients, whose sales they are seeking to streamline and bring under their own jurisdiction. All this under the guise of *wanting to protect the public from harm.*

The following text is taken from an article exploring the potential ramifications of this move:

"Imagine dropping by your favourite health food store to find it boarded up and out of business. So you go around to your local drug-mart to pick up some vitamin C, but the only dosage on the shelf is ridiculously low. The druggist informs you that 60mg is now the maximum dosage available without a prescription. So if you've been taking a mega-dosage of vitamin C to help fight heart disease or build up your immunity against cancer, you'll have to find a doctor willing to prescribe that dosage - you're no longer free to decide on your own how much of this natural vitamin you want to take.

Sounds like a nightmare? It gets worse.

Imagine that all of this is the result of new legislation imposed by lawmakers with direct ties to pharmaceutical companies - powerful companies that will use the law to create an enormous new source of profits. Now that's a real nightmare. But what makes it truly nightmarish is that, incredibly, it will soon become a reality in the United Kingdom and most of Europe - if the global pharmaceutical industry has its way." [51]

A number of health organisations are currently spearheading the fight against the pharmaceutical industry and various monopolies, as they seek to legislate against our free choice of natural nutrients. If this legislation is passed, it will directly affect **YOU** in many ways. Positive moves are afoot to thwart their attempts and a website address is

---

[51] Thompson, Jenny, "Euro Parliament Classifies Vitamins as Drugs - US Next?" Health Sciences Institute, 29th April, 2002 at: www.rense.com/general24/drgs.htm

included at the end of this book to enable you to find out more about this directive and register your protest quickly and easily.

Those cancer breakthroughs!

Sixty horses wedged in chimney!
"The story to fit this sensational headline has not turned up yet."
J B Morton

Interpreting the cancer headlines

Aside from the politicking and big business string-pulling taking place behind the scenes, our minds are also being washed with the constant froth of unfounded, emotive, headlines. **Breakthrough at UCLA!** *... yes, but with mice.* **It's in the genes!** *... another £5 million NOW will help us to isolate the gene in 2010 - perhaps.* **Excitement at latest findings!** *Buoyant opening paragraph, descending into the usual mixture of hope extinguished by caution and the obligatory appeal to the pocket.* **Cancer vaccine close!** *Yes, and close since 1976 actually.[52] But please, continue to give generously, because next time, it could be you!*

Some notable and recent examples of cancer hyperbole in the news now follow. Note the amounts of money involved, the toxicity of the treatments, and the lack of real, concrete hope in all the reports, despite the glowing headlines.

New Drug Helps Prevent Breast Tumours

BARCELONA, Spain - Recent research indicates a new hormone-blocking drug works better than the standard medicine in preventing women with early-stage breast cancer from developing tumours in the healthy breast. However, others expressed concern that the women taking Arimidex had more bone fractures than those taking Tamoxifen - an indication the new drug accelerates bone loss. "Putting women in a situation where they've got no oestrogen will just lead to skeletal collapse. Ten years of that is going to be seriously damaging," said prominent breast cancer scientist Sir Richard Peto, a professor of epidemiology at Oxford University who was not involved

---

[52] In 1971, Richard Nixon declared 'War on Cancer' and the National Cancer Institute announced that a vaccine against cancer would be available by 1976. *In These Times*, 8th-15th August 1992

in the study. "It's pretty squalid, so you can't really go long-term on something that's going to involve that." However, Coates and Peto said it may be possible to overcome that problem by giving non-oestrogen, bone-building supplements.[53]

Apart from the minor problem of skeletal collapse, isn't this just fantastic news?

British biotech company BioVex is using a genetically-altered version of the herpes simplex virus (HSV) to develop two products that may help beat a variety of cancers. BioVex was launched in 1999 by Professor David Latchman and Dr Robert Coffin, both herpes experts, with $20 million in funding. It has since formed partnerships with the drug companies Aventis and AstraZeneca. And in July 2001, it received $14 million in second-round funding.

[Spokesperson] Astley-Sparke says it will seek about $22 million in additional funds late this year. While the majority of products fail clinical trials, Astley-Sparke says the company is confident because the "scientific rationale behind these products is exceptionally strong." Still, he adds, success remains "a big if" at this early stage. Should these remedies win approval, the financial rewards would be great. Both products could have market values worth billions of dollars. While that would give BioVex's investors something to cheer about, it would give countless cancer patients something much more valuable — hope."[54]

$Billions resting on yet more 'ifs' and 'maybes'.

Genes Spotted That May Turn Breast Cancer Metastatic: *Scientists at Baylor College of Medicine have made the first steps in identifying a group of genes which may be involved in the progression of breast cancer from non-invasive to invasive. "We are at least a few years away from actually having something to translate directly to patient care," Professor Allred said. "If we do find*

---

[53] Associated Press, "New Drug Helps Prevent Breast Tumours", Thursday, 21st March 2002

[54] *Time*, "The Virus Hunters", 12th April 2002
www.time.com/time/europe/digital/sotw/0,9868,195030,00.html

genes responsible for tumour invasion, and if we can develop treatments to correct or prevent defects in them, then we have a chance to prevent lethal invasive breast cancer." [55]

Always a few years away, and always the reader is reminded just how lethal the foe and how necessary and valuable the work. The role of the geneticist in the fight against cancer is examined in more detail a little later. It's safe to say, though, that as far as conventional cancer treatments are concerned, the world is still waiting for a breakthrough that actually amounts to anything. So, with little to shout about, yet so much money being spent, where does all the money go?

Research and development

One major expenditure in all scientific pursuits is the research and development budget. Top drug companies are reported to spend, on average, about 20 percent of their revenues on research and development.[56] Cancer drug manufacturer Bristol-Myers Squibb spent over $2 billion in 2001 on R&D.[57] Every day, cancer laboratories across the world are issuing research papers to the major media outlets in support of products and product development. But do these papers always reflect pure science? With so much financial return expected on each product and with so many independent research institutions now dependent upon outside investment, it begs the question, how many of these institutions are really that independent? And who is actually funding them? To get a clearer picture, it seems that a visit to a few cancer laboratories is in order. What goes on there, I wonder?

---

[55] "Genes Spotted That May Turn Breast Cancer Metastatic", *Daily University Science News*, 21st March 2002
http://unisci.com/stories/20021/0321023.htm
[56] Tanouye, E, "Drug dependency: US has developed an expensive habit: now, how to pay for it?" *Wall Street Journal*, 16th November 1998
[57] Facts about BMS, Pharmaceutical Research Institute:
www.bms.com/research/data/factsx.html

Down at the cancer lab

"Everyone should know that most cancer research is largely a fraud and that the major cancer research organisations are derelict in their duties to the people who support them." **Linus Pauling**

In this chapter, we look at a number of issues relating to conventional cancer research. In all branches of science, most 'facts' become established as such only after a lengthy process involving input and financial support from various interested parties and allied social groups. Scientists are rarely free from outside influence. In seeking a benchmark for evaluating any scientific data that comes our way, the following advice is timeless:

"Science and research must be studied in the context of all the interested parties involved. The questions centre on determining the relative weight of the various allies in the 'fact-creating' process - e.g. funding bodies, businesses, departments of state, professions and other scientists. In analysing scientific debates, <u>one should always ask what social, institutional and political interests lie behind often apparently 'neutral' and 'technical' knowledge claims.</u>" [58]

Science critic Mel Bartley writes about the attempts made to isolate scientists from any external influences which might taint the purity and objectivity of their work. He points out that this is very difficult:

"This isolation exists only insofar as other scientists are constantly busy recruiting investors, gaining interest and then convincing people. The pure scientists are like helpless nestlings, while the adults are busy building the nest and feeding them." [59]

---

[58] University of Manchester Institute of Science & Technology (UMIST), *Research Methodology*, course handout, 1994

[59] Bartley, Mel, *Sociology of Health and Illness*, 12th April 1990, as featured in University of Manchester Institute of Science & Technology (UMIST) research methodology course handout, 1994

The cancer industry researchers have been very well fed for the last 50-60 years. But what do we have to show for it? Dr John Bailor spent 20 years on the staff of the US National Cancer Institute and was editor of its journal on cancer. He stated:

"My overall assessment is that the national cancer program must be judged a qualified failure.... The five-year survival statistics of the American Cancer Society are very misleading. They now count things that are not cancer, and, because we are able to diagnose at an earlier stage of the disease, patients falsely appear to live longer. Our whole cancer research in the past 20 years has been a total failure. More people over 30 are dying from cancer than ever before." [60]

Fraud at high level

In the seventeen years since these words were spoken, little has changed. So, where does all the money go which is allocated to all those cancer research programs? Quite literally, $£billions upon billions have been spent over the years and with nothing tangible to show for it, except a history replete with mismanagement, entrenched scientific error and fraudulent practice. Some of this fraud is being perpetrated by the most senior cancer laboratories in the world.

Our first visit is to the laboratory of Dr Robert Gallo, senior cancer researcher at Bethesda Labs in Maryland during the 1970's. Gallo had been charged with finding the virus that the orthodoxy believed lay behind cancer. In particular, Gallo was on the hunt for the virus supposedly responsible for leukaemia. His laboratory was being funded by the prestigious National Cancer Institute. The following condensed history of Gallo's highly paid quest to identify a virus for leukaemia paints a tragi-comic picture of leading-edge cancer research. Condensed from another Credence title, *World Without AIDS*, this introduction to Gallo's cancer laboratory will serve to instil a sense of caution in those who view scientific research as a purely 'neutral' pursuit.

---

[60] Dr Bailor, speaking at the Annual Meeting of the American Association for the Advancement of Science in May 1985, as quoted in Bette Overall's, "Animal Research Takes Lives - Humans and Animals BOTH Suffer", NZAVS, 1993, p.132

Gallo 'discovers' the leukaemia virus

In the belief that almost all disease was virus-driven, (it was Gallo himself who stated, *"Sometimes we virologists have a virus in search of a disease"*[61]) and after almost three years of 'experimentation' down at Bethesda Labs in Maryland, Dr Robert Gallo announced that he had isolated a virus responsible for leukaemia, which he named Human Leukaemia 23 or HL23V for short. Gallo reported his 'discovery' to the local scientific community and submitted a paper to *Science Magazine* which was published in January 1975.

Newspapers were quick to report on Gallo's 'breakthrough', but his peers questioned his claims, asking what culture he had used in which to grow the virus, how he had prepared it, and how he had gone about his experiments. Gallo would not reveal the chemistry of his culture, nor would he share the exact manner in which his virus had been isolated. Concerning the validation of scientific claims, Geoff Watts, author of *Pleasing the Patient*, reminds us of traditional scientific methodology:

> *"Researchers are required not only to publish their findings, but also to describe their method in sufficient detail to allow others to repeat the work. Indeed the repeatability of an experiment is one of the criteria by which scientists judge the claims of their peers."*[62]

Gallo's reluctance to conform to this reasonable scientific methodology served only to anger his peers. Their questions became more forcefully posed: *"Where's the leukaemia virus, Dr Gallo? And how did you preserve the cells?"*

Little fingers, little toes...
So that's where my donation goes!

With pressure mounting on Gallo to produce the necessary evidence to support his new virus, Gallo's fellow workers arrived at the lab one morning to find that the refrigerator containing the HL23V leukaemia virus and his secret culture, known only as WHE, had been

---

[61] Robert Gallo, quoted in "What if Everything You Thought You Knew About AIDS was Wrong?" AFFA Publications, 1999; see also Duesberg, Peter, *Inventing the AIDS Virus*, Regnery Press, 1996
[62] Watts, Geoff, *Pleasing the Patient*, Faber and Faber, 1992

mysteriously unplugged. Everything had now been ruined. Says Gallo of this unfortunate (but quite timely) disaster:

"We were screwed. We were only able to say, 'Honest, we had it!' and prove it to nobody."[63]

It was Robert Gallagher, a technician at Gallo's lab during this period, who later stated that they hadn't *actually* wrapped their hands around an *actual* virus; rather they had inferred its presence based on a number of intricate virological predictions.[64]

Popular medical literature of the day however made no mention of these 'minor' irregularities along the way, and credited Gallo with all the 'leukaemia breakthrough' headlines. And newspapers credit him with this discovery to this day, despite the fact that HL23V was declassified as a virus in 1980. As UK *Sunday Observer* reporter Robin Mackie blithely trotted out, *"Once a contender for the Nobel prize, for discovering the first human cancer-causing virus, Gallo...."* etc, etc.[65]

And what about Gallo's secret 'culture', known only as WHE? It was perhaps prudent of Gallo that he did not expand on its exact make-up. The initials WHE stand for 'whole human embryo'. Aborted whole foetuses, developed no further than the first three months, had various cell extractions performed upon them, the extracted cells forming the base composite for the melted HL23V. Readers comforting themselves that foetuses not exceeding the first three months are probably just underdeveloped cell matter may be shocked to discover otherwise, as the following extract from *Love Your Unborn Neighbour* reveals:

"By the sixth week from fertilisation, tiny fingers appear, followed within days by toes. At the same time the eyes develop the lens and retina and the eyelids begin to appear. Brainwaves can also be detected. At seven weeks the child has its own fingerprints, the outer ear is present and the inner ear, with its hearing and balancing mechanisms, is well established.

---

[63] Hall, Stephen, *A Commotion In The Blood*, Little, Brown and Co., 1997
[64] Ibid.
[65] *Observer Newspapers*, Resurrection of the AIDS Pioneer, 22nd December, 1996

At twelve weeks the child's features become more defined. The unborn baby can open or close the lips, wrinkle the forehead, raise the eyebrows and turn the head. The baby's sex is easy to determine. The baby measures about 90mm and weighs 45 grams and she is also sensitive to touch."[66]

This is just one example of where <u>our</u> cancer research money has been going. Three years' lucrative funding and thousands of man-hours later and finally... a cancer virus that existed only by the word of Dr Gallo. And now it had melted!

Another dud

In 1975, after more 'experiments' in the search for the leukaemia virus, Gallo informed his peers that his lab had discovered the recipe for T-cell growth culture. His peers abruptly sat up. If this were true, then many conventional cancer scientists believed this would represent a massive step towards ending the war against cancer. The administration of a strain of this factor in the patient could promote an absolute proliferation of killer T-cells, which would then make short shrift of any cancerous cells.

This time Gallo did share his recipe for human T-cell growth factor with the scientific community, submitting his research for full publication in *Science*, March 1976. Gallo subsequently received hundreds of calls from immunologists, complaining that they couldn't get the growth factor to work.[67]

Another peer-review dud.

Den of thieves

What of Gallo's team who were supporting him in this quest? What of their credentials? Lab associate Syed Zaki Salahuddin was convicted of using Gallo's laboratory credit card to purchase supplies from the NIH central stores - supplies which he then spirited out of the workplace in order to set up his own research laboratory. Having established his own lab, Salahuddin then installed his wife as director.

---

[66] "Earliest Feelings Help to Develop the Senses", *New Scientist*, 7th May 1987. Quoted in *Love Your Unborn Neighbour*, SPUC Publications, London, 1994
[67] Hall, Stephen, op. cit.

Running alongside this venture, Salahuddin also arranged for various 'private interest' items to be manufactured, all within Gallo's own laboratory, which were then sold to outside competitors.[68]

Dr Dharam Ablashi, a fellow worker at Gallo's laboratory, was recruited as a sales rep for this clandestine outfit. Salahuddin was ordered to repay $12,000 and complete 1,750 hours' community service. Gallo's second-in-command at the lab, Prem Sarin, would later find himself on trial for directing $25,000 into his own account which should have been spent hiring a lab technician. In his 'Lab Rat' article, Seth Roberts summarises the early years thus:

"Gallo's lab has been described by past and present employees as a 'den of thieves' and as being 'full of mediocrities'. In its quantity of intrigue and capricious purges, it resembles a 'medieval Italian town', says one former employee. He adds, 'I'm surprised somebody hasn't killed someone there.'"[69]

Today, despite Robert Gallo's infamous record (of which only a very small glimpse is afforded here), this gentleman is now Senior Director of The Institute of Human Virology at the University of Maryland Biotechnology Institute. He has been accepted back into the conventional fold, despite being indicted on two counts of scientific misconduct by Public Health Service's Office of Research Integrity (ORI).[70]

Same old story

And now at the Bethesda, Maryland laboratories, some 20 years later, it seems that exactly the same kind of leukaemia fraud is being perpetrated, as this report *from Physician's Weekly* indicates:

After Research Fraud: MD? Bethesda - *A genetics student's alleged fabrication could cost his PhD, but he may get an MD. The University of Michigan confirms that it is investigating Amitav*

---

[68] Oostram, Neenyah, *New York Native*, 14th August 1989, Issue 330

[69] www.virusmyth.com, December 1999

[70] A full report on the depths to which Gallo and his lab descended is found in *World Without AIDS* – a detailed expose of the fraud surrounding Gallo's supposed discovery of HIV. See section entitled 'Other Book Titles by Credence'

Hajra, a candidate in its MD-PhD program, who reportedly confessed to faking data in five published papers on the genetics of acute myelocytic leukaemia." [71]

Don't be surprised by laboratory fraud

Editor of the *British Medical Journal*, Richard Smith, presented a lecture recently, entitled *Fraud in Medical Research*. He made several relevant points:

> ➢ We should not be surprised by medical fraud. After all, it happens in other walks of life.
> ➢ By its very nature, the true extent of medical and scientific fraud is difficult to calculate.
> ➢ Most authors of studies in medical journals have conflicts of interest, yet these are disclosed in less than 1% of cases.
> ➢ Most countries do not have a coherent approach to tackling scientific fraud.
> ➢ There must be a coherent approach, in order to avoid public collapse in confidence in medical research. [72]

Writing in the UK *Guardian* on Thursday, 7th February 2002, Sarah Bosely reports that:

"Scientists are accepting large sums of money from drug companies in order to put their names to articles endorsing new medicines that they have not written - a growing practice that some fear is putting scientific integrity in jeopardy." [73]

The protectors of human health and well-being are being paid what to think and say. And as for the line, *"some fear..."*, should we not <u>all</u> fear that this behaviour is jeopardising the integrity of medicine? Said one physician in the article, *"What day is it today? I'm just working out what drug I'm supporting today."*

---

[71] "After Research Fraud: MD?" *Physician's Weekly*, 2nd December 1996. Full story at http://www.physweekly.com/archive/96/12_02_96/itn3.html

[72] Smith, Richard, "Fraud in Medical Research", lecture given, September 2001, http://bmj.com/misc/talks/fraud/sld001.htm 2001

[73] Full story, described as Professional Prostitution, at http://www.guardian.co.uk/medicine/story/0,11381,646078,00.html

This from Independent Newspapers:

False scientific research endangering the public: Doctors *are fabricating research results to win grants and advance their careers, but the medical establishment is failing to protect the public from the menace of these scientific frauds, a committee of medical editors said yesterday. Eighty cases of fraudulent research have been detected in the past four years, and 30 have been investigated in the past year. In some cases, institutions have covered up wrongdoing to protect reputations.*[74]

A devastating episode

A *Los Angeles Times* article detailed the exposure of a widespread breast cancer fraud in South Africa, which, by the time it had been uncovered, had allowed SAR 5 billion to be spent on a worthless medical intervention and had allowed around 30,000 women to be unnecessarily treated.

A Dr Bezwoda had falsely presented his results and made a number of other 'remarkable' errors in his research. He also carried out trials without approval from his university's ethics committee for research on humans. UK medical newspaper *The Lancet* described Dr Bezwoda's claims as a *"devastating episode of research fraud"*. Dr Bezwoda's dismissal was announced by the university's vice-chancellor, Mr Colin Bundy, who said:

"The university regrets this deplorable breach of ethics. We also extend a heartfelt apology to the patients involved in this research.... We will do everything possible to prevent this shocking ethical breach of individual rights of our people from ever occurring again."[75]

Convenient fictions

Who says these breaches will not occur again? Fraud, by its very nature, is largely immeasurable. The perfect fraud is the fraud that is

---

[74] *Independent Newspapers*, 13th December 2000

[75] *Sydney Morning Herald*, 13th March 2000; see also "Disappointment and Deceit in High-Dose Chemotherapy Trials", *Breast Cancer Action Newsletter*, May - June 2000: www.bcaction.org/Pages/SearchablePages/2000Newsletters/Newsletter059A.html

not detected! We have good reason to wonder what backroom research fraud might be the foundation for the qualified medical opinion being issued by our earnest oncology physician on the front line.

Dr Brian Martin has spent many years researching scientific and medical fraud. In his paper *Scientific Fraud and the Power Structure of Science*, he states:

"Another common misrepresentation of research work is exaggeration of its quality, progress and social importance. This is almost essential for a successful scientific career. A modest and honest grant application stands little chance of success: the applicant, to obtain money, must puff up the quality and importance of previous work and give a highly unrealistic assessment of the likely results of funding future work - or, as is common, request money to carry out research which actually has been completed. Most grant applications are convenient fictions.

The same applies to annual reports, media stories and other material prepared for general distribution. 'Breakthroughs' abound. Research relevant to a 'cure for cancer' covers the gamut of biological science. The quality of research is never honestly assessed. (When did you last read an annual report reporting mediocre research?) Honesty in research grants, annual reports and media reports stands about as much chance as honesty in advertising, because this sort of (mis)representation of science is, indeed, a form of advertising." [76]

Given the gloss

The pharmaceutical industry spends $13 billion per year marketing directly to doctors.[77] According to its annual report, drug company Pfizer spent 39.2% of its revenues on marketing and administration in 1999.[78] Pharmacia & Upjohn is reported to have spent about the

[76] Martin, Brian, "Scientific Fraud and the Power Structure of Science", *Prometheus*, Vol.10, No.1, June 1992, pp.83-98,
www.uow.edu.au/arts/sts/bmartin/pubs/92prom.html
[77] PR Newswire, 21st May, 2002:
www.prnewswire.com/cgi-bin/stories.pl?ACCT=104&STORY=/www/story/05-21-2002/0001732801&EDATE=
[78] Pfizer Annual Report, 1999

same.[79] Much of this money will have been spent on turning data into glossy brochure form. In 1999, Americans saw an average of nine prescription drug television advertisements a day, portraying the dual message of a pill for every ill and an ill for every pill.[80]

Dr Marcia Angell, a long-standing contributor to the *New England Journal of Medicine*, is ideally placed to caution us against reading too much into the corporate gloss. She reminds us of the commercial realities central to the drug business:

"The industry depicts these huge [marketing] expenditures as serving an educational function. It contends that doctors and the public learn about new and useful drugs in this way. Unfortunately, many doctors do indeed rely on drug company representatives and promotional materials to learn about new drugs, and much of the public learns from direct-to-consumer advertising. But to rely on the drug companies for unbiased evaluations of their products makes about as much sense as relying on beer companies to teach us about alcoholism."[81]

All manner of
senseless research funded

Perhaps one of the motivating factors behind the falsification of trial results, etc., is because there is actually very little conventional progress being made on disease, especially in the war on cancer. The pressure to *be seen* to be advancing in this war is intense. Echoing Dr John Bailor's comments, a 1986 report in the *New England Journal of Medicine* assessed progress against cancer in the United States during the years 1950 to 1982 and concluded that the overall death rate had increased substantially since 1950:

"The main conclusion we draw is that some 35 years of intense effort focused largely on improving treatment must be judged a qualified failure."

---

[79] "Drug-makers reap profits on tax-backed research", *New York Times*, 23rd April, 2000
[80] "Post-Modern Medicine", http://bmj.com/cgi/content/full/324/7342/0/i
[81] Angell, Marcia, "The Pharmaceutical Industry - To Whom is it Accountable?" *New England Journal of Medicine*, Vol.342, No.25, 22nd June 2000

The report further concluded that *"... we are losing the war against cancer,"* and argued for a shift in emphasis towards prevention, if there is to be substantial progress.[82]

Professor Michael Baum, Professor of Surgery at University College of London, recently stated:

"Mortality has barely changed since 1971. About one in four people in Britain now die of cancer. The incidence of most cancers is increasing."[83]

Mice today, straggly beards tomorrow?

Because of the pressure to *be seen to be advancing*, all manner of conventional avenues are explored, and all are handsomely funded. One wonders what amount of grant money was allocated to the following line of enquiry, taken from the UK's leading cancer publication, The *British Journal of Cancer*:

Does a Virus in Mice Cause Human Breast Cancer? *Evidence that breast cancer may develop from a virus and be transmitted from mice to humans was presented in an article for the British Journal of Cancer by Richard Sage, adjunct professor of biology, and two other scientists. The authors found that the highest incidence of human breast cancer worldwide occurs in countries where 'mus domesticus' (a type of house mouse) is the resident native or introduced species.*[84]

Being that mice are found everywhere, why not spend a great deal of time and money chasing down the link between breast cancer and the presence of the housefly, the string vest, straggly beards - manhole covers even.

---

[82] Ryan Robert, "Cancer Research - a Super Fraud?" ibid.

[83] *Daily Telegraph*, 14th March 2002

[84] "Breast cancer incidence highest in the range of one species of house mouse, mus domesticus", *British Journal of Cancer*, 82, pp.446-451, 1st January 2000

Stranglehold on research

Reinforcing the point that neither genuine cure nor genuine prevention of cancer is really being sought in these laboratories, Professor James Bennett gave a lecture to the Annual Cancer Control Society:

"Now, let's turn to the issue of research.... Part of the problem is the role that the Cancer Society plays and other health charities in their respective disease in the research process. They have a stranglehold on research. When the American Cancer Society gives money for research, the people to whom it gives money are not looking for causes of and cures for cancer. That's not the purpose of the grant. The Cancer Society gives seed grants - in other words, money to its favoured researchers, in order for its researchers to get the real bucks from the federal government or from private pharmaceutical companies. Because of this, its favoured researchers have an inside track. It's very competitive getting money." [85]

In a report entitled "Medical Demystification", Dr Sidney Singer describes conventional medical research quite unflatteringly:

"Researchers are like prostitutes. They work for grant money. If there is no money for the projects they are personally interested in, they go where there is money. Their incomes come directly from their grants, not from the universities. And they want to please the granting source, so as to obtain more grants in the future. Their careers depend on it." [86]

Does this mean that all cancer research labs are a hotbed of purposeful mischief and warped intent? Not at all. As researcher G Edward Griffin explains:

"Let's face it, these people die from cancer like everybody else.... it's obvious that these people are not consciously holding back a control for cancer. It does mean, however, that the cartel's medical

---

[85] "Unhealthy Charities, Hazardous to Your Health and Wealth": www.whale.to/cancer/bennett.html

[86] Singer, Sydney, "Medical Demystification Report", Vol.1 No.1, p.5, Medical Demystification Crusade, 1992, CA, USA

monopoly has created a climate of bias in our educational system, in which scientific truth often is sacrificed to vested interests.... If the money is coming from drug companies, or indirectly from drug companies, the impetus is in the direction of drug research.

That doesn't mean somebody blew the whistle and said "Hey, don't research nutrition!" It just means that nobody is financing nutrition research. So it is a bias where scientific truth often is obscured by vested interest." [87]

Dr Brian Martin makes a similar point:

"It could be said that the viewpoints of most scientists are not so much biased as limited: they are willing to do narrow research work whose context is set by the powerful patrons of science. The bias comes from the context, not from the conscious intent of the scientist." [88]

Conventional cancer research
Consistently narrow and imprecise?

By its very meaning, 'narrow research' is a misnomer. The two words are incompatible. Research by definition must be as wide and broad as possible, never narrow. If we devote ourselves to narrow research only, no matter how exact we might be in our methodology, we stand a very good chance of arriving at an incorrect conclusion. As W Deutscher so succinctly reminds us:

"We concentrate on consistency without much concern of what it is we are being consistent about, or whether we are consistently right or wrong. As a consequence, we have been learning a great deal about how to follow an incorrect course with the maximum of precision." [89]

Furthermore, scientists who restrict themselves to such 'narrow' research are unable to fulfil the full meaning of the term 'scientific

---

[87] Griffin, G Edward, *The Politics of Cancer*, audio cassette, American Media, 1975
[88] Martin, Brian, "Scientific Fraud and the Power Structure of Science", op. cit.
[89] Deutscher, W, *Research Methodology*, op. cit.

conclusion', adequately defined by research critics Elwood and Gallacher as follows:

"Scientific conclusions are arrived at after subjecting the available data to the most severe scrutiny and impartial criticism so as to determine those interpretations of the data that may be made on purely rational grounds." [90]

The current narrow focus by the conventional cancer industry on the gene and virus is not subjecting the wider issues of cancer to *severe scrutiny*. And the treatments offered so far fall way outside the bounds of rationality.

Personal responsibility

Inclusion of all of the above texts on scientific and medical fraud should not be interpreted as a calculated effort to undermine or dismiss scientific research altogether. Far from it. Many blessings have come about for society as a result of rigorous, uncorrupted enquiry. The texts are included merely to illustrate the fact that there may well be a very different story behind the glossily referenced paper supporting the information and/or medication your physician is prescribing for your particular condition. It is at this point that personal responsibility for healthcare takes on a new dimension.

Gavin Philips from CancerInform has a pointed attitude towards educating ourselves in the 21st century:

"The government and corporate America want to herd us all along their path and pump us full of their lies using third rate propaganda churned out by the mainstream media. We've been conditioned into allowing the idiot box and corporate public relations gurus to mold our buying habits, "news" perceptions and fill us with their advertising junk.

They are not just selling toothpaste, but mindsets as well, and the message is, "Don't worry, don't question us, we've done all the research (scientists & 'experts' $paid$ for opinions) keep all your decision-making to a minimum; BUY THIS, BELIEVE THAT! We'll do

---

[90] Ibid.

57

all the thinking, you just lie on the couch, credit card and brain at the ready to receive our junk data." [91]

In seeking to assuage a restless electorate, UK Prime Minister Tony Blair once gave a promise on education. He said that, from now on, his priorities were *"Education, education, education."* [92] (Of course, that hasn't happened.) But if there is a parallel to be drawn in this cancer story, it is that our priorities must be *'Investigation, investigation, investigation!'* When our lives are in the hands of another, as is the case with cancer medicine especially, it is no good trusting that *'they know best.'* They may not! Doubtless, there are genuine people at work within the conventional cancer institutions, earnestly seeking the answers to cancer. But when we weigh their lack of progress against the amounts of money spent so far, countless heads would have rolled long ago if this abysmal record belonged to any other public service.

The kindly gent

What then should our reaction be towards the kindly gent on the street corner, holding out his cancer charity tin? The Campaign Against Fraudulent Medical Research advises:

"The next time you are asked to donate to a cancer organisation, bear in mind that your money will be used to sustain an industry which has been deemed by many eminent scientists as a qualified failure and by others, as a complete fraud." [93]

Now that we have looked at where some of the money has been going, let's examine the institutions responsible for collecting the money.

Our money.

---

[91] Gavin Phillips, CancerInform: www.cancerinform.freewebsites.com/PCA.html
[92] The election starts here, *BBC News*, 17th February 2001
http://news.bbc.co.uk/hi/english/education/features/mike_baker/newsid_1174000/1174456.stm
[93] Ryan, Robert, "Cancer Research - A Super-Fraud?"
www.worldnewsstand.net/health/cancer2.htm

The cancer charities

*"All right, so I like spending money! But
name one other extravagance!"* **Max Kaufmann**

Martin Walker is the author of a book entitled *Dirty Medicine*.
Walker argues that such is the level of vested interests involved in
cancer charity infrastructure, that cancer research charities are part of
the problem, not the solution. Writing in the *Ecologist*, Walker reveals
some unacceptable business ties and practices behind the 'acceptable
face' of UK cancer charity interests.

*"There are over 600 cancer charities in the UK, but the three big
players – the heart of the cancer establishment – are the ICRF
(Imperial Cancer Research Fund) the CRC (Cancer Research
Campaign) and ICR (Institute of Cancer Research). They determine
the public perception of what cancer is and what can be done about it.*

*Yet all are essentially unaccountable, steeped in conservatism and
privilege, which class and power have bestowed upon the top echelons
of the British medical profession. The power of these charities is
demonstrated by how effectively they control public access to the facts
about cancer. There is no independent public review of the work of the
cancer charities, which allows them to present their own version of
events - and they do.*

*Both the CRC and the ICRF hold substantial reserves – in the mid
1990's, the ICRF's tied assets stood at £90M – most of which are
invested in industry. Even as late as the mid-90's, it was revealed that
the ICRF was 'inadvertently' investing in the tobacco industry. The
investment portfolio of the cancer charities is not publicly accessible
and consequently it is not possible for supporters to ensure that
investments have been made only in companies which are not implicit
in the production of carcinogens."* [94]

---

[94] Walker, Martin, "Your Money and Your Life?" *The Ecologist*, October 2000

Walker suggests that a good way to start rectifying conflicts of interests within the cancer charities would be to call for an immediate program of research into industrial carcinogens. He suggests that anybody who has anything to do with cancer research should be vetted for any links to carcinogen-producing companies and pharmaceutical and/or biotech industries. Walker also stipulates that cancer research scientists should spend a major part of their time researching non-chemical, non-genetic treatments and examining the environmental causes of cancer.

But this is not happening. Continues Walker:

"Apart from the continual propaganda about cigarettes, there is no public discourse about the chemical or environmental causes of cancer. And it is unlikely that the public will ever be informed about them while cancer research in Britain is dominated by a cabal of unaccountable doctors, scientists and surgeons - a 'cancer club' which garners some of its funding and much of its philosophy from an industrial infrastructure which independent scientists believe is itself a cause of rising cancer rates." [95]

A cabal? What is the level of vested interests in the average 'philanthropic' drug company? And what ties are there to the various charities? Readers will find the following information very interesting.

The board at GSK

Leading cancer drug manufacturer GlaxoSmithKline states that its global mission is to improve the quality of human life. Externally however, its board members hold senior positions with corporations that do not have mankind's best interests at heart, including directorships of alcohol, tobacco and chemical-pollutant conglomerates and various companies promoting high sugar and fat diets – all, to some degree or another, linked to human carcinogens.

At the time of writing, GSK's chairman (until 20th May 2002), Richard Sykes, is a director of Rio Tinto, a mining company with an appalling human rights record, continually exposing its workers to

---

[95] Ibid. Thanks to *The Ecologist* for permission to reproduce Martin Walker's article in full, found at the back of this book.

toxic fumes, lead, arsenic and radioactive materials, leading to cancers and other serious illness.[96] GSK deputy chairman, Roger Hurn, along with fellow directors Ian Prosser and John Young, hold key positions at chief pollutants ICI, BP Amoco and Chevron respectively. Another GSK director, Donald McHenry, resides on the board at Coca-Cola and Paul Allaire serves on the board of 'artery-sludge' giant Sara Lee. Coca-Cola is currently facing a lawsuit over its products' alleged ability to trigger type-2 diabetes, while Sara Lee features in Multi-National Monitor's "Top 10 Worst Corporations of 2001".[97]

Recently retired from the GSK board is Derek Bonham, a director at Imperial Tobacco. GSK made over £470M in 2001 from various 'stop smoking' aids. Their new product, Zyban, has recently been approved by NICE, despite it being linked to multiple deaths and injuries.[98] Fellow GSK board member Christopher Hogg, the soon-to-be appointed Chairman of GSK, was, until only recently, a director of alcohol giant Allied Domecq. His colleague at GSK is the aforementioned Ian Prosser, who is also chairman of Bass Breweries. Maybe these two gentlemen are perfectly positioned to advise GSK on how best to pitch Zofran, GSK's wonder drug to 'cure' alcoholism?[99]

---

[96] Rio Tinto: Associating with the wrong company
www.corpwatch.org/search/PSR.jsp
[97] "Corporations Behaving Badly: The Ten Worst Corporations of 2001", Russell Mokhiber and Robert Weissman http://63.111.165.25/01december/dec01corp1.html. This unflattering accolade was secured thanks to a Sara Lee management team that wilfully ignored listeria contamination at its Michigan meat-processing plant and allowed the continued production of thousands of poisonous hot dogs, culminating in at least twenty one deaths and one hundred serious injuries. At the hearing, an expert Michigan defence team, appropriately named Jenner and Block, brought new meaning to the terms 'misdemeanour' and 'technicality' and successfully 'blocked' all felony charges against Sara Lee, thus ensuring the continuation of its lucrative hot dog contract with the US Dept of Defense. For this multiple loss of life, Sara Lee was fined just $200,000.
[98] "Anti-smoking drug deaths triple" - The number of people who have died after taking the anti-smoking drug Zyban has more than tripled in a year, official figures show. By 10th January, 57 people had died following suspected adverse reactions to the drug, compared to 18 the same time last year, the Medicines Control Agency (MCA) found. 18th January 2002
http://news.bbc.co.uk/hi/english/health/newsid_1767000/1767758.stm
[99] http://www.drmirkin.com/morehealth/8572.html

GSK is also 'blessed' with the expertise of arms dealer Dr Jean Pierre Garnier, who sits on the board at United Technologies.[100] Most breathtaking of all perhaps is the fact that former executive director at GSK, Jeremy Strachan, has recently been appointed Secretary of the British Medical Association.[101]

This is a fairly representational snapshot of those who hold sway over conventional healthcare today. Another example would be the UK's premier cancer charity, Cancer Research UK, which states on their website under 'Corporate Partnerships':

"Our team has experience in developing high profile, commercially beneficial campaigns to suit the needs of our corporate partners, such as Duerr's, GlaxoSmithKline, Schroders and Tesco." [102]

The cancer club

The very people responsible for directing human health decisions with regard to cancer have key financial interests in tobacco, sugar, alcohol and pollution-causing industries – many of these products in themselves carcinogenic. These same people also have close ties with our supposedly independent cancer charities. As such, the following statement from the Cancer Research Fund, now known as Cancer Research UK, comes as no surprise – a statement which formed part of its public education document entitled *Preventing and Curing Cancer:*

"One of the biggest myths in recent years is that there is a cancer epidemic being caused by exposure to radiation, pollution, pesticides and food additives. The truth is that these factors have very little to do with the majority of cancers in this country. In fact food additives may even have a protective effect – particularly against stomach cancer." [103]

---

[100] Hughes, Solomon, "In Health and in Sickness", *The Ecologist*, October, 2001
[101] *BMA News*, 6th December 2000
[102] Cancer Research UK, "Corporate Partnerships" at http://www.cancerresearchuk.org/getinvolved/corporatepartnerships/workingtogether/causerelatedmarketing/
[103] "Cancer: Are The Experts Lying?" *The Ecologist*, March/April 1998

This statement attempts to protect petrochemicals, nuclear power, the synthetic food industry and other toxic concerns from carcinogenic enquiry. Protecting the likes of GSK perhaps?

Dying that they might live?

Writing in the UK's *Guardian*, George Monbiot says:

"Last year the Cancer Research Campaign predicted that cancer would be cured by 2050 as a result of new genetic technologies. Its website mentions pollution, but dismisses concerns with the claim that "experts think that only 5% of preventable cancer deaths may be linked to environmental factors." The CRC's 10-page press release on poverty and cancer blames inequalities in treatment for differing rates of death, but says nothing about pollution, even though the poor are far more likely to live beside dirty factories and toxic dumps than the rich.

Give them more money, the cancer charities claim, and they will find the magic formula which will save us all from a hideous death. But could it be possible that we are dying so that they might live?" [104]

Sleek cars and real estate

Across the pond to America and Professor James Bennett again:

"The American Cancer Society is an enormously wealthy organisation. It could pay every dime of its bills today and it would have over half a billion dollars in the bank, it could operate for approximately sixteen months without raising another dime from the American public. It holds immense wealth in the form of cash, certificates of deposits, stocks, bonds and particularly land and buildings. Just as one example, you can take a look at its Texas division. You wonder if it's a car dealership - it owns fifty-six automobiles. Or whether it's a real estate speculation company - it has fourteen parcels of raw land and seventeen office buildings. How

---

[104] Monbiot, George, "Purporting To Be Beating Cancer", *Guardian Newspapers*, 4th January 2001
http://society.guardian.co.uk/cancer/comment/0,8146,417727,00.html

raw land helps us find a cure for cancer or helps cancer victims is an enigma that I can't fathom." [105]

With the merger of the CRC and CRI into one larger UK charity, the Cancer Research website contains links to many large conventional institutions and continues to promote everything that is dangerous about conventional cancer treatment today.

So, what about the kindly gent with his tin?

For what it's worth, when it comes to deciding on whether or not to approach the kindly gent with his cancer charity tin, my philosophy is simple. Courtesy, a smile and a small donation (as much as it might gall on the inside!) is a small investment which usually opens the way for a productive conversation on orthodox fallibility and positive cancer treatment alternatives. At the very least, a website address can be written down on the sticker he's just given me which can then be returned to his own lapel! ☺

That the orthodoxy is fallible in a number of areas becomes even more evident as we next examine the phenomenon of cancer misdiagnosis.

---

[105] http://www.whale.to/cancer/bennett.html

Misdiagnosis

"In summoning even the wisest of physicians to our aid, it is probable that he is relying upon a scientific 'truth', the error of which will become obvious in just a few years' time." **Marcel Proust**

20% rate of misdiagnosis by doctors - *One out of every five patients who died in the medical intensive care unit at one of the nation's best hospitals were misdiagnosed by their doctors — a rate that mirrors the rates found in ICU's [intensive care units] nationwide, new research shows. Researchers assert in a report in the journal Chest that half of the misdiagnosed patients should have been treated differently, though it's hard to know whether that could have saved any lives.* [106]

Hearing those dreaded words, *"You have cancer"*, and then submitting to the orthodox regime, can be a devastating enough experience in itself. But what if you went through this experience, only to discover that it was all completely unnecessary?

You have cancer. Oh, hang on a minute...

While the above story from *USA Today* applies to misdiagnosis of disease in general, an Internet search on *'cancer misdiagnosis'* reveals a very high number of lawyers advertising their services. The level of lawyer interest in any given litigious angle is usually a good indicator of that angle's ability to pay off. In the case of cancer, lawyers have gathered thick and fast around what has been found to be a lucrative and stable source of income. The science of cancer diagnosis apparently is by no means exact.

Smartlight Mammographics is a major manufacturer of radiography and mammography equipment. The organisation admits that radiographic testing procedures are inaccurate. Amazingly, this organisation has posted links that proffer the following information: *"We expected error rates to be around 30%, but the wide range of*

---

[106] *USA Today*, 20th February 2001
http://www.usatoday.com/news/health/2001-02-20-icu-misdiagnoses.htm

results (10%-90%) was an eye-opener." and: *"Radiologists can differ substantially in their mammographic recommendations."*[107]

There are unfortunately a great number of examples where misdiagnosis has occurred in a variety of ways, with predictably disastrous consequences.

Valerie Sahar was fortunate. She was told by her doctor that a biopsy had shown she had breast cancer. It was decided to have the breast removed as well as a portion of her underarm tissue, to be followed by radiation and chemotherapy. She headed for the examining room so the doctor could check her other breast. Ten minutes later her doctor said she didn't have cancer at all and that her test results had been mixed up with those of another patient. What if this mix-up had not been noticed? The woman would have lost one breast - possibly two - and would have been subjected to radiation and chemotherapy. If she had survived the treatment, she would then have been told she was cured.[108]

Nancy Seeger, aged 56, was not so fortunate. She was only 14 years old when her mother died of breast cancer. Within five years, her mother's sister was dead of the same disease. Then, researchers developed a DNA test for the gene defect that supposedly predisposes a woman to both breast and ovarian cancer. Seeger opted for this test. When the results came back, the doctor solemnly handed her a letter which included the words *"a lifetime risk of breast cancer as high as 85 percent... risk for ovarian cancer 50 percent over one's lifetime."* The results, said the letter, had been confirmed independently.

No ovaries, but a refund
Even though she was healthy, Seeger opted for surgery to remove her ovaries. She was on the mend and already considering the removal of both her breasts too when she received yet another call from her doctor that she did not have the mutation after all. A second set of scientists had detected the error after she had donated a blood sample for research. The original lab apologised for any anxiety or stress this

---

[107] Smartlight Mammographics
www.smartlight.com/dfvcenter/misdiagnosis.html
[108] *Times Colonist*, front page, 10th September 1999, Victoria, Canada

situation may have caused and refunded her $350 fee. But Seeger could not have children.

In October 1999, she filed a lawsuit against the lab, Oncormed, and the company that later acquired it, Gene Logic. A spokesman for Gene Logic stated the company no longer performs that test.[109]

Sheila Roy is 36. She lost her marriage and two years of her life as a result of misdiagnosis and unwarranted medical intervention. In 1997, she was diagnosed with pancreatic cancer and given one year to live. She underwent aggressive treatment that included surgery, chemotherapy and radiation. She received 40 days of radiation and was given high doses of the chemotherapy drug 5FU (sometimes referred to by doctors as '5 feet under' because of its deleterious effects).

Two years after the initial diagnosis, it was discovered that the pathologist had made a mistake in interpreting test results. Medical authorities admitted the young woman had never had cancer. It is now hoped she will not develop secondary cancer as a result of the radiation and chemotherapy to which she was needlessly and carelessly subjected.[110]

Dr James Elwood

In the UK recently, a report has been released concerning the case of an elderly pathologist who misdiagnosed more than 200 cancer patients. The report was ordered after it emerged that 79-year-old Dr James Elwood, a consultant pathologist, had wrongly diagnosed more than 200 cancer patients at the Princess Margaret Hospital in Swindon. Dr Elwood had worked as a locum pathologist in three other Trusts - the Royal United Hospital Bath Trust, the Mid-Sussex Trust and Frimley Park Hospitals Trust - between 1995 and 1999.

Despite concerns being raised about his performance as early as 1995, investigations didn't start until 1999.

---

[109] Underwood, Ann, "When Knowledge Does Damage", *Newsweek*, 10th April 2000
[110] Moelaert, John, *The Cancer Conspiracy*, op. cit.

In a statement to the press, the Swindon and Community Health Council said the report was *"a damning indictment of a system that has failed to protect patients from poorly performing locum consultants."* [111]

Jennifer Rufer

The story of 22-year-old Jennifer Rufer made headlines across the US. Jennifer was treated for a cancer she never had because of 'false positive' readings from a blood test made by Abbott Labs.[112] She was awarded $16 million in June 2001, due in part to her continuous campaign over her 'diagnosis' of cancer through blood tests manufactured by Abbott Labs. Jennifer endured chemotherapy, a hysterectomy and lung surgery as a result of Abbot's errant predictive test.

Abbott Laboratories has so far refused to make the papers on these tests public knowledge and declines to acknowledge responsibility for this and other cases of cancer misdiagnosis. Abbot Laboratories also argues that there are acceptable levels of error, and cites doctors as the guilty party for not taking these factors into account.

"No matter how hard you try to educate doctors," says Abbott attorney Brad Keller, *"there are still going to be a small handful of them who are not paying attention."* [113]

Rufer's attorneys say they have as many as 15 more women who may sue Abbott Labs. As a result of her experiences, Jennifer Rufer is unable to have children.

Back here in the UK:

Cervical Cancer Misdiagnosis Shakes UK Public Confidence In Screening: *British health officials are emphasising*

---

[111] 'I'm sorry,' says bungling doctor, *Brighton Evening Argus*, 14th June 2000 http://www.thisisbrighton.co.uk/brighton__hove/archive/2000/06/14/NEWS10ZM.html

[112] Please see our 'Health Warning to Expectant Mothers' at the end of this book.

[113] Komo4 News, Seattle, 26th July 2001, More Cancer Misdiagnosis Cases, http://www.komotv.com/news/story_sr.asp?ID=12896

to a worried public that the number of misdiagnoses in cervical smear slides found at Leicester Royal Infirmary is in line with national and international test levels. False-negative cervical smear slide readings led to the deaths of 14 women and unneeded radical treatment in another 64 women in the county of Leicestershire, a seven-year audit has shown. There is speculation that perhaps one third of British women who now have a diagnosis of cervical cancer could have received wrong or misleading smear results.[114]

Seek a second opinion

If the above examples serve any purpose, it is to demonstrate that seeking a second opinion, outside of the conventional cancer circle, is a wise move. Whilst the remit of this book does not spread to the full coverage of doctor-induced injury and death, it is worth bringing to attention the fact that over a million patients are injured in US hospitals each year, and approximately 280,000 die annually as a result of these injuries. This means that the death rate of iatrogenesis (doctor-induced events) dwarfs the annual automobile accident mortality rate of 45,000 and accounts for more deaths than all other accidents combined.[115] As John Moelaert, author of *The Cancer Conspiracy*, states:

"Medicine is not an exact science like mathematics. There is an inordinate degree of guesswork involved in the diagnosis and treatment of disease, and as a result countless mistakes are made, some fatal." [116]

And further on down the line, at the doctor's surgery, Phillip Bates, the author of *Health Revolution*, suggests the following:

"Your doctor isn't an idiot, or even a bad guy – he's just the victim of his extensive and expensive education, and he believes the [American Medical Association] dogma. He reads medical journals to keep up, naturally. There's no reason for him to disbelieve the articles

---

[114] Short, Robert, "Cervical Cancer Misdiagnosis Shakes UK Public Confidence In Screening", *The Doctor's Guide Global Edition*, 7th May 2001, http://www.pslgroup.com/dg/1fa326.htm
[115] *Journal of American Medicine*, 5th July 1995, 274:29-34
[116] Moelaert, John, op. cit.

that appear in his journals about vitamin C not being effective. He must reason that if any such therapy were good, it would be reported in such journals. The individual doctor is probably not even aware that the medical journals he reads are literally controlled by the drug advertising. Don't blame your doctor for his lack of knowledge. Blame the system." [117]

The narrow view

While Credence is always careful to stress that being a doctor <u>does not</u> mean that they are part of some vast conspiracy to kill people, this does not stop those accusations from being made. The fact that qualified people (who should know better) actually hold this view is no better illustrated than in the following letter sent to me by one irate doctor:

"I have yet to see single shred of evidence the supports the conspiracy theories that abound on the web. It doesn't matter whether it's cancer treatment, aspartame, or even soybeans. Consider this: would any company seek to sell products that kill the customer? It doesn't make any sense. The scientist who discovered cisplatin was a professor of mine in university. I knew his mind and his heart. He wanted to find a cure because it had devastated someone in his family. While all chemotherapies are poisons, by extension of your logic he was creating a product that he knew would kill his family members. Does that even make sense to you?"

And further:

"But consider this: if even one person takes your recommendations not to use chemotherapy and dies anyway, you're as guilty of murder as Jack the Ripper. But more than that, you'll have failed at what you're probably trying to do: help people. Live with that. P.S. I've forgotten more than you will ever know." [118]

---

[117] Bates, Phillip, *Health Revolution,Vitamin C and Cancer*:
http://cat007.com/ccancer.htm

[118] Personal correspondence. Letter on file.

Quite depressingly, prior to writing the above letter, this doctor had already been made aware of the information in chapter 2 on cisplatin - the drug that chemotherapy experts would most want to avoid. Yet because the professor is a colleague of his and is *a well-intentioned individual*, this somehow makes it all OK. Never mind the fact that cisplatin is a corrosive carcinogen. Furthermore, anyone who questions these honourable intentions is immediately labelled a conspiracy theorist and perhaps 'Jack the Ripper'. (And presumably, by an extension of the above doctor's logic, if cisplatin, or chemotherapy in general, were to kill just one person, then the doctor advising it would also be guilty of murder.) In his book, *Hidden Persuaders*, advertising and media critic Vance Packard stated that in order for one party subtly to gain superiority over another party, that party must employ certain tactics. *"...one must pre-empt the vocabulary in order to gain the moral/political high ground."*[119]

Through emotive semantics, this doctor has unsuccessfully attempted to claim the moral high ground.

The ladder of knowledge

Nicholas Murray Butler was chief spokesman for the huge conglomerate J P Morgan and Co. Butler once stated:

"The world is divided into three classes of people: a very small group that makes things happen, a somewhat larger group that watches things happen, and the great multitude which never knows what is really happening." [120]

Lower down the ladder of knowledge, these poisonous products are being manufactured and administered by multitudes who are proud to be associated with medicines *'designed to save lives'*.

Working under such tremendous pressures every single day, doctors, nurses and physicians just do not have the time to step off the conventional treadmill and take time to catch up on contrary research.

---

[119] Packard, Vance, *Hidden Persuaders*, D Mackay & Co, 1957

[120] An Introduction to President Clinton's political mentor, Carroll Quigley. "The One Thing the Establishment Fears." Earthlink Publications, http://radiobergen.org/powergame/tragedy.html

And so, most conventional doctors fall into the category of Butler's 'great multitude'. It is far simpler and more expedient to dismiss all contrary information as fringe lunacy and conspiracy theory until such times as it appears either in a recognised conventional medical journal or as a product warning from the drug manufacturers. Then, and only then, is the information considered seriously. And even at this point, some doctors struggle to alter their prescribing habits.

Which brings us to the next thorny dilemma. Could your own doctor (with whom you may well have a trusting relationship) be in possession of certain knowledge that is critical to your case, but feels constrained and unable to share it directly with you? In other words, could your doctor knowingly keep vital information from you?

First do no harm

"The instances are exceedingly rare of man immediately passing over a clear, marked line from virtue into declared vice and corruption. There are middle tints and shades between the two extremes which render the change easy and imperceptible." **Edmund Burke**

You're out to dinner. The gathering is relaxed, the food delicious. In fact, everything is going swimmingly. And then... it starts. *"Hey, guys, Steve's the chap who's writing the book on how our doctors knowingly keep quiet about successful non-conventional cancer treatments!"* A sharp intake of breath all round and then the classic western scene: the saloon doors swing open; a dozen heads turn; the tinkling piano falters and fades; two dozen penetrative, beady eyes lock on to the stranger in town. Never mind the fact that the only thing this stranger was looking for was a relaxing night out!

Too late though. From somewhere off to the left, a weapon is drawn. *"Is that true? Do you really believe that a doctor would do that? My sister's a doctor. How can you say such a thing?"* More hands now hover nervously over their holsters. Which way will this go? Gut feeling and racing arithmetic gauge the scene in an instant. It isn't the opposition or the accusation that daunt, it's the fact that it's a crowded room and a few people could accidentally get hurt. But events have taken their own course and the one gun is now three or four, and even the table next door is taking an interest in the outcome. In thirty seconds, it's gone from bonhomie and friendly faces to *Stand-off at the Oncology Corral.* And all because of some ill-framed announcement (and in a crowded restaurant too!) that I spend most of my time informing the citizenry that doctors spend their time purposefully killing people.

Investigative journalism - Great work if you can get it

Pithy observations aside, I am grateful to Gavin Phillips of Cancerinform, who has employed the weapons of grace, time and ground rules most effectively, in order to establish the manner in which a doctor might imperceptibly stray from that Hippocratic statute: *'First, do no harm to your patient'.*

Becoming a Doctor

"For some people, this question is a stumbling block that they just cannot seem to go beyond. The question is repeated ad nauseum and in incredulous tones, as if it should not even be contemplated. What some people actually mean when they ask it is: "Doctors wouldn't suppress an effective cancer treatment so I won't look at the facts you are presenting." But, as Herbert Spencer said:

"There is a principle which is a bar against all learning, which is proof against all argument, and which cannot fail to keep man in everlasting ignorance. That principle is condemnation without investigation."

So, please proceed with an objective and questioning mind. Let me preface my answer with this. I know for an absolute stone-cold fact that at least a dozen very effective cancer treatments have been suppressed by mainstream medicine in the last 70 some years. See my research into some of these treatments and the books referenced on my site for the enormous amount of evidence supporting my conclusions.

You decided by the time you reached sixth grade that you wanted to become a doctor because you like helping people and you are very interested in the sciences. You work hard in high school and do very well on the SAT's. It's time for college. You once again study diligently and your average GPA is 3.57. You then study for the gruelling Medical College Admission Test (MCAT) required by most medical schools. Now it's the big one - medical school.

You work your tail off 14 hours a day, 6/7 days a week for 4 more years of very determined effort. Wait, you are not finished yet, but you can begin paying off those college and medical school loans of around a $150,000. Now it's time to embark on residency and specialty training. You have chosen to specialise in Internal Medicine and to sub-specialise in oncology. That's about another 5/6 years training.

Phew! You've finally made it. All the gut-busting hard work has paid off. At 31 you are an oncologist. During medical school and residency you were taught very little about nutrition/diet and absolutely nothing about so-called alternative cancer treatments. You heard a little about laetrile [Vitamin B17] from one of your professors, and he told you that there's absolutely no evidence for its efficacy and also that it can be dangerous. Believing the professor, (he must know, right?) you don't bother looking into it further. When you were staying for the weekend at a fellow student's house whose father is a doctor and the subject of alternatives came up, he told you that "...they were garbage peddled by quacks. Don't waste your time."

So, you begin treating patients, blissfully ignorant of the many treatments you are not allowed to prescribe. After several years you become increasingly disillusioned with the orthodox treatment options for cancer. You see the abysmal results you are getting, and even the people who have completed five-year remissions; the side-effects are appalling.

Over the years, several patients tell you about alternatives that had worked for a friend, so you decide to look into it. You start meeting with people who have the medical records proving that they had cancer but used different treatments and they are now cancer-free for 3/5/10 years.

After a year or so of investigation and talking with some alternative cancer therapists, you really think that there is something to this. You also find out that if the AMA/NCI find out that you even mention Hoxsey, Laetrile, 714X or antineoplastons to your patients, you face serious repercussions from the AMA. Becoming involved in unapproved treatments will result in loss of hospital privileges, and probably the loss of your medical licence, not to mention being blackballed by the American Cancer Society, ostracized by your peers and branded a "quack".

You find yourself facing a very difficult dilemma. You know chemotherapy is worthless for most cancer patients, and deadly for some, with horrendous side-effects. But everything you have worked for is at stake. You make $300,000 a year and live a very comfortable lifestyle you have certainly earned. You still owe $50,000 on those *school loans, have two kids, a five-thousand-a-month mortgage, two car loans and all the other expenses that go with your lifestyle. You are nearly 40 years old. How will you earn a living if you lose your medical licence? As you can see, reader, doctors have much to lose by prescribing medicines not approved by the medical cartel.*

What would you do?"[121]

Is this painting a picture of the doctor as an evil plotter? Not at all. Gavin Phillips' unfolding scenario paints a very human picture, highlighting one of man's basic dilemmas - pressing circumstances that can easily lead to intellectual and moral compromise. Edmund Burke's insight again:

"The instances are exceedingly rare of man immediately passing over a clear, marked line from virtue into declared vice and corruption. There are middle tints and shades between the two extremes, which render the change easy and imperceptible."

Self-selected for perfectionism

Professor Frank Davidoff is the editor of *Quality and Safety in Healthcare*. In a *British Medical Journal* article entitled "Shame: the elephant in the room", he cites the case of tolbutamide - a diabetes drug with known harmful side-effects. Why were doctors finding it difficult to listen to the evidence and change their prescribing habits, despite the dangers?

"An important clue surfaced at the annual meeting of the American Diabetes Association soon after the study was published. During the discussion, a practitioner stood up and said he simply could not, and would not accept the findings, because admitting to his patients that he had been using an unsafe treatment would shame him in their eyes....

Despite its potential importance in medical life, shame has received little attention in the literature on quality improvement - indeed, in the medical literature generally. A search on the term

---

[121] Phillips, Gavin, "Why would doctors suppress an effective cancer treatment?" www.cancerinform.org/docs.html

'shame' in November 2001 yielded only 947 references - a tiny fraction of the roughly seven million articles indexed in Medline. In a sense, shame is the 'elephant in the room': something so big and disturbing that we don't even see it, despite the fact that we keep bumping into it....

Indeed, much of the extreme distress of doctors who are sued for malpractice appears to be attributable to the shame of being sued rather than to the financial losses involved. As a related issue, who can doubt that the real agenda in the controversy currently raging over mandatory reporting of medical errors is the fear of being shamed?

Doctors may, in fact, be particularly vulnerable to shame, since they are self-selected for perfectionism when they choose to enter the profession. Moreover, the use of shaming as punishment for the shortcomings of medical students, particularly during their clinical years, and for 'moral errors' committed by registrars, such as lack of sufficient dedication, hard work, and a proper reverence for role obligations, very likely contributes further to the extreme sensitivity of doctors to shaming.

What are some of the lessons here for those working to improve the quality and safety of medical care? The first is the importance of recognising that there actually is a problem: that shame is a powerful force in slowing or preventing improvement; that unless and until shame is confronted and dealt with, progress in improvement will be slow. The second is the recognition that shame is a fundamental human emotion and is not about to go away, no matter how successful we are at handling it. Once these basic ideas are firmly rooted, the work of mitigating and managing shame can really flourish." [122]

Of the many letters this article generated in response, one letter suggested that *blame* may be a better word, and that blame be *"...directed to the researchers and the business-promoting machine of*

---

[122] Davidoff, Frank, "Shame: the elephant in the room. Managing shame is important for improving healthcare", *British Medical Journal*, 16th March 2002

the drug firms, for lack of accuracy in the work they are supposed to do on a particular drug prior to its introduction to the market."

Great prospects for the clinical trial... But where are all the patients?

In June 1999, New York City clinician Dr Nicholas Gonzalez received the largest amount of money ever allocated by the National Cancer Institute for a clinician or researcher to study an alternative treatment for pancreatic cancer. The $1.4 million grant was for a prospective clinical trial that would compare the results of Gonzalez' non-toxic, nutrition and enzyme-based treatment with conventional chemotherapy. The unusual clinical study was designed to involve 40-45 patients treated by Gonzalez and an equal number of patients receiving chemotherapy.

By mid February 2002, only 16 people were being treated on the nutritional program, with space for at least two to three dozen more. Where were the rest of the patients? Gonzalez points the finger at MDs.

"The problem has been the oncologists out in the field. And I think some of it is financial. They can make $20,000 with a course of chemotherapy for pancreatic cancer even though it doesn't work." [123]

Wherever the blame is laid, we cannot deny that in all instances, doctors are humans first, breadwinners second and doctors third.

---

[123] Chowka, Peter, 'Two years into an unprecedented study of nutrition and cancer, the truth is still out there", 15th February 2002:
http://www.naturalhealthline.com/newsletter/15feb02/gonzalez.htm

Genes and cancer

Brave new medicine?

*"Science has always promised two things not
necessarily related – an increase first in our
powers, second in our happiness and wisdom,
and we have come to realise that it is the first
and less important of the two promises
which it has kept in abundance."* **Joseph Krutch**

We have a new hope, it seems. Across all conventional medical
disciplines, we are now being told that understanding the complexities
of the gene holds the key to understanding the complexities of disease.
And nowhere does this belief hold more sway than in today's
conventional cancer treatment theory.

*"There is hope that eventually we will not only understand breast
cancer and be able to predict who will get it, but also cure it. The cure
for this disease should not require surgical-, chemotherapeutic- or
radiology-based treatment, but it will be a true cure based on the
correction of the very genes which caused all the problems in the first
place."* [124]

Thus declared Dr Miryam Wahrman, in her paper, *The Breast
Cancer Genes*. The following texts typify the conventional attitude
towards the role genetics is playing in the pursuit of a cure for cancer.

1999
*Scientists believe they have found a new gene which plays a key
role in the spread of many of the common forms of cancer. The
discovery could eventually lead to a new drug to treat common types
of cancer, such as lung, breast and colon cancer. It is expected greatly
to increase cancer scientists' knowledge of the way cancer spreads."* [125]

---

[124] Wahrman, Miryam Z, "The Breast Cancer Genes":
http://www.us-israel.org/jsource/Judaism/breast_cancer.html
[125] "Cancer Gene Breakthrough", *BBC News*, 8th January 1999:

2000

Scientists have announced the completion of a vast genetic map for humankind in a landmark step likely to revolutionise treatment of cancers and diseases, and bring profound insights about the creation of life itself. President Bill Clinton hailed the achievement as a "day for the ages. Today we are learning the language with which God created life." [126]

2001

A technique that fools cancer cells into 'committing suicide' will be unveiled by scientists in a major breakthrough against the disease. Experts claim they have developed an exciting new gene therapy which tricks cancer cells into dying without harming healthy cells in the body. It is hoped that the potentially life-saving treatment will prove effective against all common forms of cancer, including lung, cervical and breast cancer. [127]

2002

Millions of women could soon undergo genetic screening to discover if they are at risk from breast cancer after a breakthrough by scientists. A team of researchers from Cambridge University discovered that more than half of all breast cancers are likely to occur in a small group of women at high genetic risk, and screening these women could save many of the 13,000 breast cancer victims each year. [128]

And this, the very latest from *Nature*, May 2002:

Cancer arises from a stepwise accumulation of genetic changes that liberates neoplastic cells from the homeostatic mechanisms that

---

http://news.bbc.co.uk/hi/english/health/newsid_250000/250723.stm
[126] "Gene Breakthrough Could be a Cure-all", *Detroit News*, 27th June 2000: http://detnews.com/2000/health/0006/28/a01-82343.htm
[127] "Cancer Gene Brakthrough" *Today UK*, 21st November 2001: http://www.rnature.com/2001/11/21/eng2dayuk/eng2dayuk_102345_131_86915885 8899.htm
[128] "Gene Breakthrough That Will Save Women's Lives", *Daily Express*, 4th March 2002

govern normal cell proliferation. In humans, at least four to six mutations are required to reach this state, but fewer seem to be required in mice. [129]

Waiting, hoping and praying

The above examples represent only a fraction of the recent headlines surrounding information on the *genetic* link to cancer. According to a Dr Eric Fearon, a geneticist from the University of Michigan, the discovery of the blueprint of life (the mapping of the human genome) means that the speed of new medical discoveries will now be ratcheted up by a factor of 10 or even 100. [130] This observation was made back in 2000. But are we seeing the results? Can cancer be cured, eradicated even, by manipulating the human genomic map? Again, we've had lots of promises but no measurable results.

As far as mainstream thinking goes, it seems that even to think about questioning the rationale underpinning Clinton's *'language of God'* is to risk the wrath and ridicule of the 'brave new world' and of 'brave new medicine'. Rather than question some of the more worrying aspects of the cancer gene theory, most people are just waiting, hoping and praying that this new branch of research will at last bring the real breakthrough for which we've all been waiting.

And while many people will argue that it's too early to make gloomy predictions about genetic research into cancer, the more informed cancer industry critics, who are following the genetic debate, have noticed the same worrying trends emerging in this *bright, new* cancer science, as were witnessed in the *bright, new* (and now quite tarnished) cancer sciences and promises of yesteryear.

The benefits scarcely detectable

James Le Fanu, author of *The Rise and Fall of Modern Medicine*, is not impressed with the god-like status bestowed upon those who are constructing the latest genetic theories on health and disease:

---

[129] "Modelling the Molecular Circuitry of Cancer", *Nature*, May 2002:
www.nature.com/cgi taf/DynaPage.taf?file=/nrc/journal/v2/n5/full/nrc795_fs.html
[130] "Gene Breakthrough Could be a Cure-all", *Detroit News*, op. cit.

"By all accounts, 1ˢᵗ December was a momentous day in the history of science, with the publication in the journal 'Nature' of the first chapter of the 'Book of Man', snappily titled 'The DNA Sequence of Human Chromosome 22.' It is not however an easy read; its alphabet restricted to only four letters: a typical line reading TTTGAGCTGATTAGCC plus 35 million more of these same letters in the first chapter.... The information that is locked away in each and every cell is of such inscrutable complexity as to defy imagination.... This is just one illustration of a recurring feature in genetic research – the yawning gap between the key to a golden future and the reality that, in practical terms, its benefits are scarcely detectable." [131]

Ahh, yes. I think I understand now
But will I get better?

As far back as 1996, we were told that certain cancer-causing genes had been isolated.

"While efforts continue through the National Institutes of Health's National Center for Human Genome Research (NCHGR) and the Human Genome Project - the government's $3 billion, 15-year attempt to map the entire complement of human genes - the discoveries in the last few years of hereditary colon, breast, and ovarian cancer susceptibility genes stand out as major accomplishments." [132]

Six years on and now blessed as we are with the knowledge that the secrets to life, health and happiness rest on the arrangement and rearrangement of the letters T, G, A and C, readers may like to know that the colon cancer enigma has now been cracked. According to the National Centre for Biotechnological Information, after much painstaking work, the following valuable information can be offered on the human colon cancer gene:

agctaaatca gaagaaaata acaaggaaga aaaacctgat agtaagaagg
tggaggaaga cttaaaggca gacaaaccgt caagtgagga aagtgatcta gaaattgata

---

[131] Le Fanu, James, "Stop All This Fuss About Our Genes," *New Statesman*, 13ᵗʰ December 1999

[132] "Molecular Advances Offer New Tools, New Hope For Cancer Studies": www.the-scientist.com/yr1996/dec/research_961209.html

aagaaggtgc gattgaacca gacactcatg ctcctcaaga aatgggagac gaaaatgcgg agataatgga

...and also a further 10 lines of same.[133] This very library also offers helpful information on the genetic sequencing of the mouse, fly and worm. But where are the major accomplishments? How is any of this even remotely helpful for those who have been diagnosed with colon cancer?

Ross Hume Hall, chair of Dept Biochemistry at McMaster University, Ontario, has different ideas on these golden announcements, his writings on the subject so far having stood the test of time. Dr Hall has predicted that the cancer 'gene' will offer little by way of any practical benefit:

"So here we are in the late 1990's and cancer researchers still hop from one bandwagon to another. Researchers have announced the discovery of the colon cancer gene, the breast cancer gene and many more. But what does the discovery of such genes do for the patient with colon or breast cancer? Claudio Stern, a biologist at Columbia University in New York, dampens any enthusiasm. Discovering a gene, he says, is like trying to learn a foreign language from a dictionary. 'You memorize words, but know nothing of the context in which these word are used.' Look beneath the bandwagon and, of course, the driving force for discovering gene cancers becomes apparent. Not surprisingly, it's money." [134]

James Le Fanu again: *"It would be to overestimate considerably the collective intelligence of scientists to suggest they have even the vaguest idea of how this information begins to translate into 'who we are'. Geneticists must insist that what they are doing is important to guarantee the continuous flow of research funds. They endorse the image of the 'blueprint' because their claim to holding the key to deciphering this blueprint elevates their role in society to that of the*

---

[133] National Centre for Biotechnological Information:
www.ncbi.nlm.nih.gov/entrez/viewer.fcgi?val=18596098&db=Nucleotide&dopt=GenB
ank
[134] Hall, Ross Hume, "The Medical-Industrial Complex", *The Ecologist*, March 1998

shaman – the possessor of arcane knowledge no-one else can understand." [135]

Genes *R* Us

The foundations of gene theory were rocked again recently by the announcement that there might be even less human genes than originally thought. Over the years, that number has been reduced from the original 150,000 genes to about 80,000, and, recently, down to no more than 30,000. Craig Ventner is one of the geneticists responsible for publishing these intensely unpopular 'gene downsize' findings. One of the telephone calls he received as a consequence of his globally-publicised report adds the all-important *human* face to the story:

"The day after we published data pointing to the possibility of only 80,000 genes, I got this call from a US biotech boss, cursing, swearing and using all sorts of obscenities about me and my company. I calmed him down and asked him what his problem was. 'You've just announced there are only 80,000 genes, and I've just done a deal with SmithKline Beecham, agreeing to sell them 100,000 genes. Where am I supposed to get the rest, you bastard?'" [136]

Dr Barry Commoner is senior scientist at the Centre for the Biology of Natural Systems at Queens College, City University of New York, where he directs the Critical Genetics Project. In a frank paper entitled *Unravelling the DNA Myth*, Dr Commoner declares that the missing 120,000 genes should really spell the end of the gene theory construct:

"By any reasonable measure, the finding (published last February) signalled the downfall of the central dogma; it also destroyed the scientific foundation of genetic engineering and the validity of the biotechnology industry's widely advertised claim that its methods of genetically modifying food crops are 'specific, precise, and predictable' and therefore safe.[137] *In short, the most dramatic*

---

[135] Le Fanu, James, op. cit.

[136] UK *Observer*, 11th February, 2001; see also "Whatever Happened to Those Missing Genes?" www.whatareweswallowing.freeserve.co.uk/geneticsessay.htm

[137] In an article in the UK's *Big Issue* magazine, entitled "Seeds of Dissent" (15th April 2002), Andy Rowell reports on how the prestigious scientific magazine *Nature* was recently compelled, by pressure from the biotech industry, to print a retraction to a

achievement to date of the $3 billion Human Genome Project is the refutation of its own scientific rationale." [138]

As for the millions of women who may soon submit to genetic breast cancer screening – these tests will be conducted by persons who cannot even give a reasoned account of the science supporting their thesis. The ramifications for these women do not even bear thinking about, unless, of course, one can see that there is a profit to be made and one happens to be a large pharmaceutical organisation... such as...

GlaxoSmithKline... again

With a large share of the oncology products market, [139] leading pharmaceutical conglomerate GSK has definite ideas about 'educating' the wider world on the genetic approach to the cure of all disease, including cancer. The following text forms part of the GSK website on the subject:

"GSK is at the forefront of a revolution that will change the way many diseases are diagnosed and treated and the way medicines are discovered, developed and prescribed. This revolution is occurring because of advances being made in the fields of genetics and genomics

---

previous *Nature* paper on the dangers of genetically modified (GM) cross-contamination. Despite the fact that the original paper has since been validated by two other papers concerning the dangers of GM, big business has seen to it that the world's leading scientific journal has now effectively disowned the paper critical of GM. *"The Nature statement could not have come at a better time and the biotech industry is naturally gleeful. Many people are going to need that [Nature's editorial] reference,"* says Willy de Greef from Syngenta, the world's leading agribusiness company. *"Not least those who, like me, will be in the frontline fights for biotech during the Hague negotiations."* Dr Sue Mayer from GeneWatch UK says: *"It is quite extraordinary the lengths to which the biotech industry and the scientific establishment will go to discredit any critical science."*
Full story at http://members.tripod.com/~ngin/deceit3.html
And separately, in the *New York Times* (25th October 1998), an official from Monsanto, the world's leading GM food supplier, stated that the corporation should not have to take responsibility for the safety of its food products. *"Monsanto should not have to vouchsafe the safety of biotech food,"* said Phil Angell, Monsanto's Director of Corporate Communications. *"Our interest is in selling as much of it as possible. Assuring its safety is the FDA's job."*
[138] Commoner, Barry, "Unraveling The DNA Myth: The Spurious Foundation of Genetic Engineering", *Harpers*, February 2002
[139] GSK product list at www.glaxowellcome.com/prod_list.html

- advances that already are having a direct impact on the pharmaceutical industry and the provision of healthcare. Scientists are unravelling the mysteries of the relationships between genes and diseases and between genes and patients' responses to medicines." [140]

Is GSK one example among many of the drug industry capitalising on public fears of disease - building on them even? Space prohibiting, the following reference leads the reader to an article asking if society has become medicalised and diagnosed beyond reasonable expectations. The reader must be the judge. [141]

Tobacco firm to profit from cancer genes

If confirmation were needed that conventional cancer care is in the hands of profit-focused rogues, one of the world's biggest tobacco companies aims to make a great deal of money from the various diseases caused by cigarette smoking, by negotiating with biotech companies for the exclusive rights to market future lung cancer vaccines. From the UK's *Guardian*, senior health editor Sarah Bosely writes:

"The strategy by Japan Tobacco, which makes Camel, Winston, Mild Seven and the menthol cigarette brand Salem, was condemned yesterday as both cynical and dangerous. If a successful lung cancer vaccine went on the market, it would not stop smokers dying of other tobacco-related diseases, such as heart disease and emphysema. But the arrival of a vaccine, promoted by a tobacco company, would

---

[140] Genetics Research @ GSK: http://genetics.glaxowellcome.com/gsk.asp

[141] Regush, Nicholas, "Runaway Medicalisation: Challenging a Well-Entrenched Belief System". The report begins: *"I won't bore you with all the details of my messed-up ankle and knee, but I will tell you this: From the very moment that I injured myself, people were crawling out of the woodwork telling me to see a doctor. "Why aren't you seeing someone?" "I know a terrific orthopod." "You should get x-rays." "You're being foolish not getting this checked out." "I hate to tell you, man, but you really should see someone." Or they were asking me what medicine I was taking for the pain. "Are you taking Tylenol?" "You should take Aleve. It works wonders for me." Have you tried Glucosamine? It helps reduce pain and improves joint mobility." Although this attention amounted to an assault, I couldn't really blame friends for caring. They were, however, projecting their own strong dependency on medicine. And it's a dependency that has grown to the point of madness. We are medicalised from the moment of birth until death."*
Full story at http://www.redflagsweekly.com/storm_warnings.html#runaway

encourage smoking in the false belief that they could be treated. "Giving a tobacco company exclusive rights to lung cancer vaccines is like putting Dracula in charge of a blood bank," said Helen Wallace, deputy director of GeneWatch UK, which uncovered the deals.

Derek Yach, director of the non-communicable diseases division at the World Health Organisation, said: 'We tackle lung cancer by breaking the addictive grip of the tobacco industry and by taking action to help people quit smoking or never start. The last company that should control the rights to a lung cancer vaccine is one that makes huge profits from products that cause the disease.'" [142]

This inherently warped driving force in man was adequately summed by Martin Luther King Jr., who once said: *"Our scientific power has outrun our spiritual power. We have guided missiles and misguided men."* [143]

The genetics jamboree

The 2002 Oncogenomics conference is a four-day event (including banquet) being held in Dublin, Ireland. It is billed as the conference *"...to coalesce the remarkable, recent progress in regard to genome research and cancer. The conference will bring together a diverse group of dynamic speakers and participants who can together explore – in relation to human cancer – both the basic mechanisms and the potential clinical utility of the coming onslaught of genomic information."* [144]

In real terms of course, there's been no progress at all and, despite the gloss, the gathering is just another conventional jamboree, bringing together a remarkably <u>non-diverse</u> group of vested interests. Sponsors for the *Oncogenomics* event include Amgen, (the world's largest biotech company which has just purchased Immunex Corp for $16B[145]) the National Cancer Institute and The American Association of Cancer Research. Invited speakers include those from The National Human

---

[142] *Guardian Newspapers*, 12th November 2001:
www.guardian.co.uk/business/story/0,3604,591946,00.html
[143] King, Martin Luther, Jr., *International Thesaurus of Quotations*, Penguin, 1970
[144] *Oncogenomics 2002*: www.nhgri.nih.gov/CONF/Oncogenomics2002/
[145] *Investor News*, http://amgen.acquisitioninformation.com/

Genome Research Institute, Wellcome Trust (Glaxo), UK Institute of Cancer Research, Bristol-Myers Squibb Pharmaceuticals and a number of medical universities, all of whom espouse conventional cancer therapeutics and are reliant upon pharmaceutical and institutional sponsorship for their continued existence.

One such speaker at this conference is Barbara Weber, based at The University of Pennsylvania – an institution whose cancer centre (UPCC) received a 5-year grant in 2000 from America's National Cancer Institute totalling $26M, as well as funding from various industry sources totalling a further $70M.[146] So, even if Ms Weber were to hold private reservations about conventional cancer treatments, what are the chances of her jeopardising the UPHS $100M-plus sponsorship by voicing her concerns? What would happen were her keynote speech to open thus? *"I am concerned that our total lack of progress in cancer care is directly linked to our continued use of profitable mustard gas and radiation as medicine."*

As Glen Warner MD stated: *"We have a multi-billion-dollar industry that is killing people, right and left, just for financial gain. Its idea of research is to see whether two doses of this poison are better than three doses of that poison."* [147]

No critical voices

The 3rd European Breast Cancer Conference held in Barcelona in March 2002 was no different. It was organised by the Federation of European Cancer Societies (FECS), which has many links to major pharmaceutical institutions, such as GlaxoSmithKline, Rhone Poulenc and Pharmacia Upjohn, three leading cancer-drug manufacturers. Out of all the media outlets reporting the various 'breakthroughs' from that conference[148], not one newspaper reported critically on the close ties the event had to big business and the 'cancer-chemical' industry.

---

[146] "Vitamin C and the Cancer Scare":
www.whatareweswallowing.freeserve.co.uk/vitc.htm
[147] Cancer Quotes - The Cancer Page: www.whale.to/cancer/quotes1.html
[148] Associated Press, 21st March 2002: *BARCELONA, Spain – Recent research indicates a new hormone-blocking drug works better than the standard medicine in preventing women with early-stage breast cancer from developing tumours in the healthy breast. In the largest breast cancer treatment study to date, women taking Arimidex were less than half as likely as those taking Tamoxifen to develop a new*

Is cancer hereditary?

Equally interesting is the fact that with all the focus on the cancer gene and our supposed inherent predisposition to cancer, a number of scientists have offered good evidence to suggest that *hereditary cancer* plays only a tiny part in manifestation of the disease, if at all. Why aren't these voices being listened to?[149]

Campaign for Truth in Medicine

Conferences here, conferences there. Endless R&D producing countless promising headlines, and yet, all the while, the mortality statistics worsen. And still the money - our money - keeps rolling in. For those readers reacting with indignation, even outrage, over the imbalances and opportunities for abuse of power within the conventional medical infrastructure, your frustrations can be put to very good use by logging on to The Campaign for Truth in Medicine website at www.campaignfortruth.com. CTM is an organisation whose specific brief is to bring medical injustices and inequalities to wider public attention. Membership is free and details on CTM are found at the back of this book.

---

cancer in the other breast. The study, paid for by Arimidex's maker, AstraZeneca, was presented Thursday at the European Breast Cancer Conference in Barcelona, Spain. www.uniontrib.com/news/science/20020321-1213-breastcancer.html

[149] Olah, E, "Hereditary Neoplastic Diseases", *Orv Hetil*, pp.451-66, 1999, who estimated the percentage rate for hereditary cancer at 1%. Also Lindblom, A, "Hereditary Cancer", *Acta Oncol*, pp.439-47, 1999, who put the figure at 5%.

Breast cancer and mammography

"Women who are concerned about breast cancer need facts, not myths, to make their own decisions." - **Irwin D Bross**

A report from the American College of Preventative Medicine estimates that 185,000 women a year are diagnosed with breast cancer in the United States.[150] And the latest Royal Marsden Hospital 2002 web-page on breast cancer reports that 28,000 women in the UK are diagnosed with this disease annually.

Before looking at the practice of mammography in more detail, let's look at the practice of qualifying those statistics presented to us. There are more than enough doubts surrounding conventional cancer practice and especially diagnosis for us to pause a while and examine this area more carefully.

While it may be correct that 185,000 women in the United State and 28,000 women per annum <u>are diagnosed as having breast cancer</u>, how many of those breast cancer diagnoses are correct? And how dangerous is breast cancer anyway? Before coming to any premature conclusions as to the irresponsible-sounding nature of such a question, the following information on breast cancer is presented for the reader.

In a paper entitled "Dangers and Unreliability of Mammography; Breast Examination is a Safe, Effective and Practical Alternative", the authors state that the widespread and virtually unchallenged acceptance of screening has resulted in a dramatic increase in the diagnosis of ductal carcinoma-in-situ (DCIS), a pre-invasive cancer, with a current, estimated incidence of about 40,000 US citizens annually. DCIS is generally treated by lumpectomy plus radiation or even mastectomy and chemotherapy. <u>However, some 80 percent of all DCIS cancers never become invasive, even if left untreated.</u>[151]

---

[150] "Screening for Cancer": www.acpm.org/breast.htm

[151] Baum, M, "Epidemiology versus scare-mongering: The case for humane interpretation of statistics and breast cancer", *Breast J*. 6(5): 331-334, 2000

A report in the *Journal of the National Cancer Institute*, entitled "Over-diagnosis: an under-recognised cause of confusion and harm in cancer screening", stated that mammography can detect cancers that often don't progress.[152]

The one scientific fact you need to know

This next report is from PhD researcher, Irwin D Bross, who was formerly Director of Bio-Statistics at Roswell Park Memorial Institute in Buffalo NY, (Roswell Park Memorial Cancer Hospital). He wrote his thesis on breast cancer after spending some time researching the nature and outcome of the disease. Entitled "How to stop worrying about breast cancer; the one scientific fact you need to know", the main elements of his report have been reproduced below:

"What most women have is a tumour which, under a light microscope, looks like a cancer to a pathologist. Chances are, this tumour lacks the ability to metastasise - to spread throughout the body - which is the hallmark of a genuine cancer.

The world's first controlled clinical trial of adjuvant therapies for breast cancer was centralised in my department. This study produced the first important advance in the treatment of breast cancer in 50 years. It has changed the treatment of breast cancer worldwide. Unfortunately, these changes were not always for the better.

More than half of the patients diagnosed as early breast cancer had tumours that seemed to have little ability to metastasise - that were more like benign lesions rather than cancers.

Our discovery was highly unpopular with the medical profession. Doctors could never afford to admit the scientific truth because the standard treatment in those days was radical mastectomy. Admitting the truth could lead to malpractice suits by women who had lost a breast because of an incorrect medical diagnosis. The furious doctors at the National Cancer Institute (NCI) punished us for our discovery. They took our highly successful breast cancer research program away from us; they stopped funding our mathematical research; and

---

[152] Black, W C, "Overdiagnosis: An under-recognised cause of confusion and harm in cancer screening", *Journal of The National Cancer Institute*, 92(16): 1280-1282, 2000

they eventually succeeded in suppressing our findings and blocking new publications.

The Journal of the American Medical Association reported amazingly high survival rates in a Swedish study of untreated early prostate cancer, which showed 7 out of 8 of the tumours were not cancers and did not turn into cancers.[153] There is no reason for women to panic when they hear 'cancer'. Panic makes them easy victims.

There is an easy way to give California women access to the truth about breast cancer. The state of California should stop wasting $14 million a year on 'cancer research' that is useless to women, and instead spend this money on California libraries. Women should be able to go to a special alcove in any public library and get Internet access to the truth about breast cancer from grassroots breast cancer activists. Women who are concerned about breast cancer need facts, not myths, to make their own decisions.

Women should not have to depend solely on misinformation provided by persons who are in clear conflict-of-interest, such as doctors who promote the high-tech treatments for cancer and the scientists whose 'research' supports their fraudulent medical claims."[154]

That familiar orthodox pressure again?

In the UK *Times* recently, Scottish MP Margaret Ewing was reported to be facing surgery for breast cancer, after cancer was detected during a routine screening. Said Mrs Ewing at the time:

"I am facing what thousands of other women have had to face, but I do so with great confidence in the medical team and support staff, with whom I have gone through various tests."[155]

---

[153] *Journal of the American Medical Association*, 22nd April 1992

[154] Boss, Irwin D, "How to stop worrying about breast cancer; the one scientific fact you need to know":
http://home.mira.net/~antiviv/issue149.htm#HOW%20TO%20STOP%20WORRYIN G

[155] *The Times*, 13th April 2002

But was Mrs Ewing's screening accurate? Were all the right questions asked? Did Mrs Ewing have all the facts to hand? Did the screening nurse point out some of the anomalies pertaining to mammography? The confidence expressed by Mrs Ewing in the conventional paradigm is a confidence that unfortunately cannot be shared by this author. Mrs Ewing duly went into hospital on the 16th April 2002 for surgery.

The relevant contrary information on mammography had been passed on to Mrs Ewing's office for her consideration, but was deemed too uncomfortable by her staff to forward on to her. One of Mrs Ewing's aides stated that Mrs Ewing was emotionally and physically distressed, as were all the staff, and it did not seem appropriate to forward such contentious information. Sympathy is with the staff who had to make that difficult decision. But was it the right decision? Wouldn't you want to know? (Please see the appendices for *How to Present Sensitive Information on Cancer and Treatment Options*)

If more women knew

A report on false-positive breast cancer diagnosis was printed in *The Journal of the National Cancer Institute*. Included was the following:

"If more women knew how common false-positive results are, there might be less stress and anxiety while waiting to undergo further diagnostic tests, which sometimes take many weeks. Most importantly, greater educational initiatives focusing on the role of diet and lifestyle in breast cancer prevention would empower women to protect themselves rather than relying solely on early detection of the disease."[156]

The detection of a breast 'abnormality' will of course be of concern, whenever it is discovered. But awareness of the high number of false-positive diagnoses, coupled with <u>qualified</u> information as to why breast lumps aren't necessarily dangerous, <u>and do not automatically require immediate remedial action</u> (despite the pressure placed upon women to

---

[156] CF Christiansen, L Wang, MB Barton et al, "Predicting the cumulative risk of false-positive mammograms", *Journal of The National Cancer Institute*, 92:1657-66, 2000

do otherwise), will hopefully lessen the high level of alarm surrounding this issue.

Radiation risks

Moving on to the mammogram itself, at patient level, very little information is offered concerning the dangers associated with mammography. What about the radiation risks associated with this practice? This condensed report on mammography is brought to us by Dr Joseph Mercola:

"Recent confirmation by Danish researchers of long-standing evidence on the ineffectiveness of screening mammography has been greeted by extensive nationwide headlines. Entirely missing from this coverage, however, has been any reference to the well-documented dangers of mammography.

Screening mammography poses significant and cumulative risks of breast cancer for pre-menopausal women. The routine practice of taking four films of each breast annually results in approximately 1 rad (radiation absorbed dose) exposure, about 1,000 times greater than that from a chest x-ray.

The premenopausal breast is highly sensitive to radiation, each 1 rad exposure increasing breast cancer risk by about 1 percent, with a cumulative 10 percent increased risk for each breast over a decade's screening. These risks are even greater for younger women subject to 'baseline screening'.

Missed cancers are common in premenopausal women owing to their dense breasts, and also in postmenopausal women on estrogen replacement therapy.

The dangers and unreliability of screening are compounded by its growing and inflationary costs. Screening all pre-menopausal women would cost $2.5 billion annually, about 14% of estimated Medicare spending on prescription drugs."

Dr Mercola states that monthly breast self-examination (BSE), following brief training, coupled with annual clinical breast examination (CBE) by a trained healthcare professional, is at least as effective as mammography in detecting early tumours, and also safe. Dr Mercola also calls for national networks of BSE and CBE clinics to be established, staffed by trained nurses, to replace screening mammography. Apart from their minimal costs, such clinics would also empower women and free them from increasing dependence on industrialised medicine and its complicit medical institutions.[157]

It might also help to free women from the constant disinformation, posing as breast cancer statistics.

The Danish study, to which Mercola was referring, was prompted by a 1999 Swedish study that showed no decrease in cancer deaths from screening, even though mammography has been recommended there since 1985. Asian countries, which still adhere to traditional dishes of rice and vegetables with low meat and dairy intakes, still have far lower rates of breast cancer than those in the West. The report also stated that alcohol and 'hormone replacement' treatments increased risk, while exercise and plant-based diets appeared to reduce it.[158]

Dr Tim O'Shea highlights the following information on the dangers of mammography:

"This is one topic where the line between advertising and scientific proof has become very blurred. As far back as 1976, the American Cancer Society itself and its government colleague, the National Cancer Institute, terminated the routine use of mammography for women under the age of 50 because of its 'detrimental' (carcinogenic) effects." [159]

Dr Bross has more funding cut

In the 1970's, Dr Irwin Bross led an important project studying the alarming increase in rates of leukaemia. The Tri-State Leukaemia Survey, as it was called, used the tumour registries in New York, Maryland, and Minnesota to follow 16 million people. Dr Bross looked

---

[157] "More on the Dangers of Mammography", 23rd February 2002: www.mercola.com/2002/feb/23/mammography.htm
[158] Gotzsche, P C, "Is screening for breast cancer with mammography justifiable?" *Lancet*, 8th January 2000: www.cancerproject.org/nyn/breast.html
[159] O'Shea, Tim, "To the Cancer Patient", www.thedoctorwithin.com

at many factors, including family background, cause of death for parents and grandparents, the person's own health history, complete occupational history and residential history, etc. After four years of work, Dr Bross concluded that *"...the main cause of the rising rates of leukaemia was medical radiation in the form of diagnostic medical x-rays."* [160]

Dr. Bross published his results in the *American Journal of Public Health*. Immediately, the National Cancer Institute cut off his funding.

Mammography is a fraud

Dr John McDougall has made a thorough review of pertinent literature on mammograms. He points out that the $5-13 billion per year generated by mammograms controls the information that women get. Fear and incomplete data are the tools commonly used to persuade women to get routine mammograms. Says Dr McDougall:

"I went into medicine with the idea that I was going to save all of these lives with all the tricks and tools that medical doctors learned. And what I found was that very few of my patients got well. I often did harm to them. This was quite disturbing to me as a young doctor. What was even more disturbing was to find out that this failure had been fairly well documented in the scientific literature - but it doesn't fit anybody's advertising campaign.

Science says one thing and the public believes another because the public relations machine benefits the economics of the drug and medical industries. Mammography is a fraud. The 8th January 2000 issue of the Lancet carried an article stating that mammography is unjustifiable. Of the eight studies done, six of them show that mammography doesn't work, and yet the American public believes this is a time-honoured, definite way of saving their lives from breast cancer." [161]

Cancer risks from breast compression

As early as 1928, physicians were warned to handle cancerous breasts with care, for fear of accidentally disseminating cells and

---

[160] Robbins, John, *Reclaiming our Health...* op. cit.

[161] An Interview with Dr John McDougall: www.shareguide.com/McDougall.html

spreading cancer.[162] Even so, mammography entails tight and often painful compression of the breast, particularly in pre-menopausal women. This may lead to a spread of malignant cells by rupturing small blood vessels in, or around small, as yet undetected breast cancers.[163] Mammograms <u>do not</u> prevent breast cancer. Dr Tim O'Shea warns that harmless breast cancers can be made active by the compressive force of routine mammography.[164]

No benefit above self-examination

Extensive studies of breast cancer histories show no increased survival rate from routine screening mammograms. After reviewing all available literature in the world on the subject, noted researchers Drs Wright and Mueller, of the University of British Columbia, recommended the withdrawal of public funding for mammography screening, because, *"the benefit achieved is marginal and the harm caused is substantial."* [165]

The harm to which they are referring includes the constant worrying and emotional distress, as well as the tendency for unnecessary procedures and testing to be done based on results which can have a false-positive rate as high as 50%.[166]

A seven year study of 90,000 women by Professor Anthony Miller of Toronto University has shown that mammography had no impact on women aged between 40 – 49, and for women over 50, it has shown no benefit over and above what is detected by annual examinations by specialists and self-examination.[167]

In his monumental *The Politics of Cancer*, internationally recognised carcinogens expert, Dr Samuel Epstein, warns us:

---

[162] Quigley, D T, "Some neglected points in the pathology of breast cancer, and treatment of breast cancer", *Radiology*, May 1928

[163] Watmough, D J, "X-ray mammography and breast compression", *Lancet* 340: 122, 1992

[164] O'Shea, Tim, op. cit.

[165] *Lancet*, 1st July 1995

[166] *New York Times*, 14th December 1997; also O'Shea, Tim, op. cit.

[167] "Ideas", CBC, 1st February 1996

"... the US National Cancer Institute is now agreed that large-scale mammography screening programs are likely to cause more cancers than could possibly be detected." [168]

In *Radiation and Human Health*, Dr John Goffman writes:

"There will be more breast cancers induced by the procedure than there will be women saved from breast cancer death by early discovery of lesions." [169]

But as Dr John McDougall has already stated, *"... by the time a tumour is large enough to be detected by mammography, it has been there as long as 12 years! It is therefore ridiculous to advertise mammography as 'early detection'."*

Mammography and vested interests

The American Cancer Society, the world's most wealthy, non-profit institution (it has even made political contributions [170]), has close connections to the mammography industry. Five radiologists have served as ACS presidents. The ACS promotes the interests of the major manufacturers of mammogram machines and films, including Siemens, DuPont, General Electric, Eastman Kodak, and Piker. The mammography industry also conducts research for the ACS and its grantees, serves on advisory boards, and donates considerable funds. [171]

Pharmaceutical giant DuPont is a substantial backer of the ACS Breast Health Awareness Program. ACS sponsors television shows and other media productions promoting mammography; produces advertising, promotional, and information literature for hospitals, clinics, medical organisations, and doctors; produces educational films, and, of course, lobbies Congress for legislation promoting availability of mammography services. In virtually all its important actions, the

---

[168] Epstein, Samuel S, *The Politics of Cancer*, Doubleday, 1979

[169] Epstein, Samuel S, Bertell, Rosalie & Barbara Seaman, "Dangers and Unreliability of Mammography; Breast Examination is a Safe, Effective and Practical Alternative": www.iicph.org/docs/dangers_of_mammography.htm; See also "Health Concerns Related to Radiation Exposure of the Female Nuclear Medicine Patient": http://ehpnet1.niehs.nih.gov/docs/1997/Suppl-6/stabin.html

[170] www.preventcancer.com

[171] Epstein, Samuel S, Bertell, Rosalie & Barbara Seaman, op. cit.

ACS has been, and remains strongly linked with the mammography industry, while ignoring or attacking the development of viable alternatives.[172]

ACS promotion continues to attract women of all ages into mammography centres, leading them to believe that mammography is their best hope against breast cancer. According to the report, a leading Massachusetts newspaper featured a photograph of two women in their twenties in an ACS advertisement that promised early detection results *"nearly 100 percent of the time."* An ACS communications director was questioned by journalist Kate Dempsey and admitted the following, in an article published by the Massachusetts Women's Community journal *Cancer*:

"The ad isn't based on a study. When you make an advertisement, you just say what you can to get women in the door. You exaggerate a point.... Mammography today is a lucrative and highly competitive business." [173]

How about a non-complicated breast-screening alternative to replace all this 'highly competitive business'? A simple and safe program of breast self-examination is included in the appendices at the back of this book.

Those breast cancer drugs

The following *BBC News* item on breast cancer (albeit erroneous) makes reference to the drug Tamoxifen:

Breast cancer deaths plummet: Early detection has saved lives. An unprecedented fall in the number of women dying from breast cancer has been hailed by scientists. A drug, Tamoxifen, developed in the UK, appears mainly responsible for almost a 30% drop in deaths in the UK over the last decade, reported the Lancet medical journal. It is the most sudden drop in mortality for a common cancer seen anywhere in the world. [174]

---

[172] Ibid.
[173] Ibid.
[174] *BBC News*, "Breast Cancer Deaths Plummet":
http://news.bbc.co.uk/hi/english/health/newsid_753000/753821.stm

Tamoxifen

That well-worn mantra, *"early detection saves lives"*, is now seen in its proper context. No doubt, *"plummet"* will be replaced next week in an article headed *"Soar"*. More worryingly though, the BBC report failed to point out to its readers that Tamoxifen is a human carcinogen.

First, the glossy, promotional stuff

Tamoxifen (other names include Nolvadex, Tamofen and Noltam) is an anti-estrogen drug manufactured by Astra Zeneca Pharmaceuticals and is prescribed to many women with breast cancer, according to the theory that the presence or absence of estrogen and progesterone can alter the growth rate of breast cancers. Conventional theory postulates that many breast cancers are hormone-related, that is, they rely on drawing upon supplies of sex hormones to grow, particularly estrogen. On the surface of the cancer cells there are proteins called receptors.

Cancers with estrogen receptors are known as 'estrogen receptor positive' (ER positive) and are said to respond well to Tamoxifen. In these cases, the cancer is said to be hormone-dependent. Scientists believe that Tamoxifen can work to block the estrogen receptors that stimulate cancer cell growth.

Tamoxifen is usually prescribed after surgery as a defence against the cancer returning (adjuvant therapy). It is currently prescribed for between 2 and 5 years in duration, as a single daily dose of around 20 mg and, according to Cancer Information Support International:

"It is also used in women before the menopause, but this group of women more often have chemotherapy. In both groups it can help to control and even shrink the cancer, sometimes for long periods of time." [175]

And now, the research that really matters

Nowhere is it mentioned in any of the Tamoxifen promos that the World Health Organisation formally designated Tamoxifen and

---

[175] "What is Tamoxifen?" www.cancer-info.com/tamoxifen.htm

estrogen therapy as human carcinogens back in 1996, grouping these treatments with around 70 other chemicals — about one quarter of them pharmaceuticals.[176] In response to WHO's announcement, the National Cancer Institute and Zeneca Pharmaceuticals lobbied California regulators to keep them from adding Tamoxifen to their list of carcinogens. As Duncan Roades, editor of *Nexus* magazine stated:

"Here is open evidence of a government agency, chartered to find a cure for cancer, flagrantly colluding with a drug company to keep a known carcinogen on the market and keep the public from learning of its dangers.... This should have been a controversy of high order; instead it was barely reported in the press and few heard about it." [177]

One disease for another
Thanks to Dr Zoltan Rona for the following information on Tamoxifen:

The long-term safety of Tamoxifen use in healthy women has never been established. Many of Tamoxifen's side-effects are relatively benign and include hot flushes, nausea, weight gain and menstrual irregularities. Less than 20% of women taking Tamoxifen experience serious side-effects but these can be lethal or permanent.

In particular, Tamoxifen can cause uterine cancer. Cancers of the liver, ovaries and gastrointestinal tract have also been reported. A study at Johns Hopkins by Yager and Shi found that Tamoxifen is a promoter of liver cancer. When WHO announced Tamoxifen as a known carcinogen in 1996, the NCI study on this drug was abruptly curtailed, <u>but not before 33 women taking Tamoxifen at that time developed endometrial cancer.</u>[178]

Tamoxifen can also cause many hormonal imbalances and toxicities, including the development of blood clots, osteoporosis and

[176] US Department of Health and Human Services Public Health Service National Toxicology Program: http://ehp.niehs.nih.gov/roc/toc9.html
[177] Sellman, Sherrill, "Tamoxifen – A Major Medical Mistake?" www.moonlighthealth.com/library2.asp?A=45
[178] Rona, Zoltan P, "The Trouble With Tamoxifen", *Health Link*: www.selene.com/healthlink/tamoxifen.html

visual disturbances caused by corneal changes, optic nerve damage, cataracts and retinopathy (retinal damage). None of these may be reversible on discontinuing the drug. In the NCI study, 17 women who took Tamoxifen suffered blood clots in the lungs and 130 developed deep-vein thrombosis (blood clots in major blood vessels). In pre-menopausal women, Tamoxifen causes bone loss of 1.7% annually.

Side-effects such as confusion, depression, memory loss and fatigue have also been reported. Georgia Wiesner, the medical director at the Centre for Human Genetics at University Hospitals, Cleveland, said of Tamoxifen:

"You need to be clear about what the risks are so you're not trading one disease for another." [179]

It seems almost unbelievable that this drug is being prescribed today. Alongside Tamoxifen and other toxic 'medicines' manufactured by Zeneca, this company also makes herbicides and fungicides. Acetochlor, one of Zeneca's organochlorine pesticides, has been implicated as a causal factor in breast cancer and its Perry, Ohio chemical plant (the third largest source of potential cancer-causing pollution in the US) emitted 53,000 pounds of recognised carcinogens into the air in 1996. [180]

Herceptin
Herceptin (Trastuzumab) is a breast cancer chemotherapy drug, introduced by Genentech Pharmaceuticals in 1998. It is given to women with breast cancer that has metastasised (spread) to other areas of the body. A blood test has told them they have a protein in their system called HER2. It is said that Herceptin binds to cancer cells that express HER2 and slows the growth or spread of tumours. A breast cancer website sponsored by Siemens (major manufacturers of oncological and other radiography imaging devices) states:

"Many experts believe that Herceptin represents the future direction of breast cancer drugs in that it targets a particular protein of the cancer cell and prevents it from carrying out its action, similar

---

[179] Ibid.
[180] Batt, Sharon, "Cancer, Inc.", *Sierra* magazine, September-October 1999

to the new leukemia drug, Gleevec. Herceptin is given intravenously (through the vein) in an outpatient clinical setting."

But this is in direct contrast to the international warning issued by Genentech in May 2000, reporting that Hetceptin had been linked to 15 deaths and 47 other adverse reactions in patients.

Breast cancer drug blamed for deaths: *Genentech Inc. mailed a letter to doctors Thursday warning that the breast cancer drug Herceptin has been linked to 15 deaths and 47 other adverse reactions in patients. In nine of the 15 deaths, symptoms arose within 24 hours after Herceptin was administered, according to the letter. Genentech is working with the FDA to have the drug's label amended to reflect the new risks.*[181]

What could possibly be put on the label? 'Warning. Can cause symptoms leading to death within 24 hours'?

Death by doctoring

Putting paid to the idea that Herceptin is the way forward is the sad story of 26-year-old Tammy Starks, being treated with Herceptin after her breast cancer had spread. This from the US daily paper, *The Kansan:*

"One doctor told her she wouldn't live long. She underwent a complete bone marrow transplant in 1998, though it failed and the cancer remained. Then there was a ray of hope. A new doctor knew of a drug about to hit the market to help in her battle against the aggressive form of breast cancer. In 1998, the Food and Drug Administration approved the drug Herceptin, which has been shown to kill cancer cells in some women in the advanced stages of cancer....

For Tammy, the combination of Herceptin and chemotherapy worked, getting rid of the tumours in her breast, liver and lymph nodes. But six months ago, Starks' life took another turn. The breast cancer returned, this time metastasising to her brain, where she now has nine small tumours. "They can't do surgery," she said, adding that typically doctors will only perform surgery when there are three or

---

[181] "Breast cancer drug blamed for deaths", *USA Today*, 5th May 2000

less tumours. Starks, who has lost some sight in her right eye from the tumours, still receives the Herceptin once a week, though she said it has not been found to be very successful on breast cancer that has spread to the brain. She takes several chemotherapy pills every day for two weeks before she has a week off the treatment. And then there are the daily doses of pain medications and pills to prevent seizures and blood clots. Until a successful treatment is found, she and her husband Brian of seven years, and their children, Kendra, 6, and Kyle, 3, try to live a normal family life." [182]

Needless to say, readers are strongly advised to research the side-effects of all chemotherapy/hormonal drugs prescribed to them for their particular condition.

'Male-oriented' Breast Cancer Awareness Month

Breast Cancer Awareness Month in the US (and the pink ribbon campaigns here in the UK), are designed to raise public awareness of breast cancer. BCAM is held in October and is sponsored primarily by Zeneca, (a former subsidiary of Industry giant ICI), along with the American Academy of Family Physicians and Cancer Care Inc. National Breast Cancer Awareness Month is now governed by a board consisting of 17 organisations, including the American Cancer Society, the Centers for Disease Control and the National Cancer Institute.

As we have read in this and preceding chapters, public awareness of the true nature of conventional cancer care is not widespread by any means. Why can't there be a clause somewhere in Breast Cancer Awareness Month that draws attention to the fact that the whole industry is male and money-oriented? The following extract is taken from the *British Medical Journal* "Selling Sickness" debate:

"In some countries, women are invited for mammography in a letter in which the date and time of the appointment have already been fixed. This puts pressure on these women, who must actively decline the invitation if they don't want to be screened. Sometimes, women are asked to give reasons for not attending appointments, as if it were a civic duty. In leaflets, women get simple messages - that

---

[182] Full story at http://thekansan.com/stories/060800/fro_0608000010.html

cancer detected early can be cured, and early cancers can often be treated with breast-conserving surgery.

The data tell another story: no reliable evidence shows that breast screening saves lives; breast screening leads to more surgery, including more mastectomies; and estimates show that more than a tenth of healthy women who attend a breast screening program experience considerable psychological distress for many months." [183]

An unnecessary climate of fear

Writing in praise of the 'discoverers' of the supposed breast cancer gene BRCA, Dr Miryam Wahrman does acknowledge one or two drawbacks in the gene-predictive process:

"A significant dilemma which exists in regard to the BRCA genes is that the decisions to be made are not clear-cut. Inheriting either of the mutant BRCA genes may increase the likelihood of contracting cancer significantly, but not to 100%. So women must grapple with whether to undergo major surgery, or to watch and wait." [184]

Watch and wait?
Nothing short of criminal

With the advent of genetic predictors for cancer, the authority figure in the cancer equation – the oncologist - has now been given permission to pronounce a psychological, pharmaceutical and surgical curse upon healthy and unsuspecting patients. That so unsound and theoretical a knowledge-base is gaining such stature in society today is nothing short of criminal. We are mere guinea pigs. Women in particular are being herded from pillar to post and trustingly receiving diagnoses and treatments that are not only causing serious psychological and physical harm, but also a great deal of unnecessary death.

---

[183] Moynihan, Ray, Heath, Iona & David Henry, "Selling Sickness: the pharmaceutical industry and disease-mongering", *British Medical Journal Online*, BMJ, 13th April 2002
[184] Wahrman, Miryam Z, "The Breast Cancer Genes":
http://www.us-israel.org/jsource/Judaism/breast_cancer.html

In surveying the conventional breast cancer scene, in fact, in surveying the conventional cancer scene in general, one can only conclude that *death by doctoring* is alive and well in the 21st century. This author makes no apologies for the picture that has emerged with regard to conventional cancer treatment and 'care'. On the brink of the American Civil War, it was Patrick Henry who poignantly stated:

"We are apt to shut our eyes against a painful truth, and listen to the song of the siren till she transforms us into beasts. For my part, whatever anguish of spirit it may cost, I am willing to know the whole truth, to know the worst, and provide for it."

Empowering women

Were there only one side to this cancer story, then it would be a depressing read indeed. As we shall soon discover though, there is some very good news indeed on cancer in the 21st century. And fortunately, it doesn't depend on the mighty orthodoxy to deliver it! With regard to breast cancer in general, for those women facing this disease or who are worried about the prospect, the following heartening advice is offered by Dr Joseph Mercola:

Women can make a difference in eliminating breast cancer: *The breast cancer epidemic is not some great mystery. The causes of cancer are already known. Toxic diets, toxic lifestyles, toxic environments, toxic drug treatments and toxic, diagnostic techniques cause cancer. Corporations are only interested in increasing their profits and ensuring their tentacles of control, not in actual solutions. When it comes to Breast Cancer Awareness Month, women must invest their time and money into other projects, initiatives and treatments that will truly create change. Some of the most immediate steps women can take towards creating a preventative program include:*

> ➤ *Eating as many organic foods as possible – they are not only free of harmful chemicals but also have much greater nutritional value;*
> ➤ *Eliminating all commercial household cleaning products and toxic garden pesticides – replacing with safe, organic and bio-degradable brands;*
> ➤ *Drinking pure, filtered water;*

106

> ➤ *Refuse steroid hormone treatments such as HRT and the Pill - these are known to initiate and promote breast cancer;*
> ➤ *Seek out the many natural approaches to regain hormonal balance;*
> ➤ *Detoxify the body and reduce stress;*
> ➤ *Investigate safe screening techniques such as thermography, especially if you are pre-menopausal.*

Breast Cancer Awareness Month is indeed a powerful time to educate, awaken and empower women to the real causes, preventative measures and truly effective cures for breast cancer. But, let's not be duped or compromised in the process.[185]

* * * * *

We began this exploration of conventional cancer treatments by asking why it is that so many people continue to attend the conventional treatment centres, and why non-conventional cancer advice is often avoided. Having explored some of the more subtle mechanisms that keep us on the conventional path and examined the dangers associated with so many of the conventional treatments, our final chapter in part one takes a different turn. We discuss the 'alternative reputation'.

Why is it that so many people continue to believe that genuinely efficacious, non-conventional, 'alternative' treatments for illness and disease are just plain 'quackery'?

---

[185] Mercola, Joseph, "Breast Cancer Awareness Month":
http://www.mercola.com/2000/oct/29/breast_cancer_awareness.htm

The non-conventional medicine cabinet

"The desire to take medicine is perhaps the greatest feature which distinguishes man from animals." **William Osler**

Seven drops, three times a day

Aside from the wiles of the merchant and his all-pervading influence over the media and marketplace, genuine treatments for illness and disease have also always had to do battle with another entity – the well-intentioned para-healer, who unwittingly has the capacity to prove equally as threatening to the cause of genuine medicine, albeit for very different reasons.[186] The non-conventional medical marketplace seems to be largely inhabited by those who are able to deliver an admirably coherent deconstruction of the conventional medical paradigm, but who choose not to apply the same level of intelligent critique to their own often wacky nostrums and alliances.

As such, we are subjected to an equally misguided barrage of pronouncements such as, *"Submit not to the ravages of chemo. Let White Eagle purge you of those negative energies."* Visit a pyramid, a shaman, *"My sickness is a shamanic gift and calling,"*[187] a cancer 'guide', *"OK group. Eyes closed. Your cancer is receding. The lump is disintegrating. Envisage the all-consuming fire!"* A coat of mud, of seaweed or both, some radionics, this therapy, that therapy and, of course, a thousand-and-one folk remedies, Grandma's trusted 'brain tumour elixir' perhaps - a walnut kernel, perfectly preserved in rainwater, seven drops, three times a day.

Celebrities with the more serious illnesses receive these well-intentioned 'tips and tricks' by the sack-load. John Diamond was no exception.

"I've had anecdotal evidence from those who believe in voodoo, the power of the fairy people - yes, really - drinking my own p**s and

---

[186] 'Para-healer', from the word 'para': close to, alongside, near, irregular healer
[187] Kalweit, Holger, *Dream Time and Inner Space*, Shambala Publications, 1998

any number of other remedies.... I should put my faith in the Bessarabian radish, the desiccated root of which has been used for centuries by Tartar nomads to cure athlete's foot, tennis elbow and cancer, as detailed in their book 'Why Your Doctor Hates You And Wants You To Die', review copy enclosed..."[188]

Selling very well

Notwithstanding the genuine treatments available in the natural cabinet, which we discuss in Part Two, a huge number of remedies being sold as 'medicine' today contain no sensible methodology, yet perhaps not surprisingly, they are selling as well as ever. No better is this phenomenon illustrated than in the lucrative minor ailments market, where, on a daily basis across the world, untold millions in dollars, pounds, yen and Euros are being spent on pharmacologically inert mixtures and 'essences', producing truly marvellous results with illnesses from which we were going to get better anyway.

In truth, were the general public to be given clear information on the nature of self-limiting illness and the wondrous ability of a properly nourished immune system to overcome and repel almost all ills unaided, the bottom would fall out of the minor ailments market tomorrow, conventional medicine included. £95,000,000 is spent on cough mixtures alone in the UK. The *BMJ*, however, has reported a recent trial involving 2,000 participants which found that, in most cases, the mixtures were no more effective than placebo.[189] The *New England Journal of Medicine* tells us:

"90% of patients who visit doctors have conditions that will either improve on their own or are out of reach of modern medicine's ability to solve."[190]

Wishful appeal

Unfortunately though, when engaging in conversation with practitioners whose treatments fall into this category, most of the more awkward questions arising from such a discussion on self-limiting

---

[188] Diamond, John, op. cit.
[189] "Cough Mixtures under scrutiny":
http://news.bbc.co.uk/hi/english/health/newsid_1807000/1807252.stm
[190] *The New England Journal of Medicine*, 7th February, 1991

illness, etc., are usually defended, not by answering the actual question itself, but by the therapist appealing to the worthiness of his wider philanthropic goals and to *'the much greater threat to the global populace'* posed by the merchant's house, with all its toxic wares, avarice and vested interests, etc., etc.

And while these observations are accurate in many instances, presenting the weaknesses of one particular practice as evidence of efficacy for another is not a viable argument at all. Any treatment that claims therapeutic worth should be able to stand in its own right. But such is the wholesome, wishful appeal of some non-conventional literature, and so honourable are the therapist's aims, that, in most instances, the intellectual and therapeutic weaknesses are tolerated or overlooked, and he is allowed to continue his practice, unhindered by tiresome obstacles, such as intellectual consistency or quite fair demands that his practice be made 'open to fair scrutiny'.

By default, all this is having a detrimental effect on the reputation of those non-conventional treatments for illness and disease (including cancer) that are actually provably effective.

Unicorn badges to ward off head lice!

A relevant example of intellectually inconsistent cancer 'information' is found at a web-page entitled "The Future for Cancer Research". The page begins:

"Left to itself, the cancer research community will continue to explore narrower and narrower topics and make limited progress in developing a cure. This community needs to be shaken up." [191]

Few people of course, would disagree with this statement. It is a rational observation, based on a wealth of documented evidence that details the restrictive nature of conventional medical research. However, rationality is soon dispensed with as the author then directs his readers to an organisation that sells unicorn badges which, we are told, have been found to be especially useful in the fight against head lice infestations in junior school. Featured are a number of testimonies

---

[191] "The Future for Cancer Research":
http://pssst-heyu.com/antonysutton/septemberftir2.html

as to its efficacy, including one from a grandmother who swears by the badges and has ordered two more!

On the same page, the author also discusses cancer and states that future research into this disease must focus on distance healing. To prove his point, readers from anywhere in the world are invited to send in their name and email address to a practitioner who, with his special 'radionics' machine, will *psychically* and *vibrationally* tune in to the respondent and send out his *powerful healing* rays.

An impressive array of dials

Radionics is loosely based on the principles of divination and became 'electrified' divination with the advent of Dr Abraham's infamous 'Black Box' of the 1920's. Abraham's invention was apparently able to detect mental and physical disharmonies in a person, merely by scanning samples of hair, blood or saliva sent in by that person for 'special analysis'. Submitting your sample [now, just your name and email address will suffice] to today's radionics practitioners along with a fee, generally in the order of £30.00, the practitioner will feed the sample into the box, interpret the various signals emitting from an impressive array of dials, gauges and winking lights, and then return his verdict, along with a specially selected remedy.

Sceptics wishing to determine the sensibility of the snaking electrics contained in these little boxes are invariably told that removing the back upsets the delicate nature of the instruments. One firm, South West Radionics Association, told me I would not understand the full significance of the internal workings without a complete grasp of radionics theory and a background in quantum mechanics.

Healer Arthur Bailey freely confesses that a near absence of wiring in some of these instruments leaves one slightly nonplussed as to their operation, but maintains that *"...nevertheless, they do seem to work."* In his book on the subject, Mr Bailey goes on to cite the following as validation of his methods:

Whilst with a group of friends in a non English-speaking Italian restaurant, the party was having considerable difficulty deciding what to order from the unintelligible menu. Tongue in cheek, his sceptical friends suggested to Mr Bailey that he might use his 'attunement' skills to determine the most flavoursome dish.

"I got out my pendulum and dowsed down the incomprehensible list. One item in particular gave a very strong reaction. Taking courage in both hands, I ordered it. When it came, the sceptics were silenced. I had ordered by far the best item on the menu. It was delicious."[192]

But some sceptics aren't silenced

Over the years, a number of sceptics have submitted samples of blood, hair or saliva of <u>non-human</u> origin to these practitioners. Medical history abounds with glorious examples of situations where radionics operators have inadvertently revealed the true worth of their diagnostic tool. In one instance, the saliva of a young cow returned the verdict of *"an inordinate interest in women"*. In another, a reading taken from the blood of a rooster prompted the practitioner to pronounce the root of the patient's problem as *"suffering from bad teeth and a recurring sinus infection."* [193]

And no matter how well-intentioned the practitioner, should such treatments be allowed to be advertised as successful in cancer, no questions asked?

Negative brain patterns cause cancer!

Another site suggests that cancer can be reversed through hypnosis:

"We all produce cancer cells, but it is when the immune system stops receiving signals to destroy those cells that it becomes a problem. In recent discoveries, they found that certain thought patterns are harmful to the system and create lesions in the brain. By the location of the lesions in the brain you can determine the type of cancer. Once you heal the lesion, then the immune system starts getting signals again telling it to fight the cancer." [194]

---

[192] Wallace, *Anyone Can Dowse For Better Health*, Quantum Books, 1999
[193] Pfeiffer, Samuel, *Healing at any Price*, Word Publishing, 1988
[194] "Healing Cancer through Hypnosis": www.healedyou.com/Pages/cancer.html

The author, David Babb, does not indicate who the 'they' might be who discovered these 'lesions', and goes on to suggest that, through careful study of a patient's handwriting (grapho-therapy), it is possible to detect the negative brain patterns responsible for cancer. Mr Babb also offers handwriting analysis for *as little as $35.00 per session*, which might detect these cancerous negativities. Those people, whose handwriting reveals *cancerous negativity*, must then decide whether they wish to undergo Mr Babb's hypno-treatments, which are advertised as being able to correct the negativity before the cancer develops.

A gem of a remedy

Similarly, some information acquired at a recent UK health fair advertised the gem sunstone for *'cellular healing and cancer recovery'*. A leaflet being distributed advised that:

"The stones should be carried as close to the body as possible. It is best personally to pick your gemstone, but they can be purchased by mail order. The best way to pick your gemstone is to handle it. See how it feels to you - feel its energies. Never purchase a stone that does not feel right to you. Before using your gemstones, always cleanse, consecrate and empower them." [195]

Lump of earth cures cancer!
The photographs prove it

Another cancer treatment claims to be able to heal cancer by the ingestion of *supercharged* clay and/or the topical application of *supercharged* gel.

"All Intrasound products have been activated (charged) permanently with a very specific spectrum of bio-energetic energy frequencies. Immersing oneself in this Intrasound signal, through the use of the powder and the gel, raises the vibratory energy level of the body to a higher octave, resulting in the increased ability for the body

---

[195] Leaflet on file at Credence Research

to heal itself. The improvements in health that many people are getting with the Intrasound formulas are astonishing." [196]

The above practitioner 'charges' a lump of clay with a 'special frequency' emitted from his special machine and, using a hotchpotch of 'scientific papers' to prove his point, he then retails this 'highly charged' lump of earth in powdered form, at $39.00 a jar. *Intrasound* is being advertised as useful in the fight against cancer. To 'prove' the efficacy, strength and power of *Intrasound*, the site also includes some *before and after* aura photography shots. A weak, hazy aura surrounds the un-powdered individual. A photograph taken one hour after consumption of the *Intrasound* powder however and the aura is a bright, vibrant purple! [197]

Intrasound for cancer! The photographs prove it.

Buyer beware

Bringing a different perspective to bear on this subject, at a recent health fair in Manchester in the UK, I had the dubious privilege of watching an aura photography 'practitioner' at work. The 'punter' sits in a chair, whereupon he is instructed to place his hands upon a 'special surface' which apparently is a vital component in the process of 'tuning into' the aura of the individual. With the photograph taken, the punter plus colourful snap is then directed to a waiting team of aura 'consultants' who then interpret the psychedelic halo surrounding the subject's head. Advice focuses on magnificence of character, future wealth, successful relationships, all the usual stuff, but more worryingly, predisposition to disease and the steps that can be taken to avoid falling prey to the illness.

Ask no questions

I asked the practitioner what would happen if I sat for the photo, but did not place my hand upon the 'special surface' and wasn't it the case that this special surface was no more than a basic heat sensor pad, wired into the Polaroid process? [198] Non-plussed at first that a punter

---

[196] "Cancer and other healings attributed to Intrasound":
www.entersound.com/article1_2.html
[197] Ibid.
[198] A picture of this 'special plate' can be seen at:

was actually daring to ask questions, the practitioner then told me to f*** off and stop giving him grief. Having noted the speed at which he was processing the long queue of people waiting to pay the £10 for their aura photograph, his response was not altogether surprising. I estimated his wheeze was fleecing the populace at a rate of £300 per hour.

Another *'special machine'* for detecting *'special frequencies'*. All in a day's work, I suppose. A fairly good rule of thumb seems to be that if the therapy includes a machine that has a *secret, energetic* method of detecting disease, then thorough investigation is the order of the day.

Guided imagery?

There are many books and websites devoted to guided imagery and its role in the treatment of cancer. In focusing on this particular method of 'attacking' cancer, there is a danger that critiquing this approach could be construed as critiquing the benefits of a positive frame of mind. The two issues are entirely separate, as we shall see.

O Carl Simonton MD was the first modern-day imagery practitioner to promote the idea that guided imagery might be used to reverse the development of cancer. In his popular book *Getting Well Again*, he suggests the following picture to the cancer patient:

"Picture yourself reaching your goals in life. See your purpose in life being fulfilled, the members of your family doing well, your relationships with people around you becoming more meaningful. Remember that having strong reasons for getting well will help you get well, so use this time to focus clearly on your priorities in life." [199]

This is indeed a positive picture and, overall, could be of great comfort and support. But what if, alongside the imagery exercises, the patient is also receiving toxic, conventional cancer treatment? Shouldn't the dangers of this treatment at least be made known to the patient? Simonton's tape continues:

---

http://www.auraphoto.com/applications.htm
[199] Simonton, O Carl, *Getting Well Again*, Bantam Books, May 1992

"If you are now receiving treatment, picture your treatment coming into your body in a way that you understand. If you are receiving radiation treatment, picture it as a beam of millions of bullets of energy hitting any cell in its path. The normal cells are able to repair the damage that is done, but the cancer cells cannot because they are weak. (This is one of the basic facts on which radiation therapy is built.)

If you are receiving chemotherapy, picture that drug coming into your body and entering the bloodstream. Picture the drug acting like a poison. The normal cells are intelligent and strong and don't take up the poison so readily. But the cancer cell is a weak cell so it takes very little to kill it. It absorbs the poison, dies and is flushed out of your body."

Immediately, there is a problem here. Nowhere does the narrative suggest that receiving either of these treatments is exceedingly harmful. Even though Simonton wants nothing more than for the patient to overcome his or her cancerous affliction, the suggestion to the patient that they must imagine that the treatment (perhaps mustard gas, cellular radiation, or their derivatives) is effecting internal repair is a woefully ill-informed image to enforce.

Moving on through Simonton's guided imagery: "Picture your body's own white cells coming into the area where the cancer is, recognising the abnormal cells, and destroying them. There is a vast army of white blood cells. They are very strong and aggressive. They are also very smart. There is no contest between them and the cancer cells; they will win the battle." [200]

The power lies within you!
A destructive message?

All the while the patient imagines that the white blood cells are winning the battle (white blood cells being the vital part of immune system defence), they are receiving that cell-destroying conventional cancer treatment. Simonton's guided imagery is only reinforcing a lie, since both chemotherapy and radiation *deplete* white-cell counts

---

[200] Ibid.

massively. His suggestions run contrary to all the known facts about chemotherapy and survival statistics for chemotherapy recipients. To reiterate, on chemotherapy and radiation treatments, Dr Hardin Jones of the National Cancer Institute stated:

"My studies have proved conclusively that untreated cancer victims live up to four times longer than treated individuals. If one has cancer and opts to do nothing at all, he will live longer and feel better than if he undergoes radiation, chemotherapy or surgery, other than when used in immediate life-threatening situations." [201]

Mis-guided imagery?

The fact that Simonton is reinforcing an incomplete image in the mind of the individual prompts the valid question, is it misguided imagery? Another website entitled *Destroy Your Cancer* advertises visualisation audio tapes to defeat cancer. The home page includes the following statement:

"In the privacy and comfort of your home, you listen to your cassette or CD as the narrator guides you through your body, using unique visualisation techniques to watch your cancer cells and tumours shrinking smaller and smaller and smaller until they completely disappear." [202]

Simonton concludes his guided imagery session thus:

"Give yourself a mental pat on the back for participating in your recovery. See yourself doing this mental imagery exercise three times a day, staying awake and alert as you do it."

So, as the tape plays its message (that the patient's recovery and ability to shrink the cancerous cells lies within the patient's own mental powers), any person receiving and believing this message while continuing to receive the conventional treatment may well experience their battle for health being cruelly lost, while at the same time listening to a tape telling them it's possible to recover. Perhaps they're not imagining hard enough? While a positive attitude is essential in life

---

[201] Chemotherapy quotes at *The Cancer Page*: www.whale.to/cancer/quotes1.html
[202] Destroy Your Cancer at : www.destroyyourcancer.com

and even more so in times of illness, these built-in suggestions can often compound the feelings of confusion, inadequacy and self-blame for non-recovery.

Contrary to real world experience

That we are not always in control of our own circumstances is argued quite eloquently by Dave Hunt, author of the book, *America: The Sorcerer's Apprentice*, who states:

"Consider the spontaneous case with which lightning blacks out a city, a snowstorm closes a road and airports, a tornado tears off rooftops - all of this not only without any help from any human minds, but in spite of hours of seminars, subliminal suggestion tapes and positive affirmations." [203]

Once again, in talking to the practitioners of such treatments, their care and concern for the patients is obvious and they want nothing other than to see their patient recover and/or cope positively during their time of illness. Surely though, it is far better to encourage the patient to remain grounded in reality and give concise information on the nature of conventional cancer treatment and on non-toxic alternatives that actively deal with the cancer, than to reinforce positive-sounding misinformation into the patient's psyche.

And all in the same cabinet too!

While all these alternative, non-conventional 'treatments' and diagnoses (and many more like them) are most-times offered for man's highest good and from a willing heart, (and for little money in comparison to conventional treatments), this is no argument in favour of their continued use. Furthermore, it is their continued existence alongside more bona-fide, natural treatments that is causing considerable damage to the reputation of genuine medicine. We need an uncluttered cabinet. According to Donald Gould, author of *The Black and White Medicine Show*, this can only be brought about by uncluttered thinking. He warns of the dangers we invite, should we buy into the current climate of *laissez-faire* reasoning:

---

[203] Hunt, Dave, *America, The Sorcerer's Apprentice*, Harvest House, 1988

"Why not make the most of what the non-conformists have to offer and to hell with uncharitable logic? There is, I suggest, a powerful reason for rejecting this superficially attractive option. Truth is a fundamental value. If we accept uncritical thinking in one area of our lives for the sake of convenience or because of the popular appeal of a seductive myth and the short-term comfort to be gained by believing in the unbelievable, or because the false answer lets us pretend we are competently coping with a painful problem we haven't truly tackled, then we are all the more likely to adopt the same strategy in other situations, from dealing with the family, to managing the national economy, and from chairing the parish council to handling arsenals of nuclear weapons. The result is likely to be unhappy and stands a decent chance of proving a disaster. Irrational beliefs are always dangerously corrupting, even when they only relate to the cause and cure of piles." [204]

Can we blame them?

The outlandish claims being made in certain quarters of the non-conventional health marketplace are what so incensed John Diamond and continue to incense thousands today. Can we blame them for feeling this way? In need only of sensible advice and treatment, many people end up worse off in body, mind, spirit and pocket. This can very quickly lead to a *carte blanche* dismissal of all the good that genuine, natural treatments have to offer. It is my conviction that some of the errant practices posing as medicine (and the confusion arising as a result) are a contributory factor in today's general adherence to the conventional model and general dismissal of the natural medicine cabinet. As a result of this summary dismissal, thousands of people miss out on sensible treatment and will consequently perish unnecessarily.

John Diamond made the mistake of dismissing the entire non-conventional *materia medica* out of hand, stating that there was as much chance of him going down the alternative treatment route as there was of 'the Pope getting drunk on the communion wine and getting off with a couple of nuns'.[205] While his comparisons didn't

---

[204] Gould, Donald, *The Black and White Medicine Show*, Hamilton 1985
[205] Diamond, John, op. cit.

exactly aid the general cause, perhaps we can now understand some of his frustrations.

A smorgasbord under one name
Sadly, there is no clear division between the reputation of much of the unregulated alternative health industry and that of the many sensible, non-conventional treatments available today. It has all become a smorgasbord of different approaches, different values and different philosophies - all under one name. This has become a point of major concern, even to the non-orthodox regulatory bodies overseeing the complementary health movement.

Perhaps a name change is in order. Instead of conventional, alternative, complementary or whatever, is it too naïve to suggest that we should just be working towards medicine and non-medicine, full stop?

Having now had opportunity to ponder some of the weaknesses on both sides of the fence, it is hoped that an atmosphere of openness can be brought to future discussions on partnership in medical practice. Either way, critical debate should commence as soon as possible with regard to those 'helping' therapies that serve no purpose other than temporarily to distract the seriously ill.

A letter I received recently pointed the way forward quite succinctly:

"I found the references to John Diamond especially poignant. I confess to not having read his material, not wanting to engage with someone who took such a path. I now question that decision and will buy and read his book with gusto. It's so important to understand and acknowledge all sides of the argument to be able to influence."

Is cancer preventable?
We conclude Part One of this study on cancer with a statement from the World Cancer Research Fund, which tells us that a remarkable 30 to 40 percent of cancers can be prevented simply by

making healthy eating choices and adopting a healthier lifestyle.[206] This encouraging but conservative finding was established by WCRF in its 1997 report examining the role of diet in the prevention of cancer. After a review of more than 4,000 published scientific papers on the link between diet and cancer, the WCRF concluded that some of the most common cancers affecting the western world are largely preventable - providing we eat an appropriate diet.

Increasingly, we are reading from a variety of sources that a plant-based diet, rich in fruits, vegetables and unrefined cereals, provides considerable protection from cancer. In addition, certain foods and dietary components have been identified for moderation due to potential increase in cancer risk.

Part Two of this book looks at these claims in more detail. We evaluate some of those cancer treatments from the natural cabinet which do not incorporate unicorns, clay powder or chanting, which are saving and enhancing lives daily.

And we also get a glimpse of the real cancer war being waged behind the scenes. After all, if common sense and simple nutrition can indeed thwart cancer, then what on earth will become of the worldwide conventional cancer drug market, which stood at $14.8 billion in 2000, and is expected to exceed $27 billion by 2005? [207]

Now that is a lot of money.

---

[206] ANAC Report on Diet and Cancer, Australian Nutritional Advisory Council at: http://www.anac-nz.org

[207] Business Communications Co., Inc. New Developments in Worldwide Cancer http://www.bccresearch.com/editors/RB-152.html

Part 2
Great news on cancer in the 21st century!

Towards a more humane paradigm

Please note that the information in the following sections is for educational purposes only and should not be construed as medical advice. Consultation with a qualified health practitioner should always be sought in the matter of serious illness.

What is cancer?

A breath of fresh air in the debate!

Depending on who you ask, the answer to this question can be quite varied. The following texts are taken from a number of conventional cancer resources. This first one is from the popular Village Health website:

"Ultimately, a cancer can trace its history back to one single, errant cell. Each cell in our bodies is under strict instructions regarding whether to grow and divide, and whether to stay put or migrate to another part of the body. Mostly these instructions arise from the genetic instructions (DNA) within the cell itself, but cells also receive instructions from neighbouring cells." [208]

This next account of *what is cancer?* is brought to us by Covenant Health:

"Cancer is an uncontrolled growth of the cells in any part of the body. This growth interferes with the way your body normally functions.... Cancer tissues have lost their ability to 'turn off' their growth. They eventually crowd out healthy tissues, disrupting your body's ability to do what it needs to do." [209]

This from Exact Science:

"With the exception of cancers that arise from blood-forming tissues, such as leukaemia, most cancers are recognised as a swelling or enlargement in an organ or tissue of the body. These enlargements contain many cells that are different from normal cells, and undergo many changes in their genetic material, or DNA, at different times during their development." [210]

---

[208] Village Health, "What is Cancer?"
www.ivillagehealth.com/experts/ent/qas/0,11816,165919_175172,00.html
[209] Covenant Health, "What is Cancer?"
www.covenanthealth.com/features/health/cancer/canc4283.cfm
[210] Exact Science, "What is Cancer?"

And this from British Columbia Cancer Agency:

"Over time, a number of gene mutations may occur in a cell, allowing it to divide and grow in a way that becomes a cancer. Because most cancers do not happen until a cell is affected by several gene mutations, most cancers are not seen until later in life. Genes play a role in all cancers." [211]

In comparing these conventional insights into what constitutes cancer, we can see that it is defined as a genetic mutation which leads to a swelling and/or tumour or tumoural mass, either benign or malignant. The belief is that any tumoural mass must be attacked as soon as possible. Attacking the tumour supposedly attacks the cancer.

These same websites also proffer the conventional weapons. Village Health again:

*"Cancer is treatable through a number of options. **Surgery**, **radiation therapy**, and **chemotherapy** are some of the most common, However **hormone** and **biological** therapies also exist. The doctor may use one of these methods or a combination of methods for treatment."* [212]

In this next text, the US Cancer Research Institute describes what causes cancer and quite astonishingly, only reinforces the fact that high on the culprit-list is its own treatment regimen:

"Cancer is a group of over 100 diseases characterised by the uncontrolled growth of abnormal cells in the body. Normal cells can become abnormal when they are exposed to carcinogens such as radiation (for example, ultraviolet rays of the sun) or particular drugs or chemicals." [213]

---

www.exactlabs.com/cic/what_is_cancer/_index.htm
[211] BCCA, "What is Cancer?"
www.bccancer.bc.ca/pg_g_03.asp?PageID=44&ParentID=2
[212] Village Health, op. cit.
[213] Cancer Research Institute, "What is Cancer?"
www.cancerresearch.org/hbwhtcan.html

Aventis Pharmaceuticals, one of the world's leading suppliers of cancer drugs, also describes cancer as a genetic disease. It states that:

"Chemotherapy agents may also be used in combination with one another. The aim of combination therapy is to increase efficacy while maintaining an acceptable safety profile." [214]

Are we really surprised when Aventis declares that chemicals play an important role in the treatment of cancer? Across the board, this company enjoyed chemical sales in excess of $17 billion in 2001 for a variety of diseases.[215]

Quite clearly, the focus is on the tumour and the necessity for its immediate removal by chemical shrivelling or, as John Diamond described, *"pay-as-you-bleed, surgical muggings."*

A breath of fresh air!
There are many other qualified doctors and scientists who believe that cancer must not be defined as merely a tumour or mass in need of immediate removal and destruction. They say there are much wider parameters involved. We will now look at some descriptions of cancer from other professionals who do not focus upon the genetics or DNA of cancer, but upon a much simpler paradigm, namely toxic environment. This first extract is taken Dr Philip Binzel's book on cancer entitled *Alive and Well*:

"...most members of the medical profession have treated this disease using the theory that the tumour is the disease. This theory said that if you can remove the tumour or destroy the tumour, you will cure the disease. Drs. Krebs, Burk, Nieper and others said in essence: "Wrong!" These men had seen thousands of cancer patients die. They realised that 95% of these patients had been treated with surgery and/or radiation and chemotherapy. It was obvious to them that that if removing the tumour or destroying the tumour cured the disease, then these 95% would be alive and well." [216]

---

[214] Aventis Corp, "What is Cancer?" www.aventis.com
[215] www.aventis.com
[216] Binzel, Philip, *Alive and Well*, American Media Publications, 1994

In this same vein, Dr Harold W Manner writes as follows:

"In recent years a significant reassessment of the nature and causes of cancer has taken place. Cancer was formerly believed to be a localised disease, characterised by a lesion, usually in the form of a growth, which appeared at some specific part of the body. This localised lesion was thought to be the result of activity produced by an invading virus, carcinogenic agent or some form of trauma, such as a blow.

Today, there is a growing conviction among researchers and physicians that cancer is a complex disease that is the end result of a disturbed metabolism (body chemistry). It is an insidious disease that involves the entire body: the nervous system, digestive tract, pancreas, lungs, excretory organs, endocrine system, and the entire defence mechanisms. The frequent reoccurrence of a malignancy after treatment with the conventional methods of surgery, radiation and/or chemotherapy results because the basic underlying metabolic cause of the cancer is rarely considered and consequently remains uncorrected." [217]

In his book *Cancer: Why We're Still Dying to Know the Truth*, health researcher Phillip Day states:

"Another distressing fact is that medicine very often misses the plot when it comes to solving some of mankind's most serious diseases. The 'virus hunters', who dominate the grant-hungry medical research communities worldwide, see a microbe behind every serious disease. $Billions have been spent chasing down non-existent viruses for scurvy, cancer, AIDS, Legionnaires', SMON, pellagra, many other ailments, and now even BSE, the supposedly viral condition affecting cattle, its true cause now being increasingly linked to poisoning by the multitudinous organophosphates used in intensive farming today. There exists a criminal disregard for the obvious evidence that

---

[217] Manner, Harold W, *Metabolic Therapy in Cancer*, Cytopharma de Mexico, S.A, PO Box 434931, San Ysidro, CA. Dr Harold Manner was chairman of the biology department at Loyola University in Chicago during the 1970's. Because of institutional harassment over his decision to treat cancer patients with nutrition, he moved to Tijuana, Mexico, where he ran the Manner Clinic, successfully treating thousands of US cancer patients from 1982 until his death in 1992.

suggests a completely non-viral and far more simple cause for these illnesses." [218]

Cancer researcher Ernst T Krebs Jr. remarks:

"There are many chronic or metabolic diseases that have challenged medicine. Many of these diseases have already been conquered. What proved to be their solution? By solution we mean prevention and cure. What really cures really prevents. Let us think of some of these diseases that have found total prevention and hence cure.

At one time, the metabolic disease known as scurvy killed hundreds of thousands of people, sometimes entire populations. This disease found total prevention and cure in the ascorbic acid or Vitamin C component of fruits and vegetables. Similarly, the once fatal diseases pernicious anaemia, pellagra, beriberi, countless neuropathies, and the like, found complete cure and prevention in specific dietary factors, that is, essential nutrients in an adequate diet." [219]

Writing in *Alternative Medicine Definitive Guide to Cancer*, Dr Douglas Brodie states:

"Each one of us produces several hundred thousand cancer cells every day of our lives. Whether we develop clinical cancer or not depends upon the ability of our immune systems to destroy these cancer cells. That's because cancer thrives in the presence of a deficient immune system." [220]

Environment, environment, environment!

What Binzel, Manner, Krebs, Brodie, Day and many other doctors and researchers are saying is that cancer presents as a multiple-variable deficiency disease. Yes, we can remove the tumour, but if the bodily deficiencies are not corrected, then the body's defence

---

[218] Day, Phillip, *Cancer: Why We're...*, op. cit.
[219] Krebs Jr., Ernst T, *Journal of Applied Nutrition*, Vol.22, Nos.3 & 4, 1970
[220] Brodie, Douglas, as quoted in *Alternative Medicine Definitive Guide to Cancer*, Future Medicine Publishing, 1997

mechanisms are not equipped with the necessary tools to overcome the cancerous state and the original tumour and/or other growths stand a good chance of returning. Even if the tumour has been removed, our susceptibility to cancer has not.

Reiterating earlier findings, the World Cancer Research Fund reviewed more than 4,000 published scientific papers on the subject and declared that a remarkable 30 to 40 percent of cancers can be prevented by making healthy eating choices and adopting a healthier lifestyle. Supporting this view, we also read this from the American Cancer Society:

"More than $104 billion is spent on cancer, including treatment, lost productivity, and mortality costs. One third of the annual 500,000 deaths from cancer, including breast, colon, and prostate cancers, may be attributed to undesirable dietary practices."[221]

The Oxford Textbook of Medicine says:

"Good nutrition leads to health and resistance to disease; poor nutrition leads to ill-health and susceptibility to many diseases."

And the US Surgeon General has stated:

"If you are among the two out of three Americans who do not smoke or drink excessively, your choice of diet can influence your long-term health prospects more than any other action you might take."[222]

It would certainly benefit us if we were to become generally more nutritional-minded, as the following extract from Hallelujah Acres reminds us:

"Rather than helping the body to restore itself to wellness by the elimination of those things in our diet and lifestyle that created the

---

[221] American Cancer Society, "Cancer Facts and Figures", Atlanta, GA, 1994: http://www.campaignfortruth.com/nutrition.htm
[222] "The Surgeon General's Report on Nutrition and Health", US Dept of Health and Human Services, Washington DC, 1988. Available from www.hhs.gov/

problem, modern medicine seeks aggressively to fight the symptom. The way we deal with sickness today is wrong, and it produces horrible results. Not a day goes by that I do not receive dozens of phone calls and letters from people from all over the world with the most horrible stories of the results they or their loved ones have experienced after going the traditional medical route for physical problems... especially cancer....

If we would but eliminate the causes, and give the body the proper building materials, most cancers would just disappear as the body's own self-healing mechanism kicks in. In fact, cancer would never have originated in the first place if the immune system had been functioning properly." [223]

The link between all-round health and nutrition is obvious, yet conventional cancer establishments are still only devoting a small amount of their prodigious resources to the subject. For political and financial reasons, the important role nutrition plays in health and disease prevention has always been marginalised by the tumour- and chemically-focused orthodoxy. Moves are underway to reverse the rather high level of ignorance in nutrition, as this item from PR Newswire hearteningly indicates:

World renowned nutritionists conclude that vitamin and mineral deficiency is a significant public health problem: *Global vitamin and mineral deficiencies in infants and young children's diets are still a significant public health problem in both developed and developing countries. The Academy of Paediatric Nutrition, a global group of nutrition experts, gathered at the third annual meeting in London to discuss the impact these deficiencies have on child development and growth. Their remit is to discuss the latest thinking in infant nutrition and disseminate their findings to healthcare professionals and the public."* [224]

---

[223] "God Gave us Self-Healing Bodies":
www.hacres.com/printable.asp?doctype=articles&docnum=47
[224] *PR NewsWire*, 30th April 2002
more at www.mlx282.co.uk/news/020430.php

While there are even moves afoot by some conventional cancer websites to commence educating their readers on the importance of a varied and nutritious diet, there is still much more that could be done to raise awareness on these matters.

Teaching on nutrition

How seriously is nutrition and health being taught in our medical schools today? John Robbins cites statistics on Western medical and nutritional curricula in his *Reclaiming our Health*:

> ➢ Number of accredited medical schools in the United States – 127
> ➢ Number with no required courses in nutrition - 95
> ➢ Average US physician's course work in nutrition during four years of medical school - 2.5 hours
> ➢ Percentage of first-year medical school students who consider nutrition to be important to their future careers - 74%
> ➢ Percentage who, after two years of medical school, still consider nutrition important - 13%
> ➢ Percentage of US physicians who are overweight - 55%
> ➢ Percentage of US physicians who eat the recommended daily servings of fruits and vegetables - 20% [225]

Dr M R C Greenwood, President of the American Society for Clinical Nutrition (ASCN), was responsible for the following article:

Doctors Need More Nutrition Training: *Nutrition experts say American physicians are under-trained when it comes to issues of nutrition and health. Less than 6% of medical school graduates receive adequate nutrition training. "Until physicians are better trained to provide high levels of information on nutrition, Americans are missing countless opportunities to take advantage of the growing body of scientific research on the role of diet in preventing and treating disease.*[226]

---

[225] Robbins, John, *Reclaiming our Health*, op. cit.
[226] *American Journal of Clinical Nutrition*, Issue 68, 1998

Nutrition expert Dr Michael Klaper is the Director of the Institute of Nutritional Education and Research at Pompano Beach, Florida. He says:

"What's really tragic about this is that we were so busy learning how to fix broken arms, deliver babies and do all of those 'doctor' things in medical school that we considered nutrition to be boring. But after we get into practice, we spend most of the day treating people with diseases that have huge nutritional concerns that have long been essentially ignored. I frequently get calls from doctors across the country saying that their patients are asking questions about nutrition and its role in their conditions and they don't know what to tell them."[227]

It appears that medical students begin with the best of intentions, but the pharmaceutically-oriented curriculum gradually reshapes their understanding. Another good barometer for measuring the importance the conventional medical community attaches to nutrition is by sampling hospital food. Budgetary restrictions aside, in a recent letter to the *New England Journal of Medicine*, a group of researchers contends that hospital food is not healthy. Led by Dr Adam Singer of the State University of New York at Stony Brook, the researchers compiled nutritional breakdowns of meals offered to patients with no dietary restrictions in 57 university hospitals. Fifty-three of the menus failed to meet all the US Public Health Service's dietary guidelines.[228]

A colourful account of what might appear on the patient's food tray is included here:

"If you want to know what an average physician thinks about a balanced diet, look at any hospital food fed to patients, doctors, staff and visitors. Iceberg lettuce with a glob of cottage cheese and a wedge of canned pineapple. Slices of overdone and warmed-over beef that have suffered for hours in some electronic purgatory, coated with a gravy made of water, library paste, and bouillon cubes. Peas, corn and carrots, boiled. The pie is a sickening slab of beige goo, flavoured

---

[227] www.campaignfortruth.com/nutrition.htm

[228] Dembling, Sophia, *Health & Fitness News Service*, http://detnews.com/index.htmWednesday, 14th May 1997

with artificial maple sugar, in a crust of reconstituted cardboard, topped with sweetened shaving cream squirted from an aerosol bomb." [229]

Dr Andrew Saul comments on Western attitudes to diet and nutrition:

"I have seen the foolishness of conventional disease care wisdom. I have seen hospitals feed white bread to patients with bowel cancer and 'Jello' to leukaemia patients. I have seen schools feed bright red 'Slush Puppies' to 7-year-olds for lunch and I have seen children vomit up a desk-top full of red crud afterwards. And I have seen those same children later line up at the school nursery for hyperactivity drugs.

I have seen hospital patients allowed to go two weeks without a bowel movement. I have seen patients told that they have six months to live when they might live sixty months. I have seen people recover from serious illness, only to have their physician berate them for having used natural healing methods to do so.

I have seen infants spit up formula while their mothers were advised not to breast-feed. I've seen better ingredients in dog food than in the average school or hospital lunch. And I have seen enough." [230]

More red 'crud'

The following nutritional information is currently being given to parents of children being treated with chemotherapy at a large cancer hospital in Australia. Entitled *High Protein Energy Diet*, the information pack states that no special diet for children with cancer is needed, but that your child should be encouraged with a nutritious food and fluid intake. While it is important to get the child to eat and some sensible foods are suggested in the information pack, many of the recommendations proffered by the Department of Nutrition and Dietetics at the Brisbane Royal Children's Hospital fully bear out Dr Andrew Saul's *red crud* accusations. The dietary tips include:

[229] "What supplements don't have": www.mothernature.com
[230] Saul, Andrew, *Doctor Yourself* at: www.doctoryourself.com

Margarine, spread thickly.

Oil: fry foods where possible.

Cream: add to milk, breakfast cereals, desserts, custard, yoghurt, sauces and soups.

Sauces: Use gravies and sauces where possible on vegetable and meat dishes. Add sweet sauces and toppings to ice cream and other desserts.

Overcoming nausea and vomiting: Try cold, clear fluids, eg: cordial, lemonade, ginger ale, fruit juices, jelly.

For extra calories: Drink high-sugar drinks, lemonade, coke, Lucozade. Add sugar, glucose, honey, syrups as desired.[231]

Toxic onslaught - a double dose

The complete range of synthetic, 'e'-numbered, processed 'artery sludge' items that are recommended by this hospital is quite shocking. The information the dietician's department supplies makes it clear that because chemotherapy causes weight loss, body-weight must then be restored. But this weight loss is being restored with anything but proper food. How many well-intentioned parents are actually following these dietary guidelines? A child receiving chemotherapy such as the carcinogenic cisplatin is then encouraged to strengthen his/her immune system with caramel E150d, aspartame, acesulfame K, phosphoric acid, flavourings, citric acid, preservatives, E12, caffeine and phenylalanine - otherwise known as Coke; a 'fortifying' portion of reduced whey powder, hydrogenated vegetable oil, dextrose, emulsifiers, mono- and di-glyceride fatty acids, lecithin, stabilisers, sodium alginate and guagum - vanilla ice cream by any other name and topped with a generous helping of more dextrose, emulsifiers, mono- and di-glyceride fatty acids, lecithin, stabilisers and some alpha-tocopherol - chocolate-flavoured sauce – all of the above recommended by the hospital dieticians!

On the importance of <u>sensible</u> nutrition and cancer, we read this from Modern Manna:

"And God said, 'Behold, I have given you every herb bearing seed... and every tree in which is the fruit of a tree yielding seed; to

---

[231] "Going Home & The High Energy Protein Diet", information on file at Credence

you it shall be for food." Proper nutrition is vital to good health. Food that is devitalised cannot supply the vitamins and minerals it lacks. Therefore, it is of utmost importance that we choose wisely the food that goes on our table. Vegetables and fruits should be making the greater proportion of our meals, along with whole grains, beans, legumes, and seeds. Nuts can be included in small amounts. From our food, we will obtain all the elements essential for good health: vitamins, minerals, water, carbohydrates, protein, fats, and fibre." [232]

What are we eating?

Having established the importance of good nutrition in maintaining good health, the above text also mentions the word *devitalised*. This is a very important subject. Even if we pay attention to a good diet, do we always know just what we are eating? The following document was released by the US Senate:

"Our physical well-being is more directly dependent upon minerals we take into our systems than upon calories or vitamins, or upon precise proportions of starch, protein or carbohydrates we consume.... Do you know that most of us today are suffering from certain dangerous diet deficiencies which cannot be remedied until depleted soils from which our food comes are brought into proper mineral balance?

The alarming fact is that foods (fruits, vegetables and grains), now being raised on millions of acres of land that no longer contain enough of certain minerals, are starving us - no matter how much of them we eat. No man of today can eat enough fruits and vegetables to supply his system with the minerals he requires for perfect health because his stomach isn't big enough to hold them.

The truth is, our foods vary enormously in value, and some of them aren't worth eating as food.... Our physical well-being is more directly dependent upon the minerals we take into our systems than upon calories or vitamins or upon the precise proportions of starch, protein or carbohydrates we consume.

---

[232] Modern Manna, "Cancer and Nutrition": www.modernmanna.org

This talk about minerals is novel and quite startling. In fact, a realisation of the importance of minerals in food is so new that the text books on nutritional dietetics contain very little about it. Nevertheless, it is something that concerns all of us, and the further we delve into it the more startling it becomes.

You'd think, wouldn't you, that a carrot is a carrot - that one is about as good as another as far as nourishment is concerned? But it isn't; one carrot may look and taste like another and yet be lacking in the particular mineral element which our system requires and which carrots are supposed to contain.

Laboratory tests prove that the fruits, the vegetables, the grains, the eggs, and even the milk and the meats of today are not what they were a few generations ago, which doubtless explains why our forefathers thrived on a selection of foods that would starve us!

No man today can eat enough fruits and vegetables to supply his stomach with the mineral salts he requires for perfect health, because his stomach isn't big enough to hold them!

No longer does a balanced and fully nourishing diet consist merely of so many calories or certain vitamins or fixed proportion of starches, proteins and carbohydrates. We know that our diets must contain in addition something like a score of minerals salts.

It is bad news to learn from our leading authorities that 99% of the American people are deficient in these minerals [this was in 1936!], and that a marked deficiency in any one of the more important minerals actually results in disease. Any upset of the balance, any considerable lack or one or another element, however microscopic the body requirement may be, and we sicken, suffer, shorten our lives. We know that vitamins are complex chemical substances which are indispensable to nutrition, and that each of them is of importance for normal function of some special structure in the body. Disorder and disease result from any vitamin deficiency.

It is not commonly realised, however, that vitamins control the body's appropriation of minerals, and in the absence of minerals they have no function to perform. Lacking vitamins, the system can make

137

some use of minerals, but lacking minerals, vitamins are useless. Certainly our physical well-being is more directly dependent upon the minerals we take into our systems than upon calories of vitamins or upon the precise proportions of starch, protein of carbohydrates we consume. This discovery is one of the latest and most important contributions of science to the problem of human health." [233]

The year of publication? 1936! And things have hardly improved since.

Cancer: a manifestation of an antagonistic, toxic environment

Our fast-food, chemicalised, fertilised, factory-farmed society has all but lost touch with wholesome foodstuffs and those minerals necessary for maintaining good health. And we are certainly sickening for them today.

In a preface to the book, *Cancer: Nature, Cause and Cure*, Dr Alexander Berglas has this to say about cancer incidence:

"Civilisation is, in terms of cancer, a juggernaut that cannot be stopped.... It is the nature and essence of industrial civilisation to be toxic in every sense.... We are faced with the grim prospect that the advance of cancer and of civilisation parallel each other." [234]

Writing a paper entitled "The Modern-Day Scourge", Dr Mary Rodio says:

"Let's consider the similarities of 19th century America and countries where cancer is practically non-existent. For the most part, the only countries that have a low incidence of cancer are those countries where the environment is largely unspoiled and where the food is simple and unrefined. These countries are generally agricultural nations where highly processed food is uncommon. Nearly a century ago - before the arrival of chemical fertilisers - farming in America was organic. Apart from the industrial centres, the environment was relatively pristine. Cancer statistics point to the

---

[233] US Senate Document No.264, 74th Congress, 2nd Session, 1936
[234] Berglas, Alexander, preface to *Cancer: Nature, Cause and Cure*, Paris, 1957

subsequent arrival of a chemically toxic environment, over-processed foods and stress as cancer's root cause.

To better understand the possible root causes of cancer, you should know that cancer is considered an acid disease that may be generated by an over-consumption of acid foods: usually meat, dairy products, and coffee. Toxic food substances, tobacco, environmental poisons and other potential hazards may also contribute to the possibility of developing cancer. In each decade since the early 1900's, we have seen an astronomical increase in the use of harmful additives, colourings, irradiation, insecticides, fungicides, and the list could go on indefinitely, as you may well know.

Today, most of the food found in the grocery store contains refined foods, bleaching agents, chemicals, preservatives, additives, salt, sugar, etc. Refining destroys the medicinal components of food. For example, the milling process removes the wheat germ in bread that is an excellent source of Vitamin E, which is known to be a beneficial immune-enhancer. In addition, bleaching agents found in white bread also destroy Vitamin E." [235]

We can see that through our depleted, demineralised food chain, we in the West are less able to combat degenerative disease, and especially cancer.

Almost entirely cancer-free!

It is interesting to note that there are cultures around the globe today who remain almost entirely cancer-free. The Abkhasians, the Azerbaijanis, the Hunzakuts, the Eskimaux and Karakorum all live on foodstuffs rich in nitrilosides – a group of plant compounds containing Vitamin B17.

The food of these cultures consists variously of buckwheat, peas, broad beans, lucerne, turnips, lettuce, sprouting pulse or gram, apricots with their seeds and berries of various kinds. Their diet can provide them with as much as 250–3,000mg of nitriloside a day. The average Western diet, with its refined, fibreless foods, offers less than

---

[235] Rodio, Mary, "A Modern-Day Scourge", 1995:
http://radiusofgod.org/r_godcancer.html

2mg of nitriloside a day. It has also been noted that natives from these tribes consuming nitriloside-rich foodstuffs, who then move into 'civilised' areas and change their diets accordingly, are prone to cancers at the regular western incidence.[236]

Biochemist Ernst Krebs Jr spent a great deal of time studying the dietary habits of these tribes. Krebs noted in particular that: *"...upon investigating the diet of these peoples, we found that the seed of the apricot was prized as a delicacy and that every part of the apricot was utilised."* [237]

It was this observation that brought Krebs into the spotlight of cancer research, and with the spotlight came the inevitable heavy flak levelled against him by vested interests. Krebs spent many years investigating and lecturing on the anti-cancer properties of a special component contained in the seeds of the common fruits and various other natural foods. It is an amazing story, as we are about to discover.

[236] Stefansson, Vilhjalmur, *Cancer: Disease of Civilisation? An Anthropological and Historical Study*, Hill & Wang, New York, 1960
[237] Krebs, Jr., Ernst T, *Nutritional and Therapeutic Implications*, John Beard Memorial Foundation (privately published in 1964)

Vitamin B17

"For the first time since I became a nurse 23 years ago, I do not fear cancer!" **Mrs R E Bruce, RN**

Before examining the issue of Vitamin B17 in more detail, it is important we understand the terminology that has grown up around this nutrient. A number of names are being used by different people for B17. This has sometimes led to confusion.

Amygdalin
Amygdalin is a naturally-occurring substance containing Vitamin B17 and is found in a number of herbs, fruits and vegetables. Named after *amugdale* (Greek for almond), science has recorded more than 800 occurrences of amygdalin in nature. Herbs, fruits and vegetables containing the amygdalin molecule to varying degrees include apple seeds, alfalfa sprouts, apricot kernels, bamboo shoots, barley, beet tops, bitter almond, blackberries, boysenberries, brewer's yeast, brown rice, buckwheat, cashews, cherry kernels, cranberries, currants, fava beans, flax seeds, garbanzo beans, gooseberries, huckleberries, lentils, lima beans, linseed meat, loganberries, macadamia nuts, millet, millet seed, peach kernels, pecans, plum kernels, quince, raspberries, sorghum cane syrup, spinach, sprouts (alfalfa, lentil, mung bean, buckwheat, garbanzo), strawberries, walnuts, watercress, yams.

Nitrilosides
These Vitamin B17-bearing plants and fruits have long been prized for their healing properties. They appear in the herbals of nearly every great civilisation. Today's science has classified the chemistry in these plants as 'nitrilosides'. Vitamin B17 research scientist Ernst T Krebs Jr. described nitrilosides as:

"...a large group of water-soluble, essentially non-toxic, sugary, compounds found in over 800 plants, many of which are edible. These factors are collectively known as Beta-cyanophoric glycosides. We

have proposed the collective, generic term n-i-t-r-i-l-o-s-i-d-e for all such cyanophoric glycosides of dietary significance." [238]

Thanks is given to Dr Henry Rosenberg, author of "Cancer chemo(toxico)therapy revisited and alternative ways of healing", for the following condensed history of amygdalin.

The oldest known known herbal, the 'Pen Tsao Kang-Mu', attributed to the Chinese Emperor Shennung, and dating from 2700 BC, mentions its properties. The same fruits are mentioned in works by Aulus Cornelius Celsus and Scribonius Largus, dating from the early first century AD. Scribonius in particular mentions that bitter almond is effective against cancer of the bladder. The elder Pliny discusses the therapeutic effect of oil of bitter almonds on condylomatoma – an affliction of genital warts. Galen recommended almonds for liver cirrhosis, while Priscian and Empiricus used almonds to treat tumours. The great Persian apothecary and medical practitioner Avicenna used bitter almond oil to treat tumours of the uterus, spleen, stomach and liver. Maimonides, the renowned Jewish legal thinker and physician, stressed the importance of bitter almonds and beetroot as therapeutically valuable remedies.

In the 13th century, Harpestaeng, a Danish physician, used almonds mixed with honey to treat hardening of the spleen, while his contemporary, Myreposos, a Byzantine physician, used bitter almonds to treat cancers of the oral cavity. In the same century, Ibn-Al-Baitar was also using bitter almonds to treat breast cancers. Later, in the 16th century, we find a Swiss biologist called Gesner using the same almonds to treat cancer. John Gerard, who published his famous herbal in the mid 17th century in London, discusses the therapeutic properties of almond kernels and was the first to report their pain-killing (analgesic) effects.

The great Flemish herbal of the same period, compiled by R Dodoens, recommends the use of bitter almonds for 'rotting tumours'. By the 19th century, bitter almonds were an accepted treatment for cancer both on the Old Continent and in the New World. In 1845, for

---

[238] Krebs, Jr., Ernst T, "The Nitrilosides":
www.datadepo.com/cancercure/nitriloside.htm

example, the Parisian *Gazette Medicale* published an article by the Russian physician, Dr T Inosemtoff, Professor at the Imperial University of Moscow, who claimed to have successfully halted the further development of two cases of metastasised cancers using amygdalin.

Studies carried out by Sir Robert McCarrison, senior physician to the King of England at the turn of the 20th century, indicated that the Hunza tribe of Karakorum of north-eastern Pakistan hardly ever suffered from cancer. Similarly, findings by the polar explorer Stefansson demonstrated that the Eskimaux are also almost entirely untroubled by cancer as long as they live according to their native culture. Unlike most other populations, these two groups include large amounts of nitrilosides in their diet.[239]

There's Laetrile and there's laetrile

Laetrile, with a capital 'L', is an acronym for laevo-(rotary) mandelonitrile beta-glucoside, and is used to describe a purified form of the chemical amygdalin (Vitamin B17). This substance was isolated by Ernst Krebs Sr. after boiling and evaporating the component in alcohol to leave little white crystals. It was then patented by his son Ernst T Krebs Jr. in the 1950's and named Laetrile.

Laetrile without the capital

Later, different versions of Laetrile would be developed by an FDA-Johns Hopkins team in America and other research teams across the world, which the Krebs' believed were not to the same purity or standard. Although the names laetrile, Laetrile, and amygdalin are often used interchangeably, they are not the same chemical compound. The chemical make-up of Laetrile patented in the United States is different from the laetrile/amygdalin produced in Mexico. The patented Laetrile is a semi-synthetic form of amygdalin, while the laetrile/amygdalin manufactured in Mexico is made from crushed apricot pits. In explaining the chemical actions and reactions of plant substances, there is a certain tendency to slip into the language known as *'chemicalese'*. For the scientifically-minded reader, the empirical formula of amygdalin is written $C_{20}H_{27}N_{11}$. Laetrile on the other hand is

---

[239] Rosenburg, Henry, "Cancer chemo(toxico)therapy revisited and alternative ways of healing": www.karlloren.com/biopsy/book/p2.htm#amygdaline

a D-1 mandelonitrile-beta-glucuronide, and the result of breaking amygdalin into mandelonitrile and linking with gluconic acid. Laetrile's empirical formula is $C_4H_{15}NO_7$.

A simple explanation

Technical explanations naturally have their place, and there are numerous scientific texts available, some of which are referred to in this book, that will give the more scientifically-minded reader an opportunity to digest the chemical and biological properties and activities of this substance. *B17 Metabolic Therapy – A Technical Manual* is one such book, which has been produced by Credence Publications specifically for the scientific community. Details of availability are found in the appendices of this book. For the purposes of this study, I am grateful to Dr Philip Binzel for his simple layperson's account of 20th century research into Vitamin B17, which has been abridged for readers as follows:

Working on the premise that cancer is a manifestation of a mineral/nutritional deficient disease, Drs Krebs, Burk, Nieper, Contreras, Navarro and Sakai (and other researchers in the B17 research group) found that the body does have a normal defence against cancer, and they were able to describe how that defence mechanism functioned. They found that the cancer cell is coated with a protein lining (or covering) that prevented the body's normal defences from getting to the cancer cell. They found that if you could dissolve the protein lining from around the cancer cell, the body's white blood cells would destroy the cancer cell. They postulated that the dissolving of the protein lining (or covering) from around the cell was managed very competently within the body by two enzymes, trypsin and chymotrypsin. These enzymes are secreted by the pancreas. Thus, they said, these enzymes formed the first line of defence against cancer.

The researchers stated that they had also found that the body has a second line of defence against cancer in the form of a group of food substances known as nitrilosides. The cancer cell wall has an enzyme called beta-glucosidase, which, when brought into contact with nitrilosides, converts those nitrilosides into a target-specific trio of glucose, benzaldehyde and hydrogen cyanide. This trio attacks the cancer cell, while ignoring normal cell tissue. In other words, the nitrilosides become tumour-specific and the naturally-occurring hydrogen cyanide targets the cancer cells and no others.[240]

Krebs and his colleagues determined that all of us probably have cancer many times in our lives, but that our defence mechanisms, if they are functioning normally, kill off the cancer efficiently enough.

They stated that the cancer forms if there has been a breakdown in the internal defence mechanism, and while there are more than 800 foodstuffs that are nitrilosidic, the researchers found that the most rapid way to build up the nitriloside level was through the use of laetrile. They did not proclaim laetrile as a 'miracle drug' or a 'cancer cure', but merely described it as a concentrated form of nitriloside, which was able rapidly to raise the nitriloside level in the body to such a degree that the body's second line of defence against cancer was re-established.

Greatly excited at these findings, these men and others presented their information to the authorities for peer review.

And that's when all the trouble started.

---

[240] Interestingly, research is currently being carried out at Imperial College, London, under Dr Mahendra Deonerain, where scientists are examining ways of using naturally-occurring plant cyanides specifically to attack human bowel tumours. The idea came about after studying the pattern of cyanide release in the almond and cassava fruits which protects them from insect attack. See "Cyanide Targets Cancer", a BBC News report at:
http://news.bbc.co.uk/hi/english/in_depth/sci_tech/2000/festival_of_science/n ewsid_913000/913463.stm

A glimpse of war

*"One deceit needs many others, and so the
whole house is built in the air and must soon
come to the ground."* **Baltasar Gracian**

In his UK *Observer* article entitled *Quacks on the Rack*, John
Diamond summarily dismissed the natural extract of the apricot
kernel. Writing on Vitamin B17, he stated:

*"Supporters of Laetrile (vitamin B17) and Essiac, in particular,
made so much noise about their miracle cures that both have been
through the research mill on numerous occasions and found to be
useless."* [241]

As already mentioned however, Dr Dean Burk, the former head of
the Cytochemistry Department of the National Cancer Institute, and
one of its co-founders, had worked on Vitamin B17 personally. He
described this substance in very different terms:

"When we add Laetrile to a cancer culture under the microscope,"
said Burk, *"providing the enzyme glucosidase is present, we can see
the cancer cells dying off like flies."* [242]

So who do we trust in this matter? Diamond or Burk? Now we can
ask ourselves whether it was perhaps the fault of some kindly but
misguided soul who posted John Diamond an essay on the benefits of
Vitamin B17 mixed with walnut water that caused him to dismiss B17
so emphatically. Or could it be that John actually trusted the
conventional research reports he had accrued on this vitamin? By
examining the sources from where John Diamond might have got his

---

[241] Diamond, John, op. cit.

[242] Griffin, G Edward, *World Without Cancer*, op. cit. Beta-glucosidase is the enzyme
which Krebs states is heavily present in cancerous cells, which triggers the unique
cancer-destroying mechanism found in Vitamin B17. A clinical analysis of this
mechanism is found in *B17 Metabolic Therapy – In the Prevention and Control Of
Cancer* - a concise history of the research into this vitamin, including many clinical
assessments. Details on this publication can be found at the back of this book.

B17 research 'information', the uglier features of conventional cancer research – the cancer war - move more sharply into focus.

Because of the money

Cancer is big business and knowledge claims on any treatments that earn money and, conversely, on any treatments that do not earn money for the drug companies, are never neutral. Dr Ralph Moss served as the Assistant Director of Public Affairs at America's most famous cancer research institution, Memorial Sloan-Kettering, in Manhattan. He knows the cancer industry inside out. Hear what he has to say and judge for yourself the quality of the evidence against the effectiveness of Vitamin B17:

Moss: *"Shortly after I went to work* [at the Sloan-Kettering Cancer Institute], *I visited the elderly Japanese scientist, Kanematsu Sugiura, who astonished me when he told me he was working on Laetrile (B17). At the time it was the most controversial thing in cancer, reputed to be a cure for cancer.*

We in Public Affairs were giving out statements that Laetrile was worthless, it was quackery, and that people should not abandon proven therapies. I was astonished that our most distinguished scientist would be bothering with something like this, and I said, "Why are you doing this if it doesn't work?" He took down his lab books and showed me that in fact Laetrile was dramatically effective in stopping the spread of cancer."

Lee: *"So this is verified, that Laetrile can have this positive effect?"*

Moss: *"We were finding this and yet we in Public Affairs were told to issue statements to the exact opposite of what we were finding scientifically."* [243]

Unable to sit on this information, Moss later called a press conference of his own and, before a battery of reporters and cameramen, charged that Sloan-Kettering officials had engineered a massive cover-up. He provided all the supporting documents and

---

[243] Day, Phillip, *Cancer: Why We're...*, op. cit.

147

named the names necessary to validate his case. The following day he was fired for 'failing to carry out his most basic job responsibilities'.[244] Similarly, in his book *World Without Cancer*, cancer industry researcher G Edward Griffin noted:

"Every Laetrile study had been tarnished with the same kind of scientific ineptitude, bias and outright deception.... Some of these studies openly admitted evidence of anti-cancer effect but hastened to attribute this effect to other causes. Some were toxicity studies only, which means that they weren't trying to see if Laetrile was effective, but merely trying to determine how much of it was required to kill the patient." [245]

Concluding his speech at the Annual Cancer Convention at the Ambassador Hotel in Los Angeles in 1974, Ernst T Krebs Jr announced to his audience:

"If you have any questions about Laetrile, the more critical, the better, because we are dealing with solid science. We are dealing with a science that admits there is no rational alternative in the ten years that have passed since these meetings began. Nothing has come about which does anything except make more obvious that Laetrile, Vitamin B17, is the answer to cancer." [246]

Unsurprisingly, the 'evidence' to support John Diamond's claim that Vitamin B17 is useless and even dangerous is available in abundance in all of the major cancer institutions today. As Pat Rattigan, author of *The Cancer Business*, reports:

"The threat to the cancer business from effective therapies was taken very seriously from the beginning. By the 1940's the Syndicate had 300,000 names on its 'quack' files. Vitamin B17, being a unique threat due to its simplicity, attracted more concentrated attacks than all the other treatments put together: fraudulent test reports; hired,

---

[244] Moss, Ralph, *The Cancer Syndrome*, Grove Press, 1980

[245] Griffin, G Edward, op. cit.

[246] *B17 Metabolic Therapy... A Technical Manual*, compiled by Phillip Day, Credence Publications, 2002

banner-carrying pickets outside clinics; rigged juries; newspaper character assassinations; dismissal of heretic employees, etc.

The US Food and Drug Administration, orchestrating the onslaught, sent out 10,000 posters and hundreds of thousands of leaflets warning about the dangers of the toxicity of the non-toxic substance. Earlier, a Congressional Accounting Office had found that 350 FDA employees had shares in, or had refused to declare an interest in, the pharmaceutical industry." [247]

Don't take the scare stories at face value

The American Food and Drug Administration issued one such story about the death of an 11-month-old girl, supposedly from cyanide poisoning due apparently to swallowing her father's Vitamin B17 tablets. Cancer specialist and B17 advocate Dr Harold Manner takes up the story:

"...I was lecturing in Buffalo, New York and... after I had made some strong statements, a man stood up and said "Dr Manner, how in the world can you make statements like that when the FDA is making these other statements?" I reiterated that the FDA statements were lies. 'He said, "Look at this little girl in upstate New York, she took her father's Laetrile tablets and died of cyanide poisoning." Just then a little lady stood up: "Dr Manner let me answer that question. I think I am entitled to because I am that little baby's mother. That baby never touched her father's Laetrile tablets. The doctor, knowing the father was on Laetrile, marked down 'possible cyanide poisoning'. At the hospital, they used a cyanide antidote and it was the antidote that killed my child. And yet that statement will continue to appear even though they know it is a lie." [248]

Reference to this girl's 'death by cyanide', along with other uncorroborated anecdotes, are used today by the major conventional institutions to bolster their case against Vitamin B17. A request for evidence to support the information posted on the Cancer Research UK site that Vitamin B17 is a killer was denied. CRUK spokesperson Ms

[247] Rattigan, Pat, *The Cancer Business*:
www.vegan.swinternet.co.uk/articles/health/cancerbusiness.html
[248] Ibid.

Woolf, who is responsible for the information displayed on this site, said that it wasn't her responsibility to attend to such questions, and that she had deleted the message from her system. She then put the phone down.[249]

The scare stories always focus on the minute amounts of naturally occurring hydrogen cyanide supposedly found in Vitamin B17. But no mention is made in any of these stories of the wondrous mechanism governing the release of this natural form of cyanide. As with all the other nutrients, no harm has ever been shown to be done to a person ingesting Vitamin B17 in the manner nature intended. If that were the case, the plains of north-eastern Pakistan would be littered with dead Hunzakuts. They are not![250] Notice that hydrogen cyanide and an analgesic, benzaldehyde, are released only when cancerous cells are recognised by their high glucosidase content. B17 cyanide attacks cancer cells specifically and is only generated at the cancer cell site. No large amounts of glucosidase detected means no cyanide generated. There is no free cyanide 'rolling around' inside apricot kernels. Rest assured, like any vitamin, there is no evidence that Vitamin B17, ingested according to the appropriate guidelines, can kill, unless of course, one is accidentally crushed under a pallet of the stuff.

Gangster tactics

One of the first doctors to use Vitamin B17 in the control of cancer was a Dr Maurice Kowan. This landed him in court in Los Angeles. The prosecutor told the jury:

"This is not a kindly old man. This is the most thoroughly evil person the imagination can concoct.... This man has to be stopped. He is very dangerous. The way to stop him is a guilty verdict."[251]

Dr Kowan was heavily fined and, at the age of 70, sentenced to two months in prison. The justification cited by the cancer establishment for the attack on Dr Kowan was a falsified report produced by two

---

[249] Go to Cancer Research UK, Cancer Help at:
www.cancerhelp.org.uk/help/default.asp?page=2568
[250] An important point to note with B17 content is that the more bitter the taste of the kernel, the higher the content of B17. If the kernel does not taste bitter, the B17 content may be low, even negligible.
[251] Richardson, John A, *Laetrile Case Histories*, Bantam Books, 1977

doctors, Henry Garland and Ian MacDonald, in 1953. The two men, who had the fascinating credentials of being involved in surgery and radiation and also the high-profile promotion of cigarettes as a health measure, produced a report which stated that no evidence of anti-cancer changes were observed by consultants using Laetrile. This report was later found to be demonstrably fraudulent, but sadly has been quoted religiously by vested cancer interests ever since. Perhaps Fate took her revenge in an appropriate fashion in the end. Henry Garland died of lung cancer and MacDonald burned himself to death in his bed; a conflagration caused, it is believed, when a cigarette he had been smoking ignited his bed-sheets after he fell asleep.[252]

A stage-managed arrest

US physician Dr John A Richardson began to use B17 in the summer of 1971. His first patient was the sister of one of his nurses: a case of advanced malignant melanoma of the arm. She had been given around six weeks to live, with a little longer if she had the arm amputated.

"Amygdalin was administered, and almost immediately the lesions began to heal. Within two months her arm had returned to normal...."

The woman was also a diabetic who, after the cancer treatment, controlled her disease without the use of insulin. When she returned to her original doctor, he still wanted to amputate her arm. She declined the offer. The success Dr Richardson's methods enjoyed with B17 and the specially modified diet had begun to attract increasing numbers of patients.

"For the first time in my entire career, I began to see 'terminal' cancer patients abandon their stretchers and wheelchairs and return to normal lives of health and vigour.... Word of my successes with cancer patients... brought far more new patients than I could handle alone. I increased the staff.... Soon my little neighbourhood practice was converted into a busy cancer clinic with patients from many

---

[252] Day, Phillip, *Cancer: Why We're....*, op. cit.

states. The inevitable finally happened at ten in the morning, 2nd June 1972."[253]

Four cars screeched to a halt outside Richardson's clinic and disgorged ten uniformed officers. Guns drawn, they burst into the clinic, flashed a search warrant as they passed the receptionist on their way into the clinic, where they pushed the doctor against the wall and searched him 'for concealed weapons'. Dr Richardson and his two nurses were marched out past the specially-invited television cameras and were arrested under Californian 'anti-quackery' laws.

"At the time of the raid, a little girl about 7-years-old was in examination room number three. She had just begun metabolic therapy for an advanced case of osteogenic sarcoma.... Kerry had responded beautifully in terms of increased appetite, weight gain, freedom from pain and a feeling of well-being.... Normally, Kerry would have received a massive injection of vitamins, including vitamin B17.... Not being sure what kind of legal trouble I would be in, I simply cleaned and dressed her lesions and sent her home.... The little girl - as well as her parents - were greatly upset by the threatening presence of police officers. The child died three days later and there is no doubt in my mind that this death could have been postponed or avoided altogether if it hadn't been for the raid."

The concerted campaign to ruin Dr Richardson physically, mentally, financially, professionally and legally had begun. It was destined to last for years. The authorities revoked his medical licence and he was ordered to attend meetings 600 miles away in San Diego, with many of the hearings cancelled at the last minute; a procedure kept up at weekly intervals for six months.[254]

In assessing the deservedness of the 'shady' reputation bestowed upon the apricot kernel and supporting nutritional regimens, there are a great many elements to this story that point to a sustained attack by the conventional cancer industry - an attack that has continued in one form or another for the last fifty years. As mentioned earlier, with

---

[253] Richardson, John A, *Laetrile Case Histories*, op. cit.

[254] Our thanks to Pat Rattigan for the above information at: www.vegan.swinternet.co.uk/articles/health/cancerbusiness.html

global spending on conventional cancer running into the hundreds of billions annually, a naturally-occurring cancer cure of any description is an unwanted intruder. Cancer industry insider Dr Ralph Moss again, on the money involved in conventional cancer:

Moss: *"We have got a tremendous industry. Every one of those people who is getting cancer and dying of it is going to be treated, and these treatments are extremely expensive. Chemo is tens of thousands, sometimes hundreds of thousands of dollars. A bone marrow transplant, which is basically another way of giving chemotherapy, or radiation, can run to about $150,000 per person, and is almost never effective. It kills about 25% of the patients."*

Lee: *"Why carry on doing it?"*

Moss: *"Because of the money, which is tremendous."* [255]

Earning potential and locked-in financial commitments are halting the march of true cancer medicine. But, as we have seen, there are physicians who, upon arriving at this uncomfortable realisation, turn their back on their former training and decide upon the non-conventional route, sometimes speaking out to great effect.

Merchant-speak

When we understand the amounts of money involved, we can begin to understand the in-house desire to sustain a *'fact-creating'* process in support of conventional treatment. Conventional cancer treatment and research are a licence to print money. Most definitely, conventional, interested parties and institutions have colluded in a shameful anti-B17, 'fact-creating' process.

As for John Diamond's dismissal of Vitamin B17, he didn't write his comments on B17 as an intentional slur. He wasn't the forked tongue in this chain of events. He desperately wanted to live. His comments on this substance, which were read by thousands, are just another example of the damaging knock-on effect of merchant-speak. Merchant-speak on Vitamin B17 and nutritional therapy have exacted a

---

[255] Day, Phillip, *Cancer: Why We're...*, op. cit.

grave injustice upon this treatment and, subsequently, upon all who have been persuaded to think likewise.

John Diamond again, this time on some *nutter* with a magical diet:

"I was waiting my turn for zapping [radiotherapy] *one day and mentioned the ludicrousness of one diet that I'd been reading about. The radiographer agreed and said that when she had started at the hospital there used to be a nutter who, having refused radiography, would come down and rail against those sitting in the radiotherapy waiting room, telling them they should abandon evil radiation and take up his magical diet. "Criminal," I said. "You kicked him out, of course?" "Well yes," she said, "we kicked him out regularly. The only thing was, he did survive for years and the cancer did disappear." Which only goes to prove... well, nothing very much at all really, but I thought I'd pass it on in the name of fair dealing."* [256]

To continue on in the name of fair dealing, let's now hear the testimonies of those who have not been persuaded by the negative propaganda.

---

[256] Diamond, John, op. cit.

Some testimonies on B17

Philip

Phillip is 64. In April 2001, he was diagnosed with inoperable lung cancer. The oncologist showed him the x-rays that confirmed the dreaded 'shadows'. He was told to go home, enjoy his life as best he could and put his affairs in order. A week later, in a chance conversation at work, Phillip was told about Vitamin B17. He immediately changed his diet and began taking a combination of Vitamin B17 and Vitamin C. Four months later, Phillip returned to hospital for a check-up, where a new set of x-rays was taken. The shadows had completely disappeared. Says Phillip, *"I know what I saw and the doctor couldn't explain it. I'm continuing with my Vitamin B17 regime and eating about 10 kernels a day."* Phillip also pays great attention to his diet and believes that what we put into our bodies can have a dramatic effect medicinally.

Now if John Diamond's 'nutter' was just an isolated case of recovery through diet, his recovery would not, of course, constitute proof. But with Vitamin B17 and nutritional changes, we are seeing tremendous results *consistently*. Continuing on in the name of fair dealing....

William

William was diagnosed with a tumour in the oesophagus. He could not swallow food without it being liquidised. He had read about Vitamin B17 twelve months previously and had kept the article. William began taking Vitamin B17 soon after diagnosis. After three weeks, he was swallowing food a lot easier and after about seven weeks was told by his doctor that the only reason for this was because the tumour was shrinking. Says William: *"The operation to remove the tumour was cancelled and I am still awaiting the results of the latest scan. I feel fit as a fiddle. I pay attention to my diet and I thank God quite literally for Vitamin B17. It is time the NHS recognised this vitamin as an alternative to the conventional treatments. I consider that any money spent on B17 is money well spent."*

The human body has an amazing capacity to recover, if we look after it properly and supply it with the proper materials it needs for repair. Working with non-toxic, physio-friendly treatments can only work in our favour. Just look at the side-effects of Vitamin B17 as described by Edward G Griffin in *World Without Cancer*:

"B17 side-effects include increased appetite, weight-gain, lowered blood pressure, increased haemoglobin and red-blood cell count, elimination or sharp reduction of pain without narcotics, builds up body's resistance to other diseases, is a natural substance found in foods and is compatible with human biological experience, destroys cancer cells while nourishing non-cancer cells." [257]

Compare the above with the side-effects from chemotherapy and radiation, the dizziness, skin discolouration, nausea, diarrhoea, loss of hair, loss of appetite, organ failure, internal bleeding, etc., etc.

How long will it be before we find ourselves looking back on these treatments in the same way as we now look back on the blood-letting and the ammonia infusions exacted upon Charles II? Notwithstanding the often life-saving surgical removal of cancerous tissue, could there possibly be a more inhumane treatment in the 21st century than conventional cancer therapy?

Flora

Flora was diagnosed with stage 4 bowel cancer in 1999: *"Before the operation, they gave me chemotherapy, which was devastating. By the end of the course, I could hardly stand. They then removed the tumour from my bowel. I was told the cancer had spread to the liver. I was offered further chemotherapy but declined. I attended Middlesex hospital and had five sessions of laser treatment to try and contain the liver cancer followed by more chemotherapy. After the fifth time of trying to contain the cancer, they said that it was beginning to grow yet again.*

So I began an organic diet and attended the Dove Clinic for intensive Vitamin C treatment, along with other supplements. It was there that I was told about Vitamin B17. I added that to my regime.

---

[257] Griffin, G Edward, op. cit.

Over a period of time, the cancer completely disappeared from my liver. It is now February 2002 and I have been one year clear of cancer. I am maintaining my organic diet and eating about 50 apricot kernels a day, spread throughout the day. I'm 64, I've returned to work and I feel fine. Treatments such as these should at least be made known to patients by the National Health Service."

Mary

The following letter was posted to Credence head office. Mary had attended a talk in Dianella, Perth, Australia, on the subject of cancer and Vitamin B17, presented by the founder of Credence Publications, Phillip Day. Phillip's presentation was based upon the information contained in his book, *Cancer: Why We're Still Dying to Know The Truth.*

"I came out to Australia last July having been diagnosed with two malignant tumours in my left breast. I had already signed a form agreeing to an operation for mastectomy and removal of all my lymph glands. My daughter and son-in-law had insisted on my cancelling my appointment at the Royal United Hospital, Bath, UK, where I was told there was no other option.

My daughter also insisted that I came out to Australia where I saw two cancer specialists, who, after examining me and reading the medical file I'd brought from the RUH, declared a lumpectomy and removal of two lymph glands was all that was necessary. However, we decided to try radiation therapy – no surgery and no drugs.

I had just finished the 1st phase, when we went to Dianella, Perth, to hear Phillip Day speaking about cancer. We were so profoundly impressed by his splendid talk on cancer and Vitamin B17 metabolic therapy, that we brought his books, read them carefully and decided to go 'all out' on his anti-cancer diet. We all three felt so much better in health and were surprised at how energetic we felt. I still attended Bethesda Hospital for blood tests, and we were absolutely delighted to get reports of the malignant cells diminishing. Then, finally, a report that I was in full remission. There was no need to attend for any more blood tests.

So now, 10 months later, I am returning to my home in Wiltshire and will continue my apricot kernels and diet as a safe-guard against any possible recurrence of cancer. I also wish to join the Campaign for Truth in Medicine and will deal with this as soon as possible after my arrival home in UK.

The very worried and depressed person who spoke to Phillip at that Perth meeting is now a radiant, energetic 84-year-old. He has transformed my life and those of my daughter Linda and son-in-law, Henry. Yours very sincerely, Mary." [258]

Pat

"Dear Steve, I have just read your 'Death by Doctoring' article. What a powerful piece of writing. The balance of fact and personal stories paint a compelling picture. I found the references to John Diamond especially poignant. I confess to not having read his material, not wanting to engage with someone who took such a path. I now question that decision and will buy and read him with gusto. It's so important to understand and acknowledge all sides of the argument to be able to influence. So an especial thank-you for that insight. I was one of the statistics you quoted. I was diagnosed in May 1999 with aggressive lymphoma, intermediate level. I refused all conventional treatment and put together a healing plan for myself.

To me it made absolutely no sense to destroy the weakened immune system that had allowed the growth of the cancer in the first place. My plan was to inhibit the growth of the cancer, detoxify my system and boost my immunity so that my body could do its own healing. To me, that was common sense. There is no common sense in the use of chemotherapy and radiation.

Within 6 months, I was in remission; within a year, back to better health than before the cancer, and I have continued to improve ever since. I am currently getting my own book ready for publication and hope that it will help people to trust their instinct and at least question and understand the implications of going down the traditional route. I talk to so many after the treatment who say, "If only I knew then

[258] Correspondence on file at Credence Publications

what I know now." Tragically, for many, it is too late when they get to that realisation, the damage is done. Best wishes, Pat." [259]

Jason Vale

Jason recovered from three bouts of 'terminal' cancer. Today he arm-wrestles nationally in the US, is an active B17 campaigner, and hosts an Internet journal, recording day-to-day updates of the cancer sufferers with whom he comes into contact.

"I've been writing this journal and my name is Jason Vale, I've also had a 100% death-rate diagnosis and am perfectly fine now. I didn't have access to apricot seeds or Vitamin B17 back then. I just went to the store and bought cases of peaches and broke open the pits and ate the seeds out. Supposedly if you're older it helps to have the B17 [tablets] also because your body needs more help in the fight than with a younger person." [260]

Ruth Eastwood

"In April 1978, when I was 54 years old, I had a biopsy and mastectomy (in one operation). I was diagnosed with interductal adenocarcinoma of the left breast with metastases. I had bone, liver and brain scans. There were brain lesions and my liver was enlarged. The surgeon told my husband not to wait until Christmas to get the family together, as that would be too late, even if I had chemotherapy. He told me I had had this for a long time, but still wanted me to have radiation. My internist wanted me to have chemotherapy. I refused both radiation and chemo because I had already made up my mind that if I had cancer, I was going to go the B17 metabolic route.

I had been fortunate to know a lady whose cancer had spread over her whole body. She could not get out of her wheelchair. She had had all the chemotherapy and radiation they could give her, so she said the doctors sent her home to die and told her husband that she had only two or three months to live. This lady started on the Laetrile program, and soon she was out of the wheelchair. So, I had decided years before that if I ever found out I had cancer, the metabolic way

---

[259] Ibid.
[260] Day, Phillip, *Cancer: Why We're...*, op. cit.

was the way I was going to go. Since the diet is an important part of the program, I had started myself on the diet.

At that time there was a clinic in the San Francisco Bay area where I could receive my treatment. Drs Brodie and McNeel were helping Dr John Richardson in his clinic in Albany, California, across the bay from San Francisco, where Laetrile and metabolic therapy were being offered.

I am now 77 years old, feeling very good, and I am happy to say that I have had no evidence of recurrence of cancer for 23 years. At the time of my operation, there were two other women in the same hospital room as myself, both with breast cancer, both having the same surgeons. One of the patients was the same age as myself, and the other was about 10 years younger. I was given the worst prognosis, but I am the only one still alive after these many years. The youngest of the three of us died after about four years, and the one my age lived for about eight years. Also, I felt good the whole time (better than I had for years), while both of them were miserable from their chemotherapy.

Dr Brodie has had many years of experience in the treatment of cancer with alternatives and has had his share of successes. I have been following his program for all these years and I am very grateful and pleased with his care."

Anne Ryecroft

"Dear Steve, we lived in South Africa and my brother Athol was employed in the building industry for all his working life. He often worked directly with asbestos. The workmen were not given any warnings, nor were they issued with any protective clothing. He had no idea that asbestos was a deadly substance. In June 1997, my beloved brother was diagnosed with malignant mesothelioma, (a rare form of cancer of the lining of the chest caused by asbestos dust). He fought this disease with the only treatment he was offered, i.e. surgery, radiotherapy and chemotherapy. Sadly this treatment was of no help to him and in fact only exacerbated his suffering, and caused severe deterioration in his condition. He gradually became weaker and weaker until he died on 5th August 1998.

Some months after Athol's death, I developed a persistent cough that I successfully ignored. Then early in 2001 I began to experience difficulties in climbing stairs. My reaction to this was that I had become unfit and thought that I should try and exercise more. This only made the problem worse and by June of 2001 I began to feel decidedly unwell. Eventually I decided a visit to the doctor was necessary, and after a series of tests, biopsies, etc. I was finally diagnosed in early September as having malignant mesothelioma, the very same disease that had taken my brother three years earlier. This was devastating news for my whole family. When my brother, Athol, was diagnosed with the same disease we understood that this dreadful form of cancer was very rare. It seemed impossible that it could strike both a brother and a sister, but it did. It appeared that I had breathed in the asbestos dust from his clothing. My world was turned upside-down and suddenly all those things that seemed important were not important anymore.

My immediate decision was that I would not follow the same route as my brother had done, since clearly this would only hasten my death. In any case, conventional medicine could only offer me 'palliative chemotherapy', but no hope of any survival. I sent a panic e-mail to a nutritionist in South Africa for advice, as my own common sense told me that nutrition would be the best way forward. She e-mailed back with three instructions:

1. Get onto the Hallelujah Diet. (This is a diet consisting of 85% raw fruit and vegetables, carrot juice, Barley Green, and of course eliminating five foods that are known problems for cancer patients: meat, dairy, salt, sugar and white flour, as well as eliminating all processed food from the diet).
2. Try to get to the Oasis of Hope Hospital in Mexico.
3. Spend as much time with God as possible.

Well, nos. 1 & 3 were no problem, but I initially rejected no. 2. I soon began to realise that nos. 1 & 3 were not enough as my health continued to decline. But God was not going to allow me to ignore the possibility of going to The Oasis of Hope Hospital in Mexico and He kept prompting me until I could no longer ignore this. Being a single Mum with two young children to support, I had nothing like the *finances available to go there, so I said to God, "OK I'm listening now, if I am meant to go to Mexico I know that You will provide", and I put my trust TOTALLY in Him and went ahead and made the necessary arrangements.*

In all this time I was becoming weaker and weaker and it appeared that the cancer had metastasised to the liver. But God is ever faithful and the money was provided in miraculous ways. After overcoming many obstacles, including visa difficulties, and finally British Airways' initial refusal to grant me clearance for the flight because of my state of health, my 13-year-old daughter, Auriol and I finally arrived at the Oasis of Hope hospital in Tijuana, Mexico.

It was quite the most amazing experience I have ever had in my life. I knew from the moment I walked through the doors that I was in the right place. God's love permeates this remarkable hospital where everywhere you look there are colourful banners with Bible texts and wise sayings that help to create a positive attitude. Here I was not just a sick body but a person with a mind and a soul. In this hospital, they regard Jesus Christ as the Medical Director and with that one you just cannot go wrong. (There cannot be many places where your doctor will pray with you and hug you each time you meet and where they give all the glory to God.) I met so many wonderful people and forged many strong friendships that I know will last for eternity. I was immediately started on the treatment of B17 administered intravenously as well as chelation therapy, oxygen therapy and shark cartilage enemas. Of course, the nutrition program was all important too.

I came back home very much stronger, the fluid on my lung had stabilised, and so had the tumour. The two cancer spots on my liver had completely disappeared. I brought home with me 6 months' supply of the B17 that I would administer myself daily through a permanently inserted catheter in my chest, as well as other treatments with instructions to return in 6 months for a check-up and further supplies. I came home with real HOPE and knew that God was looking after me and I felt that I now had a future that I would not have had if it had been left to conventional medicine.

God again miraculously provided for the return trip in May 2002 where the doctors described my condition as 'remarkable' and I praise God for that. I am enjoying a quality of life that I could not have wished for had I not taken this step of faith and although I owe my life to B17, the ultimate glory must go to God who has masterminded all this.

I think of my brother Athol daily and feel a great sadness that we did not know about this treatment at the time he was so ill, because had we known he would have been spared a great deal of suffering and would most probably still be alive today."

Warren Hutchins

"In February, 2000, I was diagnosed with prostate and bladder cancer. Secondary cancer had spread to my lymph nodes and to both my kidneys. I went immediately onto Vitamin B17 and ate lots of paw paw. I noticed that within three days, the pain had reduced dramatically and within ten days, the pain was gone altogether. After nine weeks on the program, I sought a second opinion as to my condition and arranged CAT scans of my kidney cancers. To the doctors' astonishment, I was found to be free of cancer! They scratched their heads and just couldn't believe it. Cancer is no longer a death sentence. There is great hope for many people who undertake this program."

Laura Boomsma

In November 2001, five-year-old Laura was diagnosed with a large Wilms' tumour on her right kidney. She underwent pre-operative chemotherapy in December which saw her hair fall out. She became very sick and stopped eating. During this period, Laura's father attended a Phillip Day cancer seminar in Brisbane and learned that there were considerable dangers to human health with certain conventional cancer treatments. Laura's parents decided to stop all chemotherapy treatment immediately and Laura began a full nutritional program, including Vitamin B17. After about one month of B17 treatment, Laura was feeling much better and a scan confirmed that Laura's tumour had shrunk right down in size. In January, the hospital surgically removed the tumour and insisted on 12 sessions of post-operative chemotherapy. Laura's parents objected and said they wanted to seek alternative treatment overseas. The hospital, believing them to be 'unfit' parents, sought legal means to take Laura from them and forcibly medicate her with chemotherapy. Laura's father said he would go to jail before the authorities took Laura from them. The Campaign for Truth in Medicine became involved.

In conjunction with the Boomsma's legal team, CTM assisted in drawing up the affidavits that would be presented in court. The sheer weight of evidence contained in the affidavit against chemotherapy was enough to force the hospital to back down before the case was heard in the Queensland Supreme Court, setting a world precedent.

Free to leave Australia without having their passports seized, Laura and her father duly travelled to the UK where Laura received non-toxic, immune-boosting treatments for her condition. At the time of writing, Laura is doing very well. Said father Aaron Boomsma:

"I am just so grateful to Phillip and the mission at Credence. The change in Laura since beginning the alternative treatment has been incredible."

The above personal accounts represent only a small percentage of the B17 testimonies from around the world that attest to the life-saving benefits of this simple treatment, when coupled with suitable dietary changes. And it's a privilege to be able to say that, as far as the treatment of cancer is concerned, Vitamin B17 nutritional therapy is great news for the 21st century!

But the great news doesn't just stop at B17 and its supporting nutritional regime. Our concluding chapter examines a number of other natural cancer treatments from the natural medicine cabinet – treatments that also appear to be having an excellent effect.

Other treatments in the cabinet

*"Never does nature say one thing
and wisdom another."* **Juvenal**

VITAMIN C

The all-round benefits of Vitamin C to the human physiology have been known and utilised for centuries. In terms of its general benefits to humankind, we read the following from Dr Emanuel Cheraskin:

"There are more than ten thousand published scientific papers that make it quite clear that there is not one body process (such as what goes on inside cells or tissues) and not one disease or syndrome (from the common cold to leprosy) that is not influenced, directly or indirectly, by Vitamin C." [261]

In *Cancer: Why We're Still Dying To Know The Truth*, Phillip Day cites more specific references to cancer and the use of Vitamin C:

"Dr Linus Pauling, often known as the 'Father of Vitamin C', and twice awarded the Nobel Prize, declared that daily intakes of up to 10g of the vitamin aids anti-cancer activity within the body. Pauling was largely derided for making these declarations, but today, large doses of Vitamin C are used by many practitioners for cancer patients in nutritional therapy, who believe Pauling was right and that the popular nutrient is indispensable to the body in its fight to regain health from cancer." [262]

Scurvy and Vitamin C

According to naval records, over one million British sailors died of scurvy between 1600 and 1800. Yet for hundreds of years the cure for this gum-rotting and organ-destroying disease had already been part of the official record. Sir Richard Hawkins, the famous British

---

[261] Cheraskin, Emanuel, "The Vitamin C Connection": www.cforyourself.com/ Overview/Primer/What_C_Does/what_c_does.html
[262] Day, Phillip, *Cancer: Why We're...*, op. cit.

Elizabethan admiral, faced scurvy among his crew on a lengthy voyage to Brazil and discovered that eating oranges and lemons cured the condition immediately. However, despite reporting this phenomenon to the British Admiralty and to any physicians who would listen, this valuable knowledge perished along with Hawkins.

In the winter of 1534/5, French explorer Jacques Cartier found himself stranded when his ship became trapped in the ice in a tributary of the St Lawrence River. Soon his crew began dying of scurvy. Out of an original ship's complement of a hundred and ten men, twenty-five had already perished of the disease and many others were so sick they were not expected to recover.

The authorities did nothing

Believing that the condition was caused by bad vapours or some malignant cause to do with the 'sea airs', Cartier was astonished when local Indians showed him how to boil pine needles and bark from the white pine, later found to be rich in Vitamin C. His sailors swiftly recovered after drinking the beverage. Upon his return, Cartier enthusiastically reported this miraculous cure to medical authorities. The authorities did nothing about the information they were given, except to log it into their records.

Deaths from scurvy were so numerous in the 18th century, that by the Napoleonic Wars, more British sailors were dying from ascorbic acid deficiency than were being killed in combat. Between 1740 and 1744, British admiral, George A Anson, had set sail to circumnavigate the globe in his flagship *Centurion*. Originally starting with six ships and almost 2,000 healthy men, *Centurion* was the only ship that eventually returned. Anson reported that scurvy alone had killed over 1,000 of his men.

Such was the turmoil and embarrassment this event caused in British Admiralty circles that a naval surgeon, John Lind, became determined to find the cure for the dreaded disease. On 20th May 1747, Lind commenced an experiment which dramatically demonstrated that fresh greens and plenty of fruits eaten by scurvy sufferers produced stunning recoveries. Later experiments clearly showed that those who ate a balanced diet, fortified with these vegetable and fruit elements, did not contract scurvy.

Yet what was the reaction of the establishment? The British Admiralty and numerous other physicians, who had individually been attempting to solve the same problem and thus earn grants and fame, barely gave Lind's findings any credence. It took 48 more years and thousands of further scurvy deaths before his advice finally became official Navy quartermaster policy.

From the time the cure had become known in Europe, all it had taken to conquer scurvy was 450 years, millions of deaths, and finally the belief in a simple diet of fruit and veg.

Vitamin C and collagen

Symptoms of scurvy include bleeding gums, easy bruising and a tendency toward bone fractures. All these symptoms are a result of the requirement for Vitamin C in the development of the substance between our cells. This substance, primarily collagen, is the fibrous material that gives our tissues form and substance. Collagens are principal components of tendons, ligaments, skin, bone, teeth, cartilage, heart valves, arteries, intervertebral discs, cornea, eye lenses, in addition to the ground substance between cells.

Vitamin C protects against breast cancer

After reviewing 90 studies on the relationship between Vitamin C and cancer, Gladys Block, PhD at the University of California at Berkeley, concluded:

"There is overwhelming evidence of the protective effect of Vitamin C and other antioxidants against cancer of the breast."[263]

And Geoffrey R Howe of the National Cancer Institute of Canada reviewed 12 case-controlled studies of diet and breast cancer and noted that Vitamin C had the most consistent, statistically significant relationship to the reduction of breast cancer risk.[264] And, on the subject of the importance of mineral and vitamin supplements, a *New*

---

[263] "You can save a woman's life – and it could be your own!":
www.access2wealth.com/health/report-Save%20a%20Woman's%20Life.htm
[264] Ibid.

York Times front-page article quoted Dr Geoffrey P Oakley, Jr. at the Centers for Disease Control and Prevention in Atlanta as saying:

"We, the physicians, were mistaken not to recommend vitamin supplements to our patients for so long. We just need to admit that on this one, we were wrong." [265]

Hazel

Hazel had been given a virtual death sentence by her cancer doctor, who had told her that although there was an 86% recovery from her type of breast cancer, she was unfortunately in the smaller category. As previously noted, Hazel's chemotherapy was only making her feel terrible, and she decided that if she was to die, she would do so without further conventional treatment. Hazel began a regime of intravenously administered Vitamin C and supplements, which included Vitamin B17. She paid great attention to her diet.

She soon began to feel a great deal better. She regained her weight, her hair and her appetite. About nine months following the diagnosis, she was troubled with lower back pain and visited her doctor. He suggested a further scan based on Hazel's lower back pain, which the doctor believed was possibly the result of her cancer having spread to the base of her spine. Hazel said there was no way she was going for more chemotherapy or scans, which she believes in themselves can trigger carcinogenic activity.

Instead, Hazel supplemented her Vitamin C regime with a course of Vitamin B17 kernels, as well as maintaining a sensible diet and staying away from her conventional cancer physician. The blood count taken by her GP before Christmas read as normal. She feels very healthy and is in the process of writing a book on her experiences. She feels passionately that people need to know that there are alternative cancer treatments available and speaks to groups on this subject.

Positive Health cites a paper on the preventive effects of Vitamins A, C and E on patients with colon cancer (colorectal adenomas). Following surgery, 20 patients were given Vitamins A, C and E for 6 months; 21 adenoma patients were given placebos. Cells taken from

---

[265] Ibid.

biopsies before and during the 6-month period were evaluated for cell proliferation criteria. While there was no statistical significance in cell parameters in the placebo group, in patients receiving the vitamins, there was a statistically significant decrease in labelling in cells near the 'mucosal surface', a bio-marker of proliferation and cancer risk. The findings suggest that Vitamins A, C and E reduce cell abnormalities associated with a pre-cancerous condition.[266]

More scare tactics

The recent scare tactics surrounding Vitamin C and its supposed links to cancer are not grounded in fact. Quite simply, any good news on Vitamin C represents yet another threat to the pharmaceutical industry's considerable income from conventional cancer treatments.

Leukaemia and Vitamin C

The following testimonial appeared in a recent issue of *Alive* natural health magazine, written by Reginald Hall:

"It's a miracle! You've beaten leukaemia!" *I am 90 years old, retired 27 years. At age 82 I went to see my family doctor who was concerned about some test result findings. He sent me to the head oncologist of Credit Valley Hospital in Mississauga, Ont. The oncologist found my blood count was 80,000 and told me I had leukaemia. He said he had no prescription he could give me, but suggested I take all kinds of vitamins.*

My oncologist gave me about six months. I read in 'Nine-Day Inner Cleansing and Blood Wash', by researcher I E Gaumont and Dr Harold Buttram, about highway truck drivers with leukaemia who were treated with 12,000 mg of vitamin C daily. I decided to do 1,000 mg every two hours, 24 hours a day. I did this for two years. The night sweats left me, I started to feel good and my energy returned.

---

[266] Paganelli, G M et al. "The effect of vitamin A, C and E supplementation on rectal cell proliferation in patients with colorectal adenomas", *J. Natl. Cancer Inst.*; 84(1):47-41. 1992

In June 2000, eight years later, I returned to see the oncologist. His greeting was "Are you still here?" He took my blood count and it was 6,500. He said, "It's a miracle. You have beaten leukaemia."[267]

This next letter appears on the Cforyourself website, dedicated to furthering our knowledge on the healing powers of Vitamin C. It was sent in by Terry, who had been diagnosed with testicular cancer and had already allowed the surgeon to remove one testicle:

"Afterwards he insisted that I should have the lymph nodes removed from my under arms and groin…. I asked the doctor how much time I had to try other options. He said six months, but suggested not waiting at all, fearing that the cancer would spread. I was talking to a customer about all this a week later, and he ran home and got a book for me to read written by Linus Pauling (a two-time winner of the Nobel Prize), entitled Cancer and Vitamin C. You should get this book and read it! You will be amazed.

After reading, it I started taking 10,000 mg of vitamin C (100% pure ascorbic acid) every day until I got the only side-effect attributed to mega-dosage of C, gastritis - cramps and gas. This happened in about one month. I dropped the dose in half to 5,000 mg per day until it happened again in about another month and I dropped to 2,000 mg per day, where I remained for several months until the threat was gone. I then dropped to 1,000 mg per day which I think is good for any person to take on a regular basis.

I did not tell my doctor what I was doing and got the blood tests done as he ordered them. The flaggers dropped by half each month with the exception of the third or forth month, when they dropped to the level that is considered normal for everyone. The doctor was amazed. In fact he ordered another blood test to be sure. When I told him what I had been taking, he refused to believe it and said it was not the Vitamin C, that it would have happened anyway. This was after assuring me months before it would never happen. I am sure he doesn't want to believe a $10.00 bottle of Vitamin C can cure a $10,000.00 illness…. I could tell you more stories but I think you get

---

[267] *Alive*, January 2002 at:
http://groups.yahoo.com/group/cancer-testimonials/message/195

the point. Get the book! And after you read it you will see what I saw. It can't hurt so try it. It works!"

The final word on Vitamin B17 and Vitamin C comes from Dr Nichola Hembry, who practices at the UK's Dove Clinic, specialising in the non-conventional, nutritional and immune-boosting approaches to cancer care and treatment:

"Nutritional treatments, such as high-dose Vitamin C and B17 have been known about for years, and there are many success stories from patients lucky enough to have received and benefited from them. Research shows that levels of 400mg/dl Vitamin C in the blood can kill cancer cells by a pro-oxidative mechanism, and there is a great deal of data showing that B17 is preferentially toxic to cancer cells. The trouble is that there is little in the way of well-designed random control trial data for the use of these substances, and therefore mainstream medicine rejects them out of hand without even considering the evidence available, or even asking why these trials haven't been carried out.

It has to be said that one of the reasons is a lack of financial incentive because these substances cannot be patented. Sadly it is the cancer sufferers who lose out. Not even to have the choice of these safer, more natural treatments, even when a cancer is deemed incurable and only palliative chemotherapy or radiotherapy is offered, is in my view totally unacceptable. I have seen many patients experience an improved duration and quality of life with an integrated approach, and some go on to achieve complete remission of their disease, even when dismissed as incurable by their oncologists."

Treating cancer is not just about getting hold of Vitamin B17 and Vitamin C as quickly as possible. We need to be educated on a whole range of issues. A full list of Credence titles covering cancer diets and Vitamin B17 metabolic therapy protocols are found at the back of this book. Each has been written in an easily readable format and they make for necessary and fascinating reading!

ESSIAC TEA

"Though I worked each day from 9am to 9pm, my work was so absorbing, there was no sense of fatigue. My waiting room was a place of happiness where people exchanged their experiences and shared their hope. After a few treatments, patients seemed to throw off their depression, fear and distress. Their outlook became optimistic and, as their pain decreased, they became happy and talkative.

I could see the changes in some of the patients. A number of them, presented to me by their doctors after everything known to medical science had been tried and failed, were literally carried into my clinic for their first treatment. Later to see these same people walk in on their own after only five or six treatments more than repaid me for all my endeavours. I have helped thousands of such people. I offered the treatment at no charge." [268]

Those are the words of Rene Caisse, the woman who helped put Essiac on the Western map.

Rene Caisse

Rene Caisse was a Canadian nurse working in the early 20th century. In 1922, Rene made a discovery that changed her life dramatically. While attending to an older woman who had undergone surgery, Rene noticed scarring on the woman's breast and asked her how it came about. The woman explained that 30 years earlier she had developed breast cancer and had been led to an old Indian medicine man who told her the cancer could be cured with an herbal remedy that he knew of.

She drank the herbal mixture daily, and over time the breast tumours gradually diminished. She never had a recurrence and was 80 years old at the time Rene Caisse met her. Caisse asked the woman for the formula, remarking: *"My thought was that if I should ever develop cancer, I would use it."*

---

[268] Olsen, Cynthia, *Essiac: A Native Herbal Cancer Remedy*, Kali Press, 1999

Rene did little with the Essiac formula (Essiac is her last name reversed) until 1924 when her aunt developed stomach and liver cancer. The doctors had given her six months to live. Rene obtained permission from her aunt's physician, Dr R O Fisher, to administer the herbal tea treatment. Rene later said, *"My aunt lived for twenty-one years after being given up by the medical profession. There was no recurrence of cancer."* [269]

In 1930, the Canadian College of Physicians and Surgeons sent an agent to issue a warrant for Rene Caisse's arrest for practising medicine without a license. When the agent discovered Caisse was not only providing free services but also working only with the permission and approval of doctors, the warrant was never served. For eight years until 1942, thousands of people came for treatments; most were severely ill with cancer. Rene Caisse's mother was diagnosed with liver cancer in 1935. Rene Caisse treated her mother with Essiac and she fully recovered and lived another eighteen years until her death at age ninety of heart failure. [270]

A high recommendation

The four herbs in Essiac Tea are Sheep Sorrel, Burdock Root, Slippery Elm Bark, and Rhubarb Root. Renee Caisse died in 1978 at the age of 90. Before she died, she signed over the rights of the Essiac formula to two parties, Respirin Corp. of Toronto and Dr Charles Brusch of Cambridge, Massachusetts, director of the prestigious Brusch Clinic and personal physician to John F Kennedy.

Dr Brusch himself had cancer of the lower bowel, which completely disappeared after Essiac treatments. Dr Brusch thoroughly supported Essiac as a cancer cure and openly stated:

"I endorse this therapy, for I have cured my own cancer, the original site of which was the lower bowel, through Essiac alone." [271]

In 1977, *Homemaker* magazine initiated an investigative story on Essiac. *"Little by little, our scepticism gave way to a mounting*

[269] Olsen, Cynthia, *Essiac: A Native Herbal Cancer Remedy*, op. cit.
[270] Ibid.
[271] Ibid.

enthusiasm," two reporters wrote. They interviewed scores of former 'hopeless' cancer victims who had been cured from cancer and lived for decades after Essiac treatment. They reviewed hundreds of patients' cases. They researched the complicated anecdotal and political history and concluded that Caisse's treatment was genuine.[272]

Included here are two testimonies taken from the Credence Publication book, *The Essiac Handbook* by James Percival, details of which can be found at the end of this book.

Ellen Broderick

"In the fall of 1992, my mother, who lives in Ohio, was told that her throat and lung cancer had reached the point that she only had ninety days left to live. My sister and I began to help her straighten out her affairs. I heard about Essiac. I sent her some. She drank it for two months. On December 22, she went back to visit the doctor. He thought that she was coming in to say goodbye. When he checked her she was in total remission. I am a nurse, and I kept her x-rays as proof of her recovery."

R Kirkland

"Our family was devastated when my mother-in-law, Myrna, informed us that she had been diagnosed with cancer. In her case, it was ovarian cancer which had spread to the lymph glands and then to her lungs. It was diagnosed as inoperable and the doctors told her to get her affairs in order. After a hysterectomy, they told her she had about six months to live. The tumours in her lungs were too numerous to remove. My sister asked if there was some nutritional approach that might slow down the progress of the disease. The doctor assured her there was none. By chance, my father heard a radio program where Essiac was explained.

The remedy was so simple and straightforward that I knew my mother-in-law could take it. She took a little each night. We held our breaths. The doctor and our nurse cousin told us not to get our hopes up. Yet the weekly x-rays began indicating something they did not expect. Little by little the tumours in her lungs stabilised.... and then

---

[272] *Vancouver Sun,* 16th May, 1992

began to diminish. The nursing staff at the doctor's office reacted in awe as, week after week, the tumours began disappearing and her blood count return to normal.

A little more than a year after beginning Essiac, the doctor called to tell Myrna that she was an official miracle. Her charts showed no indication of cancer in any system. To date, five years later, there has been no recurrence of cancer."

The complete story of Rene Caisse's life and struggles is told in a book written by Dr Gary L Glum, entitled *The Calling of an Angel*. It tells of the documented recoveries of thousands of cancer patients who had been certified in writing by their doctors as incurable. Rene continued her work for 40 years until her death in 1978.

THE IMPORTANCE OF THE BOWEL
(Evacuate the premises!)

Our colon has been designed to function as a smoothly flowing expulsion system, in order promptly to flush digestive wastes from the body. We also have an in-built protection system to reduce the harmful effects of any toxic elements we might consume. When food reaches the stomach that is not wholesome, is combined incorrectly or is harmful to the body, word is immediately sent from the stomach to the mucus manufacturer, warning, *"Get busy, the enemy is on the way!"* Mucus is produced immediately and the colon and small intestine are lined with it. When the poisoned or harmful food finally enters the small intestines and then the colon, the latter is well lined with a layer of mucus, and the body does not absorb any of the poison into the bloodstream.

But with the great increase in toxicity and food processing in the 20th and 21st centuries, modern lifestyles have been taking their toll on our digestive and elimination organs. Of all the vital organs in the body, the one that suffers the most abuse from modern dietary habits is the digestive tract. Refined, processed, low-fibre foods, animal fats, a lack of exercise and an ever-increasing level of stress can all contribute to gastro-intestinal health problems:

➢ The stomach is perpetually stuffed with denatured foods taken in incompatible combinations.
➢ The liver is swollen and strained with the effort of breaking down massive intakes of sugars, animal protein and fat, as well as drugs and poisons.
➢ The pancreas increases in size owing to the constant demand for digestive enzymes to process enzymeless foods.
➢ The complete digestive system can increase in size and press against other organs. Dr Richard Schulze believes this is harmful to human health:

"I remember when my older brother got his first car. It was a 1950 Ford station-wagon. I used to be able to open up the hood, sit on a front fender with my feet and legs actually dangling inside the engine compartment and work on the engine, change spark plugs, whatever. Get the picture? Big car, big hood, little engine, lots of room. Nowadays, I open up the hood of my 2001 Ford Expedition, and every square inch under the hood is jammed, packed with engine parts, power pumps, wires, hoses, pipes and filters. It is too complex, and even if I understood it, there is NO ROOM to work on it. NO SPACE.

What is my point? I used to think our anatomy was like my brother's 1950 Ford. You know, a lung up here, a kidney down there, a bowel in the middle, with lots of room. Then, one day in school, I examined my first cadaver – and what an enlightening experience. The human anatomy is not like my brother's 1950 Ford at all. It is like my 2001 Ford. Every square inch is packed with something and everything is touching something else. This body of ours must have had an incredible engineer. Everything has its place and THERE IS NO EXTRA ROOM!

If one organ swells or gets bigger, then another organ (usually the one next to the swollen one) gets squeezed, compressed or crushed. Organs do not work so well when they are crushed and when the blood, lymphatic, nerve and general circulation get interrupted. Every organ needs good circulation to get nutrition in and waste out in order to be healthy. Squeezed and compressed organs get sick."[273]

---

[273] Schultz, Richard, "Bowel Cleansing", *Get Well* magazine, March 2002

Apart from the possible complications arising from squeezed or compressed organs, a sluggish bowel can retain pounds of old, toxic, poisonous faecal matter. Inefficient or partial elimination of waste from the body over the years causes the colon to become lined with layers of hardening material, described by some as mucoid plaque.

According to the organisation Helping People Survive:

"The average American & European intestine carries within it over 5 pounds of putrid, half-digested red meat, plus another 5-10 pounds of foul toxic mucus waste impacted for years in the folds of the colon and small intestines." [274]

A growing number of doctors believe that if these toxins are not removed from your intestinal tract, they will be reabsorbed into your bloodstream, causing a variety of health problems. Bowel cleansing can be a very effective way of detoxifying the body.

Our own personal chemical dump

The whole purpose of doing any type of cleansing or detoxification program is to get the toxins out of your fat, muscle and blood. Dr Bernard Jensen says:

"In the 50 years I've spent helping people to overcome illness, disability and disease, it has become crystal clear that poor bowel management lies at the root of most people's health problems. When we have toxic substances in the colon seeping into body tissues, it's like having a time-release poison in your bowel. It works slowly, imperceptibly wearing down the vitality, resistance and health of body tissues and organs. It's like having our own personal chemical dump that we carry around with us all the time. It's always working as long as the toxins are present, serving out their lethal micro-doses.

When the bowel becomes encrusted with non-expelled faecal material due to poor dietary habits, the absorption of vital nutrients slows down to the degree of encrustation, the energy cycle is short-circuited and a downward spiral of tissue integrity ensues. Improving

---

[274] The Colon Cleansing Story http://www.hps-online.com/bcc1.htm

the condition of your bowel will give you worthwhile dividends in renewed health, energy and vitality. It's an investment well made. Once the bowel is cleansed of accumulated waste material, the next step begins.

Giving up old habits is a very difficult thing for most people but is absolutely essential to regaining full health. The building process begins when correct, life-giving attitudes and habits take over. We can regenerate the body when we have clean tissues that are able to draw all the nutrients and chemical elements we need from the foods we eat. Coffee and donuts will not do the job; sugar and white bread won't either. If old habits are not given up, only temporary, 'flash' results will be experienced."[275]

Before considering bowel or colon or bladder surgery, why not consider a cleanse?

Dr Schulze recounts the following story about a patient of his who had gone for a routine bowel check (sigmoidoscopy) because of a history of degenerative disease and bowel cancer in his family:

"Well, sure enough, they saw it, a big cancer, they said, looking like a big mushroom, growing in his sigmoid colon, and it had metastasised (spread) and invaded into the muscle, maybe even further. He also had around 35 polyps. The doctors wanted to admit him to hospital immediately for a colon resection. They wanted to gut him and carve out at least 12 inches of his colon, probably more. He was very scared. The dad asked if he could delay the surgery for a few months while he did a bowel cleanse. The doctor said he was nuts, the herbs could be dangerous and even if they weren't, they were useless, and that a delay of a few days could be suicidal. The cancer would just grow worse, spread and kill him. The dad told me he was more afraid of the doctors and their surgery. So he decided to go on my bowel detox program.

After 8 weeks of treatment, he went back for another look by the doctor. But when the doctor looked in the colonoscope, he literally

[275] Jensen, Bernard, "Tissue Cleansing Through Bowel Management", The Angel Healing Centre at: www.angelhealingcenter.com/JensenQuotes.html

shrieked, "Oh my God, I don't believe it!" Not only were all 35 polyps gone, but the cancer looked like a dried up skeleton of a cancer. (This is exactly what cancer looks like after your body and especially your white blood cells eat up a tumour.) He said the doctor then touched the cancer skeleton with a tool through the scope and that it just fell off the bowel - it literally fell off!" [276]

The following letter was sent into the Cancercured website, testifying to Dr Shulze's approach to flushing the system:

Dr Richard Schulze tells stories about patients of his who have gone on his program, patients with cancerous colon polyps who were told they needed operations immediately. After going on raw foods, juices, herbs, and some of the other stuff he teaches, they went back to the docs and the polyps were dissolving or falling off. They didn't need surgery anymore....

I experienced my own cancer cure of sorts about 3 ½ years ago, shortly after I started a raw food diet. About three months into it (maybe 95% raw) I experienced blood in my urine. I didn't go to a doctor at first, hoping it would go away. It did, then a couple of weeks later it came back, only this time something inside of me broke loose and along with blood it came out while I was urinating. It was a spongy thing, 2 or 3 inches wide. I put it in the freezer until I could take it to a doctor.

The immediate effect was that my urine flow was stronger than it had been in years. This thing evidently had been constricting the flow. The doctor said it was a polyp from my bladder. He sent it to a lab for analysis. Later he called me to say the lab said it was cancerous, second degree (or stage 2, maybe). He wanted me to see a urologist. I didn't want to do that. Instead, reasoning that my raw foods and fasting (I did a couple of short fasts, 1- or 2-day, in that three-month period) had caused my body to eject the polyp, I increased my raw food percentage to 100%, bought the best juicer I could find, started drinking lots of fresh vegetable juice every day, getting more exercise, more sleep, sunlight, generally trying to take things easier.

---

[276] Richard Schultz, *Bowel Cleansing, ibid*

After about four months or so I decided to go to the urologist to get tested, because even though I felt OK, I was worried that maybe cancer was eating away at my bladder. The tests he did (cystoscopy, IV pyelogram) showed me to be completely cancer-free."

THE HOXSEY STORY

Of all the stories being covered in this final chapter, it is perhaps this story which provides such a rich vein of colour to illustrate the *cancer war*. Several books and two videos have been released on the Hoxsey story, and I am grateful to Daniel Haley for the following information, which has been abridged from his important book entitled *Politics of Healing, Suppression and Manipulation in American Medicine.*

In 1840, Illinois horse farmer John Hoxsey had put one of his best horses out to pasture rather than shoot him, after the vet had diagnosed a growing sore on the horse's leg as advanced cancer. But the sore began to heal and John Hoxsey noticed that each morning, the horse went directly to one particular spot, where he would graze for hours at a time. When the tumour dried up and eventually fell out, Hoxsey gathered up samples of every plant and herb in the horse's favourite corner of the pasture. This is the story of the origin of the Hoxsey treatment.

Using a formula comprising chiefly Cascara, Barberry, Red Clover, Pokeroot, Prickly Ash and Stillingia, cancer successes with these treatments were soon being reported and John Hoxsey became well-known as a cancer healer, continuing his treatments throughout the latter half of the 19th century. Upon his death, he passed on his work to his grand-son, Harry. What followed was nothing less than spectacular, in terms of results, and bloody, in terms of the cancer war.

Treat this hopeless case, then!
Okay. We will!

In the mid 1920's, things began to heat up for Harry Hoxsey and he soon found that his cancer cures were inciting the wrath and the jealousy of the medical establishment. Such was the vehemence towards him that he was refused entry to all medical colleges. Unable to train as a conventional doctor, Hoxsey sought to comply with the medical laws of the day and set up practice alongside a qualified doctor by the name of Bruce Miller. In March, 1924, Hoxsey and Dr Miller opened their clinic in Taylorville. So many patients began arriving, that within two months they had to find larger premises. In an attempt to get the AMA to look at the Hoxsey treatments seriously, Hoxsey and Dr Miller submitted to a trial, whereby a Dr Harris from the AMA proposed that they treat a clearly hopeless cancer patient, a Sgt Mannix of the Chicago Police, who had a six-inch open cancerous sore on his left shoulder. Hoxsey tells us what happened in his book, *You Don't Have To Die*:

"Dr Harris watched intently as I applied a thick coating of the yellow powder to the gaping lesion and Dr Miller put a dressing over it. We left a bottle of our internal medicine with directions that the patient receive a teaspoonful three times a day, and advised the doctor that we would be back in a week to administer another treatment. Within two weeks the surface of the pustulant sore turned black and started to dry, a sure sign that our medicine was working on the malignancy.

Within four weeks, a hard crust had formed, the cancer was shrinking and pulling away at the edges from the normal tissue. Moreover, the rapid improvement in the patient's general physical condition amazed all who saw him. He was able to sit up now, his eyes were bright and alert and the pain had vanished; he no longer needed morphine to sustain him. His appetite had returned two weeks later and he was walking around. That same day, we informed Dr Harris that necrosis (death) of the cancerous mass in the policeman's shoulder was complete, that it had separated from the normal tissue, and could be lifted out within two days."

Dr Harris then invited Hoxsey and Miller to perform the 'lifting out' operation in the hospital amphitheatre before the entire hospital staff. Hoxsey writes:

"Dr Miller removed the bandages from Sgt Mannix's shoulder. I picked up the forceps, scraped and probed the black mass of necrosed tissue. It moved freely at the perimeter but was still anchored at the base. I worked it loose, lifted it out with the forceps and deposited it on the white enamel tray provided for that purpose. And that's all

there was to the operation. Dr. Harris inspected the cavity left by the tumour. There was no sign of blood, pus, or abnormal tissue; clean scar tissue had already begun to form. 'In time it will heal level with the surrounding flesh,' I told him. Shaking his head incredulously, he declared, 'It's amazing; if I hadn't seen it I wouldn't believe it.' The entire demonstration took less than a half hour."

Twenty five years on and having cured literally hundreds of cancer patients, Hoxsey was still battling with a disbelieving and back-stabbing medical hierarchy, enduring many slanderous insults from the US cancer establishment. In February 1949, Hoxsey filed for libel against the editor of *JAMA* - a Dr Morris Fishbein, who had printed an article in a Hearst-owned Texas newspaper, the article in question entitled "Hoxsey: Cancer Charlatan".

The trial began on 16th March 1949. Hoxsey's lawyers presented fifty-seven cured patients to the court. When Dr Fishbein took the stand to denounce Hoxsey as a quack, he was forced to disclose that he had never personally administered the Hoxsey treatment and was also compelled to admit that he had never even treated a cancer patient in his life, while at the same time insisting he was an authority on the disease. He was further forced to divulge that he had never practised medicine one single day in his life, and had even failed his anatomy course in medical school.

The court found that Hoxsey had been libeled by the Hearst article. At the conclusion of the three-week trial, the judge handed the jury thirty-four issues to decide; all thirty four were decided in Hoxsey's favour. The jury ruled:

> ➢ That Fishbein's statement that "Hoxsey had more than 20 years in which to prove such virtues as might have existed in his method; such proof has never been forthcoming" was false.
> ➢ That Fishbein's statement that diagnosis had never been made by scientific methods was false.
> ➢ That practically every phrase referring to Hoxsey in the *American Weekly* article was false and tended to injure the reputation of the plaintiff and impeach his honesty,

integrity, and virtue, exposing him to public hatred, contempt, ridicule, and financial injury.

Judge Thornton's written opinion on the case should be of note to anyone interested in evaluating the Hoxsey treatment:

"This is my second jury of 12 that has found in my court that the Hoxsey treatment cures cancer. I have sat here and listened to over fifty witnesses from all walks of life who say they have been cured. They have showed their scars; they have given the names of the doctors who operated on them or treated them with x-ray or radium. I have heard the testimony of prominent and eminent pathologists, some of whom I know personally, saying that these patients were suffering from cancer before they went to Hoxsey.

I am of the firm opinion and belief that Hoxsey has cured these people of cancer. And the fact that this jury has answered all questions proves that Hoxsey has been done a great injustice and that the articles and utterances by defendant Morris Fishbein were false, slanderous, and libelous."

But still, the battles raged. In 1954, after more insinuations and distortions from the cancer establishment, Hoxsey invited ten physicians from all over the nation who assembled at his clinic for an independent, impartial investigation of his treatment. They spent two days inspecting the facilities, going over hundreds of case histories and interrogating patients and former patients. On 12th April 1954, they issued a unanimous statement, declaring:

"We find as a fact that our investigation has demonstrated to our satisfaction that the Hoxsey Cancer Clinic in Dallas, Texas, is successfully treating pathologically proven cases of cancer, both internal and external, without the use of surgery, radium or x-ray.

Accepting the standard yardstick of cases that have remained symptom-free in excess of five to six years after treatment, established by medical authorities, we have seen sufficient cases to warrant such a conclusion. Some of these presented before us have been free of symptoms for as long as twenty-four years, and the physical evidence indicates that they are all enjoying exceptional health at this time.

We as a Committee feel that the Hoxsey treatment is superior to such conventional methods of treatment as x-ray, radium, and surgery.

We are willing to assist this Clinic in any way possible in bringing this treatment to the American public. We are willing to use it in our offices, in our practices on our own patients when, at our discretion, it is deemed necessary.

The above statement represents the unanimous findings of this Committee.

In testimony thereof we hereby attach our signatures.

S Edgar Bond MD, Richmond, Indiana; Willard G Palmer MD, Seattle, Washington; Hans Kalm MD, Aiken, South Carolina; A C Timbs MD, Knoxville, Tennessee; Frederick H Thurston MD DO, Boise, Idaho; E E Loffler MD, Spokane, Washington; H B Mueller MD, Cleveland, Ohio; R C Bowie MD, Fort Morgan, Colorado; Benjamin F Bowers MD, Ebensburg, Pennsylvania; Roy O Yeats MD, Hardin, Montana."

In 1958, the Fitzgerald Report, commissioned by a United States Senate committee, concluded that organised medicine had 'conspired' to suppress the Hoxsey therapy and at least a dozen other promising cancer treatments. The proponents of these unconventional methods were mostly respected doctors and scientists who had developed nutritional or immunological approaches. Panels of surgeons and radiation therapists had dismissed the therapies as quackery, and these promising treatments were banned without a serious investigation. They all remain to this day on the American Cancer Society's blacklist of 'Unproven Methods of Cancer Management.'

By this time, the Hoxsey Clinic in Dallas had 12,000 patients and Harry Hoxsey was contemplating running for governor of Texas, a post that would enable him to appoint the state medical board and thereby get an impartial investigation into his therapy. Hordes of Hoxsey's patients flooded Washington DC, demanding medical freedom of choice. Hoxsey threatened to picket the White House with 25,000 cured patients. But the FDA and other federal agencies mounted a massive, legal and paralegal assault in response. The therapy with the potential to help cure cancer sufferers was hounded out of the United States.

In 1963, after continued pressure from the US medical fraternity, the Hoxsey Clinic finally relocated to Tijuana, Mexico, where it operates very successfully today. Space does not permit the full telling of the incredible Hoxsey story, but readers are strongly encouraged to read Daniel Haley's book, *Politics of Healing, Suppression and Manipulation in American Medicine*.

* * * * *

Successful alternative cancer treatments are by no means limited to those which have been discussed so far. Even as I write, I am mindful of the many positive testimonies from those who have followed the grape cure, Dr Joseph Gold's hydrazine sulphate, the Max Gerson approach, ellagic acid (found in raspberries, strawberries, cranberries, walnuts, pecans, pomegranates, and other plant foods), the elimination diet, mineral supplementation and other dietary/nutritional protocols. And what about this from Reverend George H Malkmus, founder of Hallelujah Acres? Revd George had just been diagnosed with colon cancer:

It was during this time of uncertainty that I turned to Lestor Roloff - a health nut, often affectionately referred to as 'Carrot Juice Roloff'. I was really in a dilemma as to what I should do for my cancer when I called Brother Roloff. His advice to me sounded strange. He advised me not to go the medical route of chemotherapy, radiation and surgery, as mom had gone... BUT SIMPLY TO CHANGE MY DIET TO RAW FRUITS AND VEGETABLES, AND DRINK LOTS OF FRESH CARROT JUICE!

Wow! That sounded too simplistic! But it sure sounded better than the medical route which I had pretty well decided not to pursue. So, overnight I changed from a meat-centred, cooked and processed food diet with plenty of sugar desserts, to an all-raw diet with lots of carrot juice. I stayed on this total raw diet for approximately one year. I didn't eat any cooked food during that year... just raw fruits, raw vegetables and one to two quarts a day of freshly extracted, raw carrot juice.[277]

The results were spectacular! Almost immediately I started to get well! In less than one year, my tumour had totally disappeared. It simply got smaller and smaller until it was gone. But that was not all. In less than one year, every physical problem I had been experiencing also disappeared! Such physical problems as haemorrhoids, hypoglycaemia, severe allergies and sinus problems, high blood pressure, fatigue, pimples, colds, flu... even body odour and dandruff were gone! Totally healed!

In the years that have followed - and I am over 60 years old at this writing - I have not experienced as much as a cold, sore throat, upset stomach, been to a doctor or taken as much as an aspirin. It is so thrilling, at my age, still to be able to play football, basketball and softball with the boys, jog five miles with ease, and have more energy, endurance and stamina than I had when I was 20 years old." [278]

Where does one end? It is purely a matter of space. Readers are encouraged to take what they can from this book and if necessary, look further, always remembering that golden rule, *investigate, investigate, investigate!*

The question often asked of me is this, *"Steve, what would you do if you were diagnosed with cancer?"* For those interested in this answer, I have included some useful pointers over the following pages.

---

[277] Repeated studies have shown the anti-cancer benefits of beta-carotene, the precursor to Vitamin A, when combined with a wide spectrum of phyto-nutrients derived from an organic, raw, living, wholefood diet. For concrete strategies on what to do with your food, see the highly recommended Credence recipe title *Food For Thought*. Details are at the back of this book.

[278] Malkmus, George & Michael Dye, *God's Way to Ultimate Health : A Common Sense Guide for Elimination of Sickness Through Nutrition*, Hallelujah Acres Publishing, April 1997, www.yourlifesource.com

The end? Or just the beginning?

If I had cancer...

The motivating factor behind *Great News on Cancer in the 21st Century* is to bring a sense of realism to the subject of cancer, as well as REAL HOPE. Throughout the writing of this book, I have been acutely aware of my own slender mortality and that, thankfully, I have not had to face a cancer diagnosis of my own. Were I to do so, I believe that my experience and understanding of the subject would lead me to pay great attention to the following points.

➢ Unless life-saving surgery is needed, immediate submission to the usual conventional pressures is not necessary. <u>In almost all cases, there is time enough to think things through.</u>

➢ I would be thankful that the cancer had been diagnosed and would seek to verify the diagnosis before taking any further steps.

➢ I would not consider chemotherapy or radiation treatment. I believe it is the wrong approach. My immune system will need to be at its functional best and treatments that damage my immune system do not make any sense. Chemotherapy and radiation treatments can severely damage the immune system.

➢ I would concentrate on my diet and pay special attention to rebuilding the body by introducing the minerals, enzymes, vitamins and trace minerals that are missing in our denatured diets. I would include foodstuffs in my diet that are rich in nitrilosides as detailed in this book. I would cut out all refined sugar, dairy, additive and synthetic products and avoid the foods discussed in the appendix section at the back of this book. An excellent guide on how to reorganise your diet and supplementation along the lines we have discussed is Credence's *Food for Thought* - the strap-line to this invaluable read: *"Fabulous food that won't kill you!"*

➢ I would concentrate on decreasing the amount of harmful toxins I allow into my life, from personal care products to considering the home/workplace environment.

➢ I would aim to exercise and get fresh air regularly.

- I would expect the experience to cause me to appreciate in a much deeper way the many every-day blessings in my life that can so often go unnoticed. As John Diamond said of family and friends, *"He who didn't realise what a boon an unimpaired voice was, who ate his food without stopping to think about its remarkable flavour, who was criminally profligate with words, who took his wife and children and friends for granted - in short, he who didn't know he was living."* And finally
- I would endeavour to draw closer to my family and friends and to our loving God, for His support and from Whom all blessings flow in the first place!

And so...

In conclusion, I am conscious of the fact that, throughout this book, conventional medicine has had a harsh spotlight shone upon it. However, there are many elements of conventional medical practice that are saving and enhancing lives every day, not least in some methods of diagnosis, pre-emptive surgery, replacement surgery, pain management and in acute and emergency medicine. As with all true medicine, may the good continue and may the bad be open to complete reappraisal.

I hope this book has given the reader a clear frame of reference and that it has served as a legible map with which to navigate the cancer jungle.

And finally, I do so wish I'd been given the opportunity to meet John Diamond because I reckon we'd have got on like a house on fire. Who knows what might have happened as a result?

Thank you for reading.

Appendices

A thesis presented to the Anglo-American Institute of Drugless Therapy by Dr Henry Rosenberg, 1990

This thesis comprised a collection of papers on the carcinogenic effects of chemotherapy which featured the following studies:

HAQUE, T., LUTCHER, C., FAGUET, G., TALLEDI, O., Chemotherapy-associated acute myelogenous leukemia and ovarian carcinoma, Am. J. Med. Sci., Sept. - Oct. 1976; 272 (2): 225-228;

JOCHIMSEN, P.R., PEARLMAN, N.W., LAWTON, R.L., Pancreatic carcinoma as a sequel to therapy of lymphoma, J. Surg. Oncol., 1976; 8 (6): 461-464;

SEIDENFELD, A.M., SMYTHE, H.A., OGRYZLO, M.A., UROWITZ, M.B., DOTTEN, D.A., Acute leukaemia in rheumatoid arthritis treated with cytotoxic agents, J. Rheumatol., Sept. 1976; 3 (3): 295-304;

ROBERTS, M.M., Acute leukemia after immunosuppressive therapy, Lancet, 9 Oct. 1976; 2 (7989): 768-770;

KUIS, W., DE KRAKER, J., KUIJTEN, R.H., DONCKERWOLCKE, R.A., VOUTE, P.A., Acute lymphoblastic leukaemia after treatment of nephrotic syndrome with immunosuppressive drugs, Helv. Paediatr. Acta, Jun. 1976; 31 (1): 91-95;

NAESS, K., Cancer of the pancreas chemically induced. Can drugs play a role? (Norwegian), Tidsskr. Nor. Laegeforen, 10 Jun. 1976; 96(16): 949;

STECHMILLER, B., WIERNIK, P.H., SHIN, M., SATTERFIELD, J., Metastatic teratocarcinoma following chemotherapy. Maturation to a mass pathologically indistinguishable from a mediastinal enteric cyst, Chest, May 1976; 69 (5): 697-700;

JAFFE, N., Late side effects of treatment: skeletal, genetic, central nervous system and oncogenic, Pediatr. Clin. N. Am., Feb. 1976; 23 (1): 233-244;

MEADOWS, A.T., D'ANGIO, G.J., EVANS, A.E., HARRIS, C.C., MILLER, R.W., MIKE, V., Oncogenesis and other late effects of cancer treatment in children, Radiology, Jan. 1975; 114 (1): 175-180;

SCHWARZ, J.H., CANELLOS, G.P., YOUNG, R.C., DEVITA, V.T. Jr., Meningeal leukaemia in the blastic phase of chronic granulocytic leukaemia, Am. J. Med., Dec. 1975, 59 (6): 819-829;

TERRACINI, B., Il ruolo di alcuni farmaci nell'ezioologia dei tumouri delle vie urinarie, Cancro, 1973; 26 (3): 185-188;

LI, F.P., CASSADY, J.R., JAFFE, N., Risk of second tumours in survivors of childhood cancer, Cancer, Apr. 1975: 35 (4): 1230-1235; CARTER, S.K., Second tumours complicating cancer therapy, Haematol. Bluttransfus., 1978; 22: 41-44;

BOIVIN, P., Les leucémies induites par la radiothérapie ou par la chimiothérapie peuvent-elles êtres prévues? Nouv. Presse Méd., 9 Sept. 1979; 7 (29): 2533-2534;

LEGLER, F., Karzinogenese durch Schadstoffe aus der Umwelt, Pharmaka und Ernährungsgewohnheiten, Oeff. Gesundheitswes., Oct. 1978; 40 (10): 653-662;

SCHULER, D., Iatrogenic carcinogenesis (Hungarian), Orv. Hetil., 10 Sept. 1978; 119 (37): 2239-2243; ROSNER, F., Is chemotherapy carcinogenic?, Cancer, Jan. Feb. 1978; 28 (1): 57-59;

PENN, I., Malignancies associated with immunosuppressive or cytotoxic therapy, Surgery, May 1978; 83 (5): 492-502;

NIEWEG, H.O., Iatrogene leukemie, Nederl. Tijdschr. Geneesk., 25 Mar. 1978; 122 (12): 398-401; MULDER, N.H., HOUWEN, B., Behandelen en vooruitzien. Acute leukemie na behandeling van een andere kwaadaardige ziekte, Nederl. Tijdschr. Geneesk., 25 Mar. 1978; 122 (12): 385-399;

ERSKINE, J.G., WANG, I., HUTTON, M.M., Chronic granulocytic leukaemia developing upon a follicular lymphoma, Br. Med. J., 19 Nov. 1977; 2 (6098): 1329;

CADMAN, E.C., CAPIZZI, R.L., BERTINO, J.R., Acute non-lymphocytic leukaemia: a delayed complication of Hodgkin's disease therapy: analysis of 109 cases, Cancer, Sept. 1977; 40 (3): 1280-1296; CHABNER, B.A., Second neoplasm a complication of cancer chemotherapy, N. Engl. J. Med., 28 Jul. 1977, 297 (4): 213-215;

KURTIDES, E.S., Breast cancer, chemotherapy and second malignant neoplasms, J.A.M.A., 4 Jul. 1977; 238 (1): 28-29;

WOLF, M.M., COOPER, I.A., DING, J.C., Hodgkin's disease terminating in acute leukaemia: a report of seven cases, Austr. N. Z. J. Med., Aug. 1979; 9 (4): 398-402;

KAHN, M.F., ARLET, J., BLOCH-MICHEL, H., CAROIT, M., CHAOUAT, Y., RENIER, J.C., Leucémies aigues après traitement par agents cytotoxiques en rhumatologie. 19 observations chez 2006 patients, Nouv. Presse Méd., 14 Apr. 1979; 8 (17): 1393-1397;

PENN, I., Leukaemias and lymphomas associated with the use of cytotoxic and immunosuppressive drugs, Cancer Res., 1979; 69: 7-13;

JOUET, J.P.,HUART, J.J., BAUTERS, F., GOUDEMAND, M., Leucémies aigues complicant la maladie de Hodgkin. Cinq nouvelles observations, Nouv. Presse Méd., 17 Feb. 1979; 8 (8): 613-614;

DANO, K., FORCHHAMMER, J., Carcinogenesis and drugs (Danish), Ugeskr. Laeger., Aug. 1981; 143 (35): 2246-2247; FARBER, E., Chemical carcinogenesis, N. Engl. J. Med., 3 Dec. 1981; 305 (23): 1379-1389;

STEWART, A.L., WILKINSON, P.M., Rapid onset of acute myeloid leukaemia following radiotherapy and chemotherapy for metastatic seminoma of the testis, J. Cancer Res. Clin. Oncol., 1981; 100 (1): 109-111;

HOOVER, R., FRAUMENI, J.F., Jr., Drug-induced cancer, Cancer, 1 Mar. 1981; 47 (5 Suppl.): 1071-1080;

BLANC, A.P., GASTAUT, J.A., SEBAHOUN, G., DALIVOUST, P., MURISASCO, A., CARCASSONNE, Y., Naissance d'une leucémie aigue au décours d'un traitement immunosupprésseur par le chlorambucil. Une observation, Nouv. Presse Méd., May 1981; 10 (21): 1717-1719;

CORDIER, J.F., TOURAINE, R., Cancers épidermoides du poumon chez un patient traité pour cancer aplasique à petites cellules. La chimiothérapie favorise-t-elle le développement de cancers d'un autre type histologique?, Nouv. Presse Méd., 9 May 1981; 10 (21): 1713-1716;

ASBORNSEN, G., GODAL, H.C., MYHRE, K., Acute myelogenous leukaemia after cytostatic therapy in breast cancer (Norwegian), Tidsskr. Nor. Laegeforen, Feb. 1981; 101 (6): 387-388;

PENN, I. Immunosuppression and skin cancer, Clin. Plast. Surg., Jul. 1980, 7 (3): 361-368;

CHAN, K.W., MILLER, D.R., TAN, C.T., Osteosarcoma and acute myeloblastic leukaemia after therapy for childhood Hodgkin's disease - a case report, Med. Pediatr. Oncol., 1980; 8 (2): 143-149;

MAHOMED, Y., MANDEL, M.A., CRAMER, S.F., MICHEL, B., Squamous cell carcinoma arising in pemphigus vulgaris during immunosuppressive therapy, Cancer, 15 Sept. 1980; 46 (6): 1374-1377;

DOHY, H., GENOT, J.Y., IMBERT, M., D'AGAY, M.F., SULTAN, C., Myelodysplasia and leukaemia related to chemotherapy and/or radiotherapy: a haematological study of 13 cases. Value of macrocytosis as an early sign of bone marrow injury, Clin. Lab. Haematol., 1980, 2 (2): 111-119.

Full list available at
http://www.karlloren.com/biopsy/book/p1.htm#chemo

Breast self-examination
A simple program for women

Breast self-examination and clinical breast examination (CBE - breast examination done by a healthcare provider) are useful in the early detection of breast changes and breast cancer. The following lists represent the most common signs, symptoms and examples of physiological changes but is not all-inclusive.

Stand before a mirror. Look at both breasts to note anything unusual - changes in shape, protruding veins, discoloration, or any other change from normal. Look for a discharge from the nipples, puckering, dimpling, or scaling of the skin.

Check for changes in contour or shape of your breasts. Watching closely in the mirror, clasp your hands behind your head and press your hands forward.

Next, press your hands firmly on your hips and bow slightly toward the mirror as you pull your shoulders and elbows forward. This completes the portion of the breast self exam in front of the mirror.

Some women do the next part of the exam in the shower; your fingers will glide easily over soapy skin. Raise your left arm. Use three or four fingers of your right hand to feel your left breast firmly and thoroughly. Beginning at the outer edge, press the flat part of your fingers in small circles, moving the circles slowly around the breast. You can begin at the outer edges of the breast and gradually work towards the nipple, or vice versa. Be sure to cover the whole breast and include the area between the breast and the underarm, including the underarm itself. You are feeling for any unusual lumps or mass under the skin.

Gently squeeze the nipple and look for a discharge. Report any discharge or unusual lumps to your doctor.

- Repeat this same process lying down so that the breast becomes flattened, making it easier to feel lumps or other masses.
- Repeat the exam on your right breast, both standing up and lying down.

Visual and palpable changes

A visual change could be general changes in shape, nipple changes and skin changes. A palpable change is a discrete lump or thickening of the breast that can be felt upon physical examination. This is the most common symptom of breast cancer. The lump may be tender but most often it is painless. Any abnormality, lump or thickening found during a BSE should be reported to a physician right away. Palpable changes include: a lump or mass, an area of (tissue) thickening, an expressible discharge, an axillary lymph node enlargement.

BSE is easy to learn and to do. Statistics show that most breast cancers are actually discovered by women themselves. Ideally, BSE should be conducted once a month. If a woman is still menstruating, she should inspect her breasts approximately seven to ten days after the beginning of menstruation, when they are not swollen and tender. If she is no longer menstruating, she should still perform regular monthly examinations; the first day of each month is often an easy-to-remember schedule.

Post-mastectomy, lumpectomy or breast reconstruction self-examination

If you have had a mastectomy, a lumpectomy or breast reconstruction, you should feel your chest area, paying close attention to the scar and tissue surrounding it. Raise your arm on the un-operated side; or the opposite side if you have had surgery on both sides (bilateral); and using your opposite hand, place three or four fingers at the top of the scar. Press gently using the circular motion described above. Examine the entire length of the scar. You are looking for lumps, bumps, hard spots or thickenings. As with your breasts, familiarity with your scar(s) or reconstructed breast(s) will make it easier for you to recognise any changes and report them to your doctor.

What to Check For

The best way to discover abnormal breast lumps is to know what is normal for your breasts; then, if a problem develops, you can spot it immediately. Remember, most women's breasts have a bumpy texture and the upper portion is usually the lumpiest. Essentially, what you are looking for are persistent lumps that do not disappear or change size after menstrual cycles. These are dominant lumps, appearing suddenly and remaining. Abnormal breast lumps will vary in size, firmness and sensitivity. They may be hard or irregular with sharp edges. Still others appear as thickened areas with no distinct outlines. Some lumps are painful and tender. Pain is not ordinarily a sign of breast cancer, however, and may just indicate the development of a breast cyst. Sometimes, natural underlying anatomic structures, such as breast glands, the breastbone or ribs, can be mistaken for lumps. A firm ridge in the lower curve of each breast is normal. Do not worry about making a mistake. Always report suspected lumps to your doctor. It never hurts to be wrong but it can definitely be damaging and even fatal to ignore a cancer. The bottom line is: **when in doubt, check it out!***

Thanks to the Women's Information Network Against Breast Cancer at http://www.winabc.org/selfexam.html and to Health A-Z.com at http://www.healthatoz.com/atoz/breast/breastexam.html

*And remember, when going to your physician, you are entitled to ask questions! You now have a more informed view.

How to present sensitive information on cancer and treatment options

Presenting or distributing controversial information on cancer is often, a very delicate issue. Information on the nature of chemotherapy (plus some healthy alternatives) was recently posted to a number of parents with children who had been diagnosed with various forms of cancer. It provoked a variety of responses. One letter drew attention to the feelings of the parents at a time like this. Part of it ran as follows:

"I am concerned at the way you have thrust this information upon people who quite clearly are having a very tough time. W.... and J.... are making decisions that they believe are right for their daughter, with the help of the medical profession. I'm sure that they will have already explored all avenues of the treatments available, be it alternative or conventional. With your website, you are virtually giving the parents no choice but to feel guilty about the course of treatment that they have chosen for their child. Their lives must be traumatic enough right now without having outside influences trying to contradict their decisions."

Was this an intrusive way of introducing the dangers of chemotherapy? According to the case history information on the little girl, her operation is imminent and is to be followed by an intensive regimen of chemotherapy and ongoing radiation treatment. What does one do for the best? When it comes to the sharing of potentially life-saving information, where do the etiquette boundaries lie? What is the best way of presenting information such as this? Is there a best way? Interestingly, another letter I received from the same group began:

"Funny how this report ended up on my pc, just as I was being asked to help with some fund raising for Cancer Research...."

Aaron Boomsma, the father of five-year-old Laura, who was recently diagnosed with a Wilms' tumour of the kidney, is in no doubt. Such was the severity of chemotherapy prescribed to Laura, that her hair fell out and she was violently sick for many days. As soon as Aaron and his wife heard the well-founded, contrary information on chemotherapy, they brought an immediate halt to their daughter's conventional treatment and came to the UK, where Laura received non-toxic treatment and responded tremendously. Says Aaron:

"For me, it was quite simple. I was presented with the information. I did some independent research for myself and very soon found out that the hospital treatments we had been talked into for Laura were exceedingly dangerous. I am so thankful that I was given information that made me question the path we were on."

Personally speaking, I find great encouragement from speaker D L Moody, who said of truth: *"The best way to tell if a stick is crooked or not is not to spend time arguing over the matter, but simply to lay a straight stick beside it."*

Whilst you're never going to please all people all of the time, I think it just comes down to how you lay that stick down. And if you are going to lay it down, lay down some positive alternatives too!

Your Money and Your Life?
Examining the Cancer Charities
Martin Walker

Everybody knows what causes cancer. Bad diet; too much sunlight; cigarettes; faulty genes – and, of course, that virus which crops up near nuclear power installations. Modern science has told us so, and now it must tell us how it can be cured. But are we getting there? Diligent research, largely carried out by Britain's cancer charities, means that a cure for cancer is probably now nearer than ever.

That, at least, is one side of the cancer story; the side you can hear from establishment scientists, drugs companies and media science correspondents. But the other side is hidden from history and the public record. For, in truth, we do not know what the main causes of cancer are, nor why the disease is escalating. Apart from the continual propaganda about cigarettes, there is no public discourse about the chemical or environmental causes of cancer. And it is unlikely that the public will ever be informed about them while cancer research in Britain is dominated by a cabal of unaccountable doctors, scientists and surgeons – a 'cancer club' which garners some of its funding and much of its philosophy from an industrial infrastructure which independent scientists believe is itself the cause of rising cancer rates.

For cancer 'research' in Britain is a misnomer. As science and medicine have become increasingly interlocked with industry, the motivation, initiative and funding for preventative cancer research has all but dried up. Throughout the post-war years in Britain, industry, government and science have tried to tackle the cancer epidemic by searching for miracle cures rather than investigating causes; by playing with gene sequencers rather than looking at environmental pollution; by taking industry's money rather than looking at its record. The conclusion today is inescapable: Britain's cancer research charities are part of the problem, not the solution.

The 'cancer establishment'
There are over 600 cancer charities in the UK, but the three big players – the heart of the 'cancer establishment' – are the Imperial Cancer Research Fund (ICRF), the Cancer Research Campaign (CRC)

and the Institute of Cancer Research (ICR). All are involved in the United Kingdom Co-ordinating Committee on Cancer Research (UKCCCR). The philosophical and scientific approach of this cancer establishment is frighteningly narrow. Its interest in researching environmental or chemical causes of cancer appears negligible. The great weight of its research is consumed with the deeply fashionable idea that unravelling the human genome will provide the solution to all human illness, cancer included – despite the fact that, on the highest estimates, no more than 5 per cent of cancers are considered to be hereditary.[279]

These three charities preserve a near-monopoly over the whole field of cancer in the UK. They determine the public perception of what cancer is and what can be done about it. Yet all are essentially unaccountable, steeped in conservatism and the privilege which class and power have bestowed upon the top echelons of the British medical profession. Between them, they have been gradually and intermittently losing the war against many cancers for almost a century.

The Imperial Cancer Research Fund (ICRF)

The Imperial Cancer Relief Fund was launched in 1902 with a £30,000 appeal – a 'scheme for investigating the cause, prevention and treatment of cancer' – by an independent group of physicians from the Royal College of Surgeons and the Royal College of Physicians. From the 1920's onward, the ICRF became essentially a public company and, in 1939, a charity.

The original London laboratory of the ICRF was staffed until the late 1950's by only nine scientists, whose annual expenditure in 1950 was around £41,000. After the building of a £2m laboratory in Lincoln's Inn Fields in 1963 however, the Fund grew rapidly. By the mid-1990's, it was receiving around £59m annually in donations,

---

[279] Olah, E, [Hereditary Neoplastic Diseases] in *Orv Hetil.* 1999; 140: pp.451-66. Although all cancers might be described as genetic, inasmuch as they are the consequence of altered DNA, opinion varies as to the levels of genetic predisposition to a variety of cancers. Olah suggests only 1 per cent of cases have a hereditary genetic component (which even then he suggests usually have to be triggered by environment or lifestyle co-factors) while Lindblom and Nordenskjold put the figure at around 5 per cent. Also Lindblom, A, Nordenskjold, H, Hereditary Cancer, *Acta Oncol*, 1999; 38: 439, 447

spending £50m on research and £10.5m on administration. Its assets, in investments, mortgages and property ownership stood at almost £90m.[280] Today the ICRF boasts over 40 research groups based at Lincoln's Inn Fields, a laboratory in Hertfordshire which houses 10 research groups, and an additional 35 clinical units and research groups based in National Health hospitals and universities around the country. It employs over 1,000 scientists, doctors and technicians. In the year 1996-97, it spent over £56m on research.

An article in the *Sunday People* in the weeks after the opening of the Lincoln's Inn Fields laboratory was a foretaste both of the kind of tame journalism it would attract and the fostering of public guilt that was to characterise the ICRF over the next three decades. The writer estimated that the new laboratories would cost £700,000 a year to run, leaving a £620,000 shortfall for the Fund. The money to run the new cancer research laboratory could not, the article stated, come from the government. If it did, 'the State would want to keep a strict eye to see how its money was being spent.... the scientists themselves do not want this'. The paper then exhorted readers to send money to help the Fund 'beat cancer' within ten years – 'or even less'; money which could only come 'from you and me and the chap next door'.

The money duly came from the public's purses and wallets, as it has done ever since. After all, we all want to help 'beat cancer'. But how well has the ICRF done in that fight? According to its own fact sheet, Imperial Cancer Research Fund Past and Present, the Fund does not consider preventative research or trials of carcinogenic chemicals to be a priority. Of the 110 units, departments and laboratories cited in the ICRF 1998 Scientific Report, not one deals with chemical or environmental carcinogens, and only three look at preventative issues.

Why should this be? As with all the major cancer charities, the answer has to do with money – and, more specifically, the question of who funds the Fund, which is explored later in this article.

The Institute of Cancer Research (ICR)

The Institute of Cancer Research (ICR) is an Associate Institute of the University of London, linked to the Royal Marsden NHS Trust. The

---

[280] Charity Commission papers on the Imperial Cancer Research Fund

Institute is not a charity, and so for a long time was unable to raise funds in the same way as the ICRF and the CRC. In 1991, however, it found a way around this, by setting up its own charity, Breakthrough Breast Cancer. By 1998, the charity had raised over £15m, which it spent building the Toby Robins Breast Cancer Research Centre at Sutton, Surrey.

Breakthrough is a different kind of cancer charity. Apparently popular, accessible and trendy, from the beginning it had close ties to the fashion and cosmetics industry (its biggest campaign was sponsored by Avon cosmetics), with very public support from models, actors and pop stars. This superficial populism makes no difference to its approach, though – it does exactly the same work as the other cancer charities, conducting no significant research into environmental or chemical causes of breast cancer. More than that, Breakthrough provides a public face for major drugs companies to sell their own approach to cancer treatment.

The setting up of Breakthrough solved more than funding problems for the ICR. When it gained a popular base it also gained trial subjects for the ongoing trials which the ICR was carrying out with the drug tamoxifen. Breakthrough's main drugs company sponsor is Zeneca, the pharmaceutical breakaway from ICI which developed tamoxifen. Breakthrough provided Zeneca with access to the House of Commons, when the charity provided a secretary to the All Party Parliamentary Group on Breast Cancer, a group composed solely of Members of Parliament. Through them, Breakthrough is able to control breast cancer information in parliament. This strategy ensures, as intended, that the All Party Parliamentary Group focuses on screening and treatment of cancer while ignoring its environmental or chemical causes.

The Cancer Research Campaign (CRC)
The British Empire Cancer Campaign, launched in 1923, became the Cancer Research Campaign (CRC) in 1980. Although smaller than the ICRF, by the mid-1990's, the CRC had an annual income from donations of £59m, a research allocation of £64.7m and assets of £25m.[281]

---

[281] Charity Commision papers on the Cancer Research Campaign

Professor Gordon McVie, current director-general of the CRC, is a major cancer research apparatchik, and one of the two key players in the cancer research industry over the last two decades. McVie is probably best known for his absurd attempts to seduce children into eating vegetables. After Medical Research Council studies revealed that a diet rich in vegetables might reduce cancer rates, Professor McVie commissioned the Iceland Group to come up with brightly coloured or interestingly flavoured vegetables. In April 1997, cheese-and-onion flavoured cauliflower, chocolate coated carrots, pizza flavoured sweetcorn and peas tasting like baked beans hit the streets. Sales plummeted and Iceland soon withdrew the delicacies from its shelves. McVie came out of the affair looking distinctly silly.

McVie's vegetable brainwave is a good model by which to assess the approach of the CRC, and the big cancer charities in general. For orthodox cancer research is often concerned with changing the nature of things in order to adjust to problems created by contemporary society, rather than going to the root of the problems.

The UK Co-Ordinating Committee on Cancer Research (UKCCCR)

The UKCCCR, set up in 1984 by the CRC, the ICRF and the Medical Research Council (MRC), seems to exist to serve the interests of the most powerful established research charities. Theoretically, it is supposed to co-ordinate the work of major cancer charities. In reality, its purpose seems to be to endorse cheques garnered by the big charities from mainly industrial funders.

The UKCCCR has around 15 main subcommittees, almost all of which are concerned with running clinical trials of various drugs produced by the pharmaceutical companies which fund them. Member organisations earmark funds received to be used under a sub-committee of the UKCCCR. In turn the UKCCCR lends its name to research for which the ICRF, the CRC and the ICR have received money. In essence, the function of the UKCCCR appears to be to give credibility to research paid for by drug companies, with which the ICRF, CRC and ICR do not wish to be publicly or charitably associated.

Spinning a Line

The power of these charities is demonstrated by how effectively they control public access to the facts about cancer. There is no independent public review of the work of the cancer charities, which allows them to present their own version of events – and they do.

In the 1960's, the Imperial Cancer Research Fund was talking of curing cancer within ten years. Almost 40 years later, in January 1999, the *Sunday Mirror* ran a typical contemporary cancer article, based upon the results of the EUROCARE II study[282] and a booklet published by the CRC.[283] It was headlined, 'How we're winning the war on cancer'. At the top of the article, like a supermarket price ticket, was a table: 'Stomach cancer down 40%, Cervical cancer down 20%, Lung cancer down 5%, Oesophagus cancer down 5%, Child cancer cure rate 65%, Testicular cancer cure rate 90%, Breast cancer cure rate 60%, Skin cancer cure rate 97%...' In the middle of the article was a quote from Professor Gordon McVie of the Cancer Research Campaign:

"These million people [treated for and survived cancer over the last ten years] *are alive because the results of research are at long last reaching the NHS. The wealth of investigation that has been taking place is coming to fruition."*

This article was typical of the current reporting of cancer research and treatment. The approach has commonly identifiable parts; the shock troops are unverifiable statistics with no contextual moorings such as gender, age, occupation or class. While we are told that stomach cancer is 'down' 40 per cent, cervical cancer 'down' 20 per cent, lung cancer 'down' 5 per cent and oesophagus cancer 'down' 5 per cent, we are not told that any such reductions in fact have little to do with the cancer research charities. Such vacillations are governed almost entirely by lifestyle, fashion, occupational trends and carcinogenic product marketing.

---

[282] Coebergh J W W, Sant M, Berrino F, Verdecchia A, eds. "Survival of adult cancer patients in Europe diagnosed from 1978-1989", the EUROCARE II Study. *Eur J Cancer* 1998; 34 (special issue): 2137
[283] Cancer Research Campaign. Survival – England and Wales, 1971-1995 (CRC Factsheet 2). London: Cancer Research Campaign, 1999

Inevitably, such articles fail to tell the reader whether the cancers quoted as having rising cure rates represent a high or low percentage of overall cancer cases; nor is the reader given any idea how many other cancers are rising while having no treatment success. In fact, only one of the cancers cited in this particular article – breast cancer – is traditionally associated with high mortality rates, and some have always been successfully 'cured' with surgery.

Finally, the argument is always neatly concluded with bald, simplified assertions about 'prevention': too much sun, sex, cigarettes and a poor diet. Taken as a whole, this approach to propaganda avoids any reference to air pollution, chemical food additives, pesticides, alcohol or any occupational carcinogens whatsoever – into which research is rarely if ever conducted by these organisations. They have dumbed-down the debate on prevention and stifled the debate on causes.

In June 1997, the ICRF and the CRC scrambled to attack a Macmillan Cancer Relief Report which suggested that cancer rates would go on rising into the 21st century. Such views, though, are not unusual; in fact it is usually the CRC and the ICRF which hold the minority opinion on cancer rates. In January 1980, *The Times* reported that:

"More than £25 million a year is spent on cancer research in Britain, but the death rate from the condition has changed little since the war.... Research seems to have little effect in reducing the death rate from the four big killers; cancer of the lung, large intestines, breast and stomach."

This remains as true now as it was 20 years ago.

Doing the Business

So who funds the cancer establishment? Who funds the research of the top doctors and scientists who consistently refuse to investigate wider environmental causes of the disease? The answer goes a long way to explaining why the top cancer charities behave as they do.

In Bed with Industry

When asked about funding, the bigger charities point to their fund-raising pie charts, which show that their major funding comes in individual covenants and donations, with only relatively minor amounts given by corporate sponsors. Yet this is to miss the point; for the big cancer research charities are steeped in an industrial culture which can serve to hide serious conflicts between the need for preventative research and the needs of industry.

Both the CRC and the ICRF hold substantial reserves – in the mid-'90's the ICRF's tied assets stood at £90m – most of which is invested in industry. Even as late as the mid-'90's it was revealed that the ICRF was 'inadvertently' investing in the tobacco industry. The investment portfolio of the cancer charities is not publicly accessible, and consequently it is not possible for supporters to ensure that investments have only been made in companies which are not implicit in the production of carcinogens.

The major charities also give the impression of being completely separate from the pharmaceutical industry, by processing their money through 'joint' organisations like the UKCCCR. Money for research into nuclear power and cancer, for example, given by the nuclear industry, is passed on to the UKCCCR, of which the ICRF and the CRC are partnership members. The UKCCCR has a very low public profile, and charitable contributors wishing to find out about its work or its funding often find it very difficult. Another group, the Clinical Trials Service Unit at Oxford, to which the ICRF and the British Heart Association are linked, accepts millions in research grants from pharmaceutical companies to research different therapies.

For some years now, the top charities have been competing like any other 'service provider' for corporate cash. Both the Cancer Research Campaign and the Imperial Cancer Research Fund invest heavily in creating 'Corporate Partnerships'. Tellingly, they sell their involvement with commerce and industry not on the grounds that companies will be helping to prevent or cure cancer, but that the companies themselves will profit from being aligned with the charity – as this quote from a Cancer Research Campaign document sent to business demonstrates:

"Supporting the CRC makes good business sense: Companies expect tangible and quantifiable returns from their work with charities. We can demonstrate the success of our commercial packages – successes that can make a real difference to sales, corporate image and teambuilding in your business."[284]

The CRC's enticement to partnership is brazen. Nor is the charity shy about offering its brand image to commercial companies, telling companies: *"86 per cent of consumers are more likely to buy a product that is associated with a cause. The most appealing 'causes' to consumers are health and medical research."*[285]

The ICRF is even more bullish in selling its partnership deals. Its website extols entrepreneurs to: *"Make a difference to your business through increase in sales. We have proved that working with ICRF can improve sales results."* Practising what it preaches, the ICRF currently works in 'partnership' with CGU Insurance, NM Rothchild, Siemens, Marks and Spencer, Tesco and Nike. The charity boasts to its partners that it enjoys a 97 per cent 'approval rating' amongst the UK's adult population; it is the image-booster par excellence for the average multinational.

Another point of conflict involves the boards and committees of the main cancer charities. A number of these committee and board members come from industries which themselves have a long and poor record on cancer. The Chairman of the CRC, for example, is R D C Hubbard, who for 10 years, from 1965-74, was on the board of Cape Industries, then a major manufacturer of the carcinogen asbestos.

Recently, the charities themselves have been branching out into business, and investing public money in the companies which will produce the drugs and diagnostic aids which they have researched. Early in 1999, for example, ICRF announced that it was to buy a £2.5m stake in Antisoma, a biotech company floated on the Pan-European Stock Exchange in 1998 and the London Stock Exchange in 1999. Antisoma's only product is a treatment for ovarian cancer developed by

---

[284] Cited on CRC website. Source: *In Business with Charities*, 1992, NCH Action for Children
[285] Business in the Community, 1996, cited on CRC website

the ICRF. In such ways, the charity/industry nexus keeps itself moving in smooth circles.

Sloganeering

Though much of their funding now comes from business, the cancer charities are still adept at tugging at the public heartstrings – with a view to opening the public purse. Scarcely a month goes by without one or another of them launching a 'major appeal' to raise public money.

Such appeals have become more and more sophisticated over the decades. The charities now spend substantial amounts simply developing new slogans for these campaigns, such as the ICRF's recent 'Turning science into hope', or the misleading 'Finding cures, saving lives'. The charities have found, however, that the most effective slogans are those which insist that 'you' can make a difference. 'Working together, we can achieve so much more' claims Breakthrough Breast Cancer. 'Cooperation is the key to success' insists the Leukaemia Research Fund, which also promises that it is 'Spending your money wisely'. Yet it is virtually impossible for the public to find out how 'wisely' the LRF – or any of the other established cancer charities – are spending their money, for none of them offers a detailed prospectus, a general meeting or voting rights to subscribers, beneficiaries, workers or interested parties.

Destroying the Opposition

The cancer establishment's refusal to research environmental and chemical causes of cancer could, perhaps, be seen as a crude sin of omission. But its determined and continual assault on all and any 'alternative' therapies and practitioners reveals the charities in their true colours – as footsoldiers for the chemical industry and the conventional medical establishment.

Such 'quackbusting' is not new. The cancer establishment, especially those leading figures involved with the ICR and the Royal Marsden Hospital, the ICRF and the CRC, have played a leading part in attacking alternative treatments for almost a century. By 1924, the ICRF was defining one of its primary roles as policing the alternatives:

"The knowledge thus obtained [by the ICRF] *has helped to dissipate the atmosphere of hopelessness which formerly existed and has profoundly influenced the diagnosis and the treatment of cancer. It has also served to protect the public against spurious claims which have been made concerning the cause or the cures of the disease."* [286]

The high point of scientific medicine's assault upon alternative approaches to cancer was the 1939 Cancer Act, which coincidentally came into being in the same year that the ICRF was granted its Royal Charter and Charitable Status. The Act forbade, on pain of draconian punishment, anyone other than a qualified doctor, involved in work with cancer, from speaking about the causes or the treatment of cancer. From that point on, the cancer establishment and its partners in industry launched an all-out war on alternative approaches to cancer, which is still being fought today.

The Big Guns

A good example of this war, one of many similar tales, is the story of what happened to the Bristol Cancer Help Centre in 1991. That year, at a press conference, the ICRF and the CRC announced the results of research they claimed to have carried out into the 'therapeutic outcome' of the regime at Bristol Cancer Help Centre, an organisation dedicated to treating cancers with alternative means. The research concluded that women who attended Bristol after having breast cancer diagnosed were three times more likely to die as a result of their illness than women who had conventional treatment.

But the 'research' was not what it seemed. Although the researchers were supposed to carry out two studies, one on survival and the other on quality of life, they failed even to begin the quality of life study and announced the 'results' of the survival study only 18 months into a 5-year schedule. It was later found that the results of the preliminary study were bogus. The researchers had, for example, taken their sample from attendees at Bristol, even if these subjects had not been involved in the Bristol therapy. They had also failed to acknowledge that many of the Bristol attendees studied had previously had – failed – conventional surgery.

---

[286] 1924 report on the work of the ICRF in the Charity Commission file on the ICRF

It was later revealed that one of the research team, an eminent oncologist, had also been a committee member of Healthwatch, an organisation set up with the main aim of debunking alternative treatments. The head of the study and the report's principal author, Dr Clare Chilvers, has since declared an interest in Zeneca, the company which produces tamoxifen, the anti-breast cancer drug.

Although the Bristol study was roundly condemned by statisticians, other researchers and Bristol Clinic attendees, and despite the fact that the publication of the research damaged many people's lives, it was three years before the CRC and the ICRF offered an apology. In January 1994, the Charities Commission censured both the CRC and the ICRF for the study, and consequently Professor McVie and Sir Walter Bodmer, the directors of the two charities at the time.

On this rare occasion, the wrongs done by the cancer establishment to their smaller rivals were made public. Sadly, though, this is the exception. Faced with the power of the big cancer charities, many alternative practitioners simply collapse.

What Can Be Done?
The big cancer research charities have become the self-appointed watchdogs over emerging forms of treatment and the censors of campaigns which place the emphasis in cancer research upon the environment and chemicals. Instead of being academically independent and intellectually curious, cancer research scientists are now hand-in-hand with the very industrial system which has turned modern life into a maze of risk. The big cancer charities' effective monopoly is unaccountable to the people who fund them with voluntary contributions or the representatives of those who leave them bequests. Although they dictate NHS policy on cancer, they are unaccountable to parliament or the public.

Clearly, something has to change, and there are several areas that must be tackled.

Cleaning up Funding
Since the 1980's, government in Britain has scaled back on public funding for scientific research; the consequent trend in research has

been for those agencies which distribute large research budgets to enter into partnership with industry in order to secure shrinking funding. As a consequence, there has been a steady movement of research away from the accountable public sector into the unaccountable private sector.

The power and independence of the cancer charities owe a lot to the continuing unwillingness of government to become involved financially and scientifically in cancer research. Only by removing the dependency of cancer researchers on private money can research become honest again. There are several potential ways of doing this. Research could become the responsibility of the State, and be allocated a budget, dispersed through an autonomous agency similar to the Medical Research Council. Or genuinely independent organisations, placed under much tighter regulation than at present, could be allowed to flourish. There are other options too; but the crucial thing is that this topic is opened for public debate.

Assuring Accountability

Cancer research has to be dragged from the grip of vested interests and returned to the more creative appraisal of genuinely independent academics, scientists and intellectuals. There are relatively simple ways of doing this. For example, anyone who has anything to do with cancer research should be vetted for links with carcinogen-producing industries. Office-holders and scientists working in cancer research should have to make a public declaration of all their interests in pharmaceutical or biotech companies. These declarations, together with staff salary figures, should be made publicly available. All cancer research scientists should also have to spend a major part of their time on non-chemical, non-genetic treatments or environmental causes of cancer.

Pursuing Prevention

Crucially, though, we need to ensure that genuine research into the real causes of cancer – and thus into genuine prevention – can take place. A wide-ranging program of research into industrial carcinogens should become a priority of cancer research, while the literature on previously tested industrial carcinogens should be reviewed and regulated. All cancer research should be locked into the regulatory process, so that as soon as carcinogens are recorded or discovered, the appropriate regulatory agency acts upon this information.

Statistical information about all cancers, including epidemiological statistics and those on causation – however inconclusive – should be compiled and published in a variety of different forms by an independent body to which the public has access. There should be a frequent public scientific, academic and financial audit of all cancer research, by an independent regulatory review body. The report of this audit should be debated in the House of Commons annually, at which time a yearly cancer research strategy should also be debated.

National Health Service treatment for cancer should also be deregulated and 'freed-up'. Experimental 'alternative' therapeutic work on cancer should be detached from the odium of criminalisation, while remaining within established regulatory boundaries and allowed into hospitals. Trusts throughout the country should be encouraged to explore community-based therapeutic initiatives.

The research, prevention and treatment of cancer is too important to be left in the hands of a small number of unaccountable scientists, funded by industry money and the voluntary sector. Cancer sufferers in Britain have paid too high a price for the indulgence of science and its utopian search for a universal elixir. They have also been kept in the dark for too long about the real price of technological and industrial progress. It is time for the cancer establishment to give up its secrets.

Martin J Walker is the author of six books, including Dirty Medicine. Anyone interested in investing in the publication of his next book – The Gatekeepers, a history of alternative cancer care in Britain, should contact him at Slingshot Publications, BM Box 8314, London WC1N 3XX

What's really behind the EU Directive on vitamins and minerals?

Here in the UK and in other European countries, legislative moves are being made by various governmental agencies to control public access to vitamins and minerals. Europeans are fast becoming aware of one of those moves, in the form of the EU Directive on Food Supplements – a bill which seeks to gain control over some 300 vitamins, minerals and herbs and reclassify many of them as prescription drugs. And in the US, the Federal Trade Commission (FTC) has recently set up an initiative called Operation Cure-All. The stated aim of OCA is:

".. to use Internet both as a law enforcement tool to stop bogus claims for products and treatments touted as cures for various diseases and as a communication tool to provide consumers with good quality health information." [287]

As in Europe, the US government wishes to take control of the non-pharmaceutical health market. There is to be a crack down on fraudulent health information on the Internet. The stated aim? *To protect the consumer from possible harm.*

But is there another reason behind this overtly philanthropic move? Rufina James suffers from a serious medical condition, which is helped enormously because of her present ability to access the necessary vitamins and minerals. Without them, she would be in trouble. Ruth has taken the time thoroughly to examine the Federal Trade Commission's 'Operation Cure-All' in a broader context. Her report on the subject makes for necessary reading.

---

[287] Operation Cure All at http://www.ftc.gov/opa/1999/9906/opcureall.htm

The Sinister Truth Behind Operation Cure-All

by Rufina James

www.therealessentials.com

What's really behind Operation Cure-All? Is it just the US Food and Drug Administration (FDA) and FTC taking their power too far? Or is there a deeper, more sinister purpose to this campaign?

How could a country that prides itself in its freedom of speech, freedom of choice, and freedom of information be facing such severe restrictions in health freedom and dietary supplements? Haven't the people made their will known? Didn't our government pass the Dietary Supplement Health & Education Act of 1994 to insure our right to health supplements?

Indeed, our government did. But the FDA and FTC have found ways to get around that. The laws put in place to protect us are being ignored. And what's worse is that those laws are about to be superceded, if the powers that be have their way.

A Means to an End

You see, Operation Cure-All is just a tactic, a vehicle, in a much bigger overall plan. It is a result of 'Codex Alimentarius' (meaning food code) - a set of regulations that aim to outlaw any health information in connection with vitamins and limit free access to natural therapies on a worldwide scale.

What's Behind Codex?

Behind the Codex Alimentarius Commission is the United Nations and the World Health Organisation working in conjunction with the multinational pharmaceutical cartel and international banks. Its initial efforts in the US with the FDA were defeated, so it found another ally in the FTC. Now Codex, with the FTC and the pharmaceutical cartel behind it, threatens to become a trade issue, using the campaign of Operation Cure-All to advance its goals.

Codex began simply enough when the UN authorised the World Health Organisation and the Food and Agriculture Organisation to develop a universal food code. Their purpose was to 'harmonise' regulations for dietary supplements worldwide and set international safety standards for the purposes of increased trade; to standardise labelling and regulatory requirements between countries to facilitate increased international trade. Pharmaceutical interests stepped in and began exerting their influence. Instead of focusing on food safety, Codex is using its power to promote worldwide restrictions on vitamins and food supplements, severely limiting their availability and dosages.

Real Goals of Codex

To bring about international 'harmonisation.' While global harmony sounds benign, is this the real purpose of this plan? While the stated goal of Codex is to establish unilateral regulations for dietary supplements in every country, the actual goal is to outlaw health products and information on vitamins and dietary supplements, except those under their direct control in the US. These regulations would supercede domestic laws without the American people's voice or vote in the matter.

How Can it be Possible?

Americans gasp at the thought. It goes against everything America stands for. Many believe this can't be possible. The truth is, it's not only possible, it's required by the Codex agreement.

In fact, under the terms of the Uruguay Round of GATT, which created the World Trade Organisation, the United States agreed to harmonise its domestic laws to the international standards. This includes standards for dietary supplements being developed by the United Nation's Codex Alimentarius Commission's Committee on Nutrition and Foods for Special Dietary Use.

The Uruguay Round Agreements carry explicit language clearly indicating that the US must harmonise to international standards:

"Members are fully responsible under this Agreement for the observance of all provisions.... members shall formulate and implement positive measures and mechanisms in support of the

216

observance of the provisions.... by other than central government bodies." [WTO TBT Agreement at Article 3.5]"

In other words, the federal government must not only <u>change federal law</u>, but must also require state and local governments to change their laws to be in accordance with international law.

Not only that, Codex is now enforceable through the World Trade Organisation (WTO). If a country disagrees with, or refuses to follow Codex standards, the WTO applies pressure by withdrawing trade privileges and imposing sanctions. Congress has already bowed to this pressure several times and so have the governments of many countries.

While the exemption clauses USC 3512(a)(1) and (a)(2) were created supposedly to protect our laws from harmonisation to international standards, they have proven totally ineffective. The United States has already lost seven trade disputes, in spite of the exemption clauses. Due to the enormous pressures put on it by lobbyists from multinational corporations (who contribute millions to congressional campaigns), Congress bowed to pressure and changed US laws.

It appears our government is being manipulated one way or another to serve the goals of the UN, the World Health Organisation and the World Trade Organisation. Food control equals people control - and population control. Is this beginning to sound like world government and one-world order? Could this be the real goal behind Codex?

The United States, Canada, the Europeans, Japan, most of Asia, and South America have already signed agreements pledging total harmonisation of their laws including food and drug laws to these international standards in the future.

What Codex will Bring

What can we expect under Codex? To give you an idea, here are some important points:

> Dietary supplements could not be sold for preventive (prophylactic) or therapeutic use

217

> Potencies would be limited to extremely low dosages
> Only the drug companies and big phytopharmaceutical companies would have the right to produce and sell the higher potency products (at inflated prices)
> Prescriptions would be required for anything above the extremely low doses allowed (such as 35 mg for niacin)
> Common foods such as garlic and peppermint would be classified as drugs or a third category (neither food nor drugs) that only big pharmaceutical companies could regulate and sell. Any food with any therapeutic effect can be considered a drug, even benign everyday substances like water
> Codex regulations for dietary supplements would become binding (escape clauses would be eliminated)
> All new dietary supplements would be banned unless they go through Codex testing and approval
> Genetically altered food would be sold worldwide without labelling

According to John Hammell, a legislative advocate and the founder of International Advocates for Health Freedom (IAHF), here is what we have to look forward to:

"If Codex Alimentarius has its way, then herbs, vitamins, minerals, homeopathic remedies, amino acids and other natural remedies you have taken for granted most of your life will be gone. The name of the game for Codex is to shift all remedies into the prescription category so they can be controlled exclusively by the medical monopoly and its bosses, the major pharmaceutical firms. Predictably, this scenario has been denied by both the Canadian Health Food Association and the Health Protection Branch of Canada (HPB).

The Codex proposals already exist as law in Norway and Germany where the entire health food industry has literally been taken over by the drug companies. In these countries, vitamin C above 200 mg is illegal as is vitamin E above 45 IU, vitamin B1 over 2.4 mg and so on. Shering-Plough, the Norway pharmaceutical giant, now controls an echinacea tincture, which is being sold there as an over-the-counter drug at grossly inflated prices. The same is true of ginkgo and many other herbs, and only one government-controlled pharmacy has the right to import supplements as medicines which they can sell to health food stores, convenience stores or pharmacies."

It is now a criminal offence in parts of Europe to sell herbs as foods. An agreement called EEC6565 equates selling herbs as foods to selling other illegal drugs. Action is being taken to accelerate other European countries into 'harmonisation' as well.

Paul Hellyer in his book, *The Evil Empire*, states:

"Codex is supported by international banks and multinational corporations, including some in Canada, and is in reality a bill of rights for these banks and the corporations they control. It will hand over our sovereign rights concerning who may or may not invest in our countries to an unelected world organisation run by big business. The treaty would make it impossible for Canadian legislators, either federal or provincial, to alter or improve environmental standards for fear of being sued by multinational corporations whether operating in Canada or not.

This will create a world without borders ruled by a virtual dictatorship of the world's most powerful central banks and multinational companies. This world is an absolute certainty if we all sit on our hands and do nothing."

This is the future the FDA and FTC are striving to bring us via Codex harmonisation. Is this a future we are going to accept or prevent?

Why Target the Internet?

It is no accident that the FDA and FTC are targeting Internet health sites through Operation Cure-All. We are standing in the doorway of an unprecedented revolution - the information revolution brought about by the Internet.

Now all people everywhere have the ability to learn about anything that interests them with just a few clicks. History has shown that informed, educated people change civilisations - they change the flow of thought and the flow of money. They can even change the direction of a country. When similar transitions have happened in the past, the powers that existed did not give up willingly. The Catholic Church fiercely protected its practice of selling "indulgences' as a forgiveness of sin. When the practice was abolished, the Catholic Church lost a great deal of power and money.

When the printing press was invented, books were banned and printers were imprisoned by the authorities, who feared an educated public could not be governed. In the same way, the medical monopoly (and the UN) now fears that a public educated in health and privy to the shortcomings of modern medicine cannot be controlled. Loss of control means loss of revenue and power. And they are doing everything they can to stop progress so they can contain their losses and strengthen their power.

The printing press changed the world. Can you imagine what life would be like today if the book-banners had their way? But because the printing press won, society progressed and freedom was embraced. The Internet is changing the world in an equally significant way. While the entire Internet can hardly be suppressed, the pharma-cartels and their backers are looking to protect their interests by restricting as much information as they can on the Web.

Will we, the people, win out again, or will the UN and the World Health Organisation agenda and the pharmaceutical cartel change the course of history and take us back to the 'dark ages' of medicine?

Please visit www.laleva.cc/indexeng.html and sign the petition against the restriction of vitamin and mineral sales. It takes thirty seconds to complete and it is so important.

The *Food For Thought*

- Eat properly constituted, organic percentage consumed in its natu are provided in our companion gu
- The ideal balance is: 80% alka Closer attention to this area reve comprise 90% acid/10% alkali. Not
- Try to limit meat components to n ...% of the total diet. Also, reduce dairy intake. Eliminate both if sick.
- Fish, deep and cold caught, is good, excepting those listed below.
- Hydrate the body (4 pints of clean, fresh water a day).
- Detoxify (eat fruit before noon on an empty stomach). A full account of what to do can be found in *Health Wars*.
- Reduce meat and dairy intake (eliminate if sick).
- A basic supplement program (see '*Food For Thought*').
- Exercise (to get everything moving!).
- Rest.
- Reduce environmental toxicity (dangerous jobs, using toxic chemicals, radiation, etc.).
- Use safe personal care products.
- Use safe household products.

Foods to Avoid

- Pork products (bacon, sausage, hot-dogs, luncheon meat, ham, etc.) With today's intensive farming methods especially, these products are high in nitrites, and are known homotoxins, which can cause high blood urea. They can also help form dikitopiprazines – a metabolic chemical by-product, which has been linked to brain tumours and leukaemia.[288]
- Scavenger creatures (inc. ALL shellfish and other carrion-eaters – see Leviticus 11 in the Bible). Carrion-eaters, pork and shellfish in particular, concentrate toxins of other animals in their tissues, which we then consume to our

---

[288] Day, Phillip, *Food for Thought*, Credence Publications, 2nd Ed., 2002; "Adverse influence of pork consumption on human health", *Biologic Therapy*, Vol. 1, No. 2, 1983

ent. The same goes for the elimination organs of mercially raised animals, such as liver and kidney, which can be high in drug and pesticide residues.

Aspartame/saccharin, artificial sweeteners. These are known mental impairment problems and cancer risks.

➤ Refined sugar/flour/rice. Restricted amounts of wholegrain bread are OK. Use only wholegrain rice. No sugars should be consumed other than those contained naturally in whole foods.

➤ Hydrogenated & partially hydrogenated fats (margarine).

➤ Junk (processed) food, including fizzy sodas and other soft drinks containing sugar, artificial sweeteners or phosphoric acid, which are drunk out of aluminium cans.

➤ Fat-free foods. Essential fats are essential!

➤ Olestra, canola, soy, etc. Avoid fake or synthetic fats. Soy, in its unfermented state (meat and milk substitute products), disrupts the hormone (endocrine) system, blocks the absorption of calcium and magnesium, and acts like estrogen in the body. Small usage of fermented soy products (soy sauce and miso) is OK.

➤ Polluted water (chlorinated or fluoridated – see *Health Wars* section, entitled 'Water Under the Bridge').

➤ Caffeine products.

➤ Excessive intake of alcohol products.

➤ Excess salt. It's better to spice food with ground kelp to maintain a healthy iodine intake.

The Four Pillars of Mental Health

➤ Eliminating allergies
➤ Maintaining blood sugar balance
➤ Avoiding toxins and pollution
➤ Ingesting optimum nutrition[289]

For a full analysis of 'food as it should be', see *Food For Thought*, the food recipe companion to this book and others in the Credence stable (see 'Other Books by Credence').

---

[289] Day, Phillip, *The Mind Game*, Credence Publications, 2002

Contacts! Contacts! Contacts!

If you wish to purchase more copies of this book or find out where you may obtain any of Credence's other book and tape products, please use the contact details below. Credence has local sales offices in a number of countries. Please see our website at www.credence.org for further details on how to contact them:

UK Orders: (01622) 832386
UK Fax: (01622) 833314
www.credence.org
e-mail: sales@credence.org

Health Review magazine

What other book entitles you to a free magazine subscription and regular e-mail updates completely free? If you have not received these and have purchased this book, contact us on the above numbers.

Eclub bulletins

Twice each month, the Campaign for Truth in Medicine sends out the EClub Internet bulletin to thousands of subscribers worldwide. This highly informative e-mail newsletter is available FREE to customers who have purchased this book or who have requested EClub. This online bulletin contains the latest news and research on cancer, heart disease, mental health and other vital health topics. DO NOT BE WITHOUT THIS GREAT RESOURCE! If you wish to subscribe, log on to the Campaign site at www.campaignfortruth.com and click the 'Join CTM' tab to complete your free application.

Credence Publications
PO Box 3
TONBRIDGE
Kent TN12 9ZY
England
infopack@credence.org

Other book titles by Credence

Scared Sick of Cancer? Don't Be.
Get the Facts... and then get
on with your life!

CANCER: WHY WE'RE STILL
DYING TO KNOW THE TRUTH
by Phillip Day

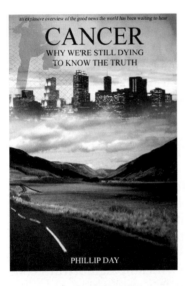

For more information on the truth behind cancer and Metabolic Therapy, our world-famous book, *Cancer: Why We're Still Dying to Know the Truth* is the excellent starting point. This overview title exposes the ongoing establishment cover-up over the failure of traditional cancer treatments and explains Metabolic Therapy (Vitamins B17/A&E/C/enzymes), the controversial treatment for cancer and its prevention. This book further details the amazing track record of nutrition and its role within the simple, combined protocol of Metabolic Therapy. Whether you have cancer, or are exercising prevention for you and your family, **PLEASE** get educated on this vital issue today.

Title: Cancer: Why We're Still Dying to Know the Truth
by Phillip Day
First published in April 1999 by Credence Publications
Available at www.credence.org

B17 METABOLIC THERAPY IN THE PREVENTION AND CONTROL OF CANCER

- a technical manual -

compiled by Phillip Day

From the desks of some of the world's leading cancer scientists comes the empirical proof of Vitamin B17 and its co-factors in the treatment and prevention of cancer. These explosive findings have been the cause of the real cancer war, where vested interests have moved to vilify and denigrate nutrition in order to protect their highly lucrative cancer incomes.

> **B17 METABOLIC THERAPY**
>
> in the prevention and control of CANCER
>
> a technical manual
>
> compiled by
> PHILLIP DAY

- ➤ Find out why 18 'primitive' cultures do not get cancer in their isolated state.
- ➤ What three nutritional components have been found vital in the prevention and the treatment of cancer?
- ➤ What can you do to change your diet in ways which will give you maximum protection from cancer and other associated ailments?
- ➤ Why do animals not get cancer in the wild, yet succumb to it when 'domesticated' by humans?
- ➤ Discover the amazing research of Professor John Beard of Edinburgh University and American Biochemist Ernst T Krebs Jr which shows what cancer actually is. Remove your fear of this disease forever.
- ➤ Why are huge budgets continually spent on 'fighting the war against cancer' when this information has been in the public domain for 50 years?
- ➤ Examine the actual technical theses and trials carried out by doctors and scientists that validate this amazingly simple protocol.

> Find out what you can do today to join the global movement to eradicate cancer from the 21st century!

Phillip Day: *"Now comes the empirical information for doctors, scientists and laymen alike, which can be used at a local, state or global level to eradicate cancer and its heartache from the human race forever. Each of us has a chance today to be great – to remove far from us the greed, entrenched error and ignorance that has allowed cancer to flourish like an evil bloom in our midst. In a sense, cancer will remain around only as long as it takes humankind to achieve that rare level of maturity, when he will treasure his own well-being and that of his friends and loved ones above the tempting lure of wealth, prestige and renown."*

Title: B17 Metabolic Therapy – A Technical Manual
by Phillip Day
First published in 2002 by Credence Publications
Available at www.credence.org

HEALTH WARS
by Phillip Day

PRESS RELEASE: Western healthcare is now the third leading cause of death in Britain, according to a UK health research organisation. England-based Credence Research, citing statistics which demonstrate that drug-dominated medicine is now the third leading killer in most industrial nations, warns that the true death toll may be far higher than even its reported figures.

Credence Chief Executive Phillip Day states: *"225,000 Americans are killed every year by Western healthcare, according to the American Medical Association. In Britain, the official figure of 40,000 is in reality far higher, if you examine the proper markers.*

226

1 in 5 Australians will be killed every year by their doctors, through incorrect drug-prescribing, botched medical procedures, infections in hospitals and, the main killer, <u>correct</u> drug prescribing. This worldwide allopathic catastrophe is well known to the authorities who, in reality, are unable to do much about it within the current healthcare system, for the reasons we report."

Credence, whose recently released publication, Health Wars, deals with this unsettling phenomenon, states: *"90-95% of the diseases currently killing populations, at least in the industrial nations, are nutritional deficiency and/or toxin related conditions, such as heart disease, cancer, diabetes and stroke. To understand completely why medicine continues to fail with these problems, and worse, be guilty of its own unique slaughter of the citizenry, one need look no further than the fact that doctors receive almost no formal training in nutrition. Thus, doctors are not trained to understand the underlying metabolic problems of at least 90% of diseases, which can be treated effectively, even in their late stages, or completely prevented, using simple, and unfortunately un-patentable nutrition."*

On the toxin disease front, the medical establishment is equally dismissive and trivialises the real chemical and environmental causes, according to Credence. To illustrate why this happens, Day points out that the very industry responsible for producing and selling chemicals, which routinely kill and maim the public, also manufactures the public's medicines. *"Don't expect the chemical industry to gain a morality on this issue overnight. It is hamstrung by stark conflicts of interest. The urgent call for reform needed to prevent further tragedy on the scale we face must come from the public itself."*

On Credence's recently released book, Day declares: *"The purpose of 'Health Wars' is to highlight these problems and to urge citizens to pressure their governments for immediate reform. Compounding its failures, British healthcare has ironically been brought to its knees by the crippling costs of the very drugs and treatments, which have been, and continue to be, the main instigators of these frightening death statistics. Credence has been looking at mortality. But how many citizens out there have been crippled or maimed by healthcare practices, such as vaccinations, errant drug prescribing and unnecessary surgeries? Recent reports show that the NHS must* *budget every year for at least £2.8 billion in compensation claims alone. That's enough to build and fully staff 28 new hospitals <u>every twelve months</u>."*

Credence states that medical science has known for years that the answers to heart disease, cancer, stroke and other illnesses lie completely in nutrition and lifestyle changes, not radical surgeries, toxic drugs or radiation. To prove this point, the company cites at least 18 cultures alive today who do not apparently suffer from these health problems. *"Interestingly,"* Day elaborates, *"we tend to call these peoples 'primitive' and 'less developed'. But they know enough about nutrition to ensure that they survive in sterling health, in many cases to over 100 years of age. The authorities know this too, and do nothing. Why? Because Western healthcare today is a multi-trillion-dollar industry worldwide, and you cannot pay CEO salaries and shareholder dividends using apples, oranges and chemical-free, organic vegetation."*

Day believes that health reform is inevitable, and that the public can do much to precipitate the process by getting educated and politically active: *"A proper healthcare industry must have nutritional education at its heart,"* he states. *"This is the most basic body science. We are what we eat. But the people will have to fight a war with their industrial and political peers first, in order to secure the return of their unalienable right to drink fresh, uncontaminated water, to eat fresh, uncontaminated food and to breathe fresh, uncontaminated air."*

Title: Health Wars
by Phillip Day
First edition published June 2001 by Credence Publications
Available at www.credence.org

TOXIC BITE
by Bill Kellner-Read

Most people go to the dentist at some point in their lives, and many go regularly. But who really questions what happens when we are in the dentist's chair? Can we be sure that we are receiving the best, long-term treatment for such an important and necessary part of our body?

Finally there's a new book that demystifies dentistry and lets you take control of your own dental health. *Toxic Bite*, by British dentist Bill Kellner-Read, gets to the bottom of some startling questions:

➢ Could your gum disease be responsible for heart disease or stroke?
➢ What products are we using every day that contribute to wider toxic illnesses?
➢ And what about those extractions? Do we really need that tooth pulled?
➢ Should we really be extracting children's teeth for orthodontic correction?
➢ What are the longer-term consequences of having less teeth in our mouth?
➢ What about the other correctional work being carried out today?
➢ Is there a link between nutrition and gum disease?

You might not have toothache. But what about back-ache, neck-ache, jaw-ache, migraine or those constant blinding headaches? It may well be an underlying dental problem that is contributing to wider systemic disease, chronic pain and discomfort in your body.

For the best in toxin-free tooth, mouth and body care, read *Toxic Bite* - the latest addition to the Credence roster of top-selling healthcare titles.

Title: Toxic Bite
by Bill Kellner-Read
First published in 2002 by Credence Publications
Available at www.credence.org

FOOD FOR THOUGHT
compiled by Phillip Day

Need a guide on where to go with your food? What better way to embrace the dietary concepts laid down in *The Mind Game, Cancer: Why We're Still Dying to Know the Truth* and *Health Wars* than to obtain a copy of our official recipe book.

This delightful guide takes you through the main concepts of acid/alkali, Vitamin B17 dishes, the proper combining of foods, the problems with meat and dairy in excessive amounts, fruit consumption techniques, smart foods, a host of detox menus, 5-10% meat and dairy recipes, snacks, pro-active sickness dieting, children's dishes and proper supplementation. Whether you are suffering or just want to make a change for your extended future, sensible nutrition comes to life in *Food For Thought*, bringing you the most delicious foods that WON'T KILL YOU!

Title: Food for Thought
Compiled by Phillip Day
First published in August 2001 by Credence Publications
Available at www.credence.org

PLAGUE, PESTILENCE AND THE PURSUIT OF POWER

by Steven Ransom

Almost every day, it seems, we are hearing reports of some 'highly infectious' disease breaking out somewhere across the world - the recent flu pandemics, AIDS decimating Africa, tuberculosis on the rise again, measles, and meningitis on the increase. And in the animal kingdom, we've seen Bovine Spongiform Encephalopathy (BSE), poultry flu, swine fever, more BSE and now foot and mouth, wreaking havoc across our countryside. One could be forgiven for thinking that we are quite literally surrounded by virulent illness. But not everything is as it seems – not by a long way.

In this book, we discover that these so-called 'epidemics' are NOT the deadly illnesses we have been led to believe by our respective governments, national papers and news programs. With all the above-mentioned illnesses, the facts being disseminated have been grossly misleading, accompanied, in many instances, by a deliberate intent to scare and deceive. Welcome to the shocking world of the politically manufactured epidemic - the 'psycho-plague'.

The formula is quite simple. Using the mainstream media as their chosen vehicle for change, powerful vested interests are deliberately instigating national and international fearsome headlines. Through these channels, the problem – the epidemic – the psycho-plague, is manufactured. A crisis has now been firmly embedded into the mind of the populace. **"We must have a solution!"** we cry. Lo and behold, a governmental/corporate solution is speedily proffered.

In reality, the epidemic needing 'swift state intervention' has been nothing more than a Trojan Horse either for creating immense profit for various pharmaceutical industries or, as we shall discover, for ushering in unsavoury, global super-state ideology. Throughout this whole process, we are being taught what to think about health and disease, but not how.

In examining the facts laid out before us, we soon realise that our battle is not so much against pathological disease, as against corrupt and self-serving desires, birthed in the minds of man. This book contains the supporting evidence to make this case. You are invited to consider the evidence for yourself.

But this book also maps out a positive way forward. For, in discovering the true nature and causes of these 'epidemics', a longer lasting remedy can now be planned for the future.

Plague, Pestilence and the Pursuit of Power is dedicated to those who want to find out what really goes on behind the closed doors of Big Business and Big Government and to those who wish to see truth reign in conventional science and medicine.

Title: Plague, Pestilence and the Pursuit of Power
by Steven Ransom
First published in June 2001 by Credence Publications
Available at www.credence.org

WORLD WITHOUT AIDS

by Steven Ransom & Phillip Day

World Without AIDS dismantles one of the world's greatest fears and lays bare the deceit, fraudulent science and needless fearmongering that lie at the heart of this supposed global epidemic. Over ten years in the making, this impeccably researched book gives an eye-opening account of what vested interests can get away with, given a trusting public, an almost limitless supply of money and scant scruples. It also explains the non-existence of HIV, the bankruptcy of the HIV test, the real causes of immune suppression, the AIDS-devastating-Africa myth and the appalling dangers of the establishment-approved medications prescribed to those who have been written off as 'HIV positive'.

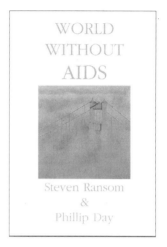

Title: World Without AIDS
by Steven Ransom and Phillip Day
First published in June 2000 by Credence Publications
Available at www.credence.org

* * * * *

HEALTH WARNING TO EXPECTANT MOTHERS

If you have recently become pregnant, you will be recommended to take an HIV test as part of a standardised, ante-natal care package.[290] This test is highly inaccurate and remains scientifically unproven. It should be refused on the following grounds.

1) All manufacturers of these tests include the following or similar disclaimer with their test kits: "At present, there is no recognised

---

[290] Refer to "Review of antenatal testing services", NHS Regional Office, London, UK Dept of Health." Recommending the HIV test became UK national policy in July 1999, and is now mandatory in some US states.

standard for establishing the presence or absence of antibodies to HIV-1 and HIV- 2 in human blood."[291]

2) The reason for this disclaimer is because the AIDS test does not measure the presence of a virus.[292] The AIDS test has been designed to detect levels of antibody activity in the blood. Antibody activity in the blood stream is a normal occurrence in humans, but is being misinterpreted by the AIDS test as indicative of the presence of HIV.

3) As a result of this misinterpretation, healthy individuals are being wrongly diagnosed as HIV positive. Since this information has come to light, in excess of 60 different medical conditions have been recorded that can give rise to a false HIV positive reading. These separate conditions include flu, flu vaccination, malaria, tetanus vaccination, Hepatitis A and B, Hepatitis vaccinations, alcohol and drug use, recent viral infections and even pregnancy.[293] Receiving a spurious but emotionally devastating diagnosis of HIV positive will prompt your doctor to recommend a course of anti-HIV drugs. Known as protease inhibitors or anti-retrovirals, these drugs are highly toxic. They have the well-documented capacity to harm the mother, and also severely to deform and even kill the unborn child. [294]

The current level of spending on AIDS drugs in the Western World is phenomenal. So too are the profits enjoyed by the AIDS drug manufacturers. As a result, the information contained in this advisory leaflet is largely being ignored by the medical establishment. Sadly, this is not an unexpected reaction. The pursuit of profit at the expense of

---

[291] The above disclaimer is included in all Abbott 'AXSYM' Aids tests at the time of writing, the world's leading supplier of AIDS test kits.

[292] Monetary rewards offered to leading organisations within the scientific community by concerned organisations for reasonable evidence that HIV exists remain uncollected.

[293] Johnson, Christine, *Continuum Magazine*, September 1996. Maggiore, Christine. *What if Everything You Knew about AIDS was Wrong?* An Alive and Well Publication, April 2000. Ransom & Day, *World Without AIDS*. Credence Publications, July 2000. www.credence.org

[294] Kumar et al, *Journal of Acquired Immune Deficiency Syndromes*, 7; 1034-9, 1994. JAMA Journal of American Medical Association, Jan 5th 2000, Incidence of liver damage. *World Without AIDS*. AZT and enlarged craniums in infants. Refer to www.virusmyth.com for a more comprehensive list of scientific references which catalogue the damage caused by AIDS drugs.

health, the wilful employment of flawed medical procedures, the administration of dangerously toxic drugs to expectant mothers, the disregard for the plight of thousands upon thousands of wrongly diagnosed people, and a refusal by the medical establishment to listen to sound contrary evidence or to admit medical negligence - all these are the hallmarks of that once-respected drug, thalidomide. Do not allow either yourself or your child to face the possibility of becoming another heartbreaking medical statistic.

THE ESSIAC HANDBOOK
By James Percival

In 1923, a Canadian nurse, Rene Caisse, came upon an ancient Ojibway Indian herbal concoction that appeared to have remarkable powers to offer the sick. In the years since, thousands of patients, many considered beyond hope, have testified that this simple, natural treatment saved their lives where modern medicine had failed. Read the story of Essiac, the remedy that defied disease.

Title: The Essiac Handbook
by James Percival
First published in June 2001 by Credence Publications
Available at www.credence.org

THE MIND GAME

by Phillip Day

Every new year brings incredible new inventions, new advances in technologies, new medicines, further discoveries in physics, chemistry and the other sciences. There are also new political challenges and military threats. News channels such as ABC, CNN, the BBC and Sky report 24 hours a day on the problems besetting this complicated, restless and fretting planet. Credence Research monitors this prodigious output; our publications division prepares reports and publishes books on these subjects. Our lecturers travel and host public meetings around the world to share this vital information.

But *The Mind Game*, it must be said, has been my most extraordinary and challenging project to date. I believe, after you have finished reading this book, that you also will agree that there are no greater or more important issues facing us as a civilisation than those under discussion in these pages. I speak to thousands of citizens a year during the course of my own touring. Almost to a man, woman or child, my audiences are worried about the world around them. They are at present known as the Silent Majority.

Author and researcher Bruce Wiseman writes: *"Outside our windows, the peaceful streets of years past now harbour violence. In some neighbourhoods, gunfire pierces the night. Police helicopters fly overhead, scanning yards and alleys for runaway criminals.*

We worry about our children. Once-quiet schools are now hothouses of drug-trafficking, promiscuity, and vice unimaginable in days gone by. We hear of an ever declining literacy rate, dwindling test scores, and of graduates who can't even find their home city on a map. We wonder how they will ever make it in the adult world.

In our homes, at our jobs, on our television screens, we see that the once-clear line between right and wrong has become grey and hazy. Virtue is held up to ridicule. The honest man is viewed as a fool. Criminal behaviour is now excused under the banner of 'irresistible impulse' and 'diminished capacity'.

Hardly anyone would argue with the statement that <u>something</u> has been eating at the moral fabric for decades now.... No one questions that there is a palpable, destructive force. In the United States, for example, people are at each other's throats over it. Liberals blame it on conservative policies, right wingers rebuke the left. Many in the religious community have held the entertainment industry accountable." [295]

The Silent Majority

The Silent Majority of the public sees these things, yet has remained silent up to now. These are ordinary, decent citizens who have grown exasperated with the ineffectiveness and corruption of their political system. Many have registered their protests by refusing to vote. Others are frustrated at the media for eschewing its collective responsibility to evaluate the social problems we really face. Most people, as we will learn later, have not the slightest idea which ends the press really serves. Dumbfounded, we look on as our newspapers, TV and cinemas feed us a steady, putrid fare of sex, violence, money and the shenanigans of the famous, instead of promoting the common-sense approaches that could heal our nations, restore our health services and stabilise our societies.

Psychiatry

Psychiatry is one science in particular that comes under scrutiny in my book. At first glance, most would not even acknowledge the incredible changes psychiatric and psychological theories have had on our world. Yet we shall see that they have permeated our courts, our police, our hospitals, our movies and TV, our schoolyards, our governments and even our homes. Who would consider for one moment that psychiatry could have played such a fundamental role in

---

[295] Wiseman, Bruce, *Psychiatry – The Ultimate Betrayal*, Freedom Publishing, Los Angeles: 1995, pp.5,6

the development of politics, education, entertainment, war and medicine?

Off the Rails?

Many have concluded that mankind itself must be going insane. Indeed, we are told, at no other time in human history has a greater segment of society been diagnosed 'mentally ill' than today. Our nations' governments, schools and courts appreciate this, which is why they are veritably aswarm with armies of politically correct legislators, administrators and the inevitable battalions of psychologists, psychiatrists and other 'mental health' experts. One could expect that with such an impressive arsenal of professional expertise on call, victory itself would be assured. Who would possibly consider for a moment, in their right mind, that these might conceivably be the very same armies responsible for all the chaos?

Thomas Szasz

Dr Thomas Szasz is an interesting individual. He is Professor of Psychiatry Emeritus at the State University of New York at Syracuse and Lifetime Fellow of the American Psychiatric Association. Although reaching the pinnacle of his profession, Dr Szasz has repeatedly denounced psychiatry as *"...probably the single most destructive force that has affected American society within the last fifty years."* An author of 23 books, including *The Myth of Mental Illness*, described by *Science* magazine as *"bold and often brilliant"*, the Hungarian-born specialist has covered, in his writings, every type of abuse carried out by his profession. Szasz pronounces psychiatry guilty, not only of gross abuses of power and human rights over its patients, but also for the far-reaching, deleterious effects its philosophies have had on society throughout the world:

"Psychiatry is a part of the general liberal ethos.... Everybody is a victim, everybody has special rights, no responsibilities. This psychiatric view has so completely infiltrated [global thinking], people don't even think of it as psychiatry." [296]

---

[296] Citizen's Commission of Human Rights (CCHR) Interview with Dr Thomas Szasz, 17th September 1993

The *Mind Game* Mission

This book traces the origins of psychiatry - this 'science of the mind' - and lays bare the startling and unsettling history of the Trojan Horse that has taken up residence in our midst. Part 1 of my book deals with psychiatry itself, while Part 2 examines the major 'mental disorders' from their true and vital standpoint. And it is here that the good news about our predicament is truly seen. Is there really such a thing as 'mental disease', or is the reality for us and our societies altogether more straightforward and, most importantly, manageable?

There is great news here for those concerned about Alzheimer's, Parkinson's, ADD/ADHD, schizophrenia, anorexia, multiple sclerosis and a host of other disorders. For the millions who wrestle with these problems and issues daily, help is at hand. My task in the pages to follow is to report to you the leading research on these issues from the mouths of the specialists themselves, so the reader may make up their own mind on how to proceed from here.

For those unsettled and perplexed by the predicaments of the modern world and why seemingly nothing is being done about them, the journey we will shortly take will explain the nature of Wiseman's *"palpable, destructive force"*, and how it has gained so much power over us. More to the point, my new book will discuss measures whereby the public may retake control over much of what has been given up or taken away. If you are sympathetic to the mission of this book, then take heart, for there are millions of people who think the same way you do. I believe, if we are to pass on to our children a future world that contains any legacy at all of decency, honesty and a moral compass, then we must discuss and resolve the answers to the ultimate question that faces our world today:

"What on Earth is Going On?"

Title: The Mind Game
by Phillip Day
Published by Credence Publications 2002
Available at www.credence.org

The Campaign for Truth in Medicine

"a force for change"

What is CTM?

Campaign for Truth in Medicine is a worldwide organisation dedicated to pressing for change in areas of science and medicine where entrenched scientific error, ignorance or vested interests are costing lives. Its ranks comprise doctors, scientists, researchers, bio-chemists, politicians, industry executives and countless members of the world public, all of whom have made one observation in common. They have recognised that, in certain key areas of global disease, drug treatments and overall healthcare philosophy, the medical, chemical and political establishments are pursuing the wrong course with the maximum of precision, even when their own legitimate and erudite scientific research has illustrated the dangers of pursuing these courses.

CTM Backs its People's Charter

CTM's People's Charter catalogues these key problem areas - for example AIDS, cancer, mental health, heart disease and vaccinations - where the preponderance of evidence demonstrates severe cause for concern over deadly errors in basic science, resulting in needless loss of life. CTM's charter also highlights industry's every-day use of potentially harmful contaminants and biohazards, such as toothpaste's sodium fluoride, shampoo's sodium lauryl sulphate and cosmetic's propylene glycol, which have long been linked to long-term serious health risks and death. CTM's purpose is to present this damning evidence to its members, to the public at large and to the establishments and individuals involved in these errors, in order to press for immediate change and cessation of their use for the benefit of humanity. The People's Charter is periodically amended to reflect current issues and new areas of concern.

CTM Stands for Truth

For decades members of the public and a significant proportion of their medical and scientific professionals have become increasingly angry and frustrated at what they see as establishment indifference and even downright hostility towards much-needed changes in healthcare, especially in areas where the proven solution is substantially less profitable than the current status quo.

Promoting the Truth

CTM believes in promoting the truth in these matters, thereby exposing those morally bankrupt and compromised politicians, corporations and individuals responsible. This method of action is viewed as a top priority. CTM is dedicated to pushing for immediate change, in order that immediate relief from many of the diseases and their causes, currently afflicting us, may be implemented, the remedies for which, in certain cases, have been a matter of existing scientific knowledge for decades.

The Journal of the American Medical Association (JAMA) implicitly reports that western healthcare, along with its drugs, treatments and hospitals, is now the third leading cause of death in the United States, next to heart disease and cancer. If we examine this astonishing fact, also highlighted by US consumer advocate Ralph Nader in the early 1990's, we come to realise that the Western healthcare paradigm is adopted by almost all developed nations and many other developing countries around the world. Thus this tragic statistic of iatrogenic death can be fairly considered to be global in application.

This would be serious enough on its own, yet the true extent of this orthodox medical catastrophe is unfortunately far more devastating. Western medical establishments are in possession of key life-saving information that can immediately and drastically reduce current and future global incidences of cancer, heart disease, AIDS and other treatable, non-fatal conditions. But in almost all cases these institutions have chosen neither to adopt these measures, train their healthcare practitioners in these practices, nor publicise the latter to a generally trusting world populace. Thus these government personnel and their associated medical luminaries, who have wilfully kept this life-saving information from their doctors and the public, may justifiably be exposed for becoming the leading cause of death across the planet today.

CTM Stands For Direct Action

CTM believes that, in certain cases, legitimate direct action is warranted against these institutions and individuals to halt their wilful and harmful actions and hold them to account. In these circumstances, CTM calls upon its membership to organise and act in a unified, lawful and mature fashion to bring these matters to the attention of the mass communications media, government leaders and heads of state through demonstrations and other appropriate action. CTM is dedicated to being part of the people's movement in this regard; a powerful and irresistible force for change, compelling vital reform TODAY for a safer and healthier world for our children and children's children.

CTM is Free From Vested Interest Funding

Through its network of worldwide professional contacts, CTM has constant access to well-researched information on key health issues. CTM brings its members highly readable and jargon-free information, such as that contained in this book.

CTM Has All the Necessary Contacts

...at local and central government/corporate level, responsible for particular health legislation and legislative change. Names, addresses, contact details and relevant template letters are supplied with all CTM newsletters.

CTM is a Health Advocacy Organisation

with purpose and direction. It is a conduit through which the individual minority voice can become a powerful and respected, collective majority voice for change.

What You Can Do Now

CTM invites you to visit its website to learn more about how you can join this worldwide movement FOR FREE and receive regular bulletins and further information on these fascinating subjects as they develop. Be part of a different future. One that celebrates life!

Campaign for Truth in Medicine
PO Box 3
Tonbridge
Kent
TN12 9ZY UK
e-mail: info@campaignfortruth.com
www.campaignfortruth.com

Index

Z

Notes

Notes